What I Would Tell Her

28 Devoted Dads on Bringing Up, Holding on to
and Letting Go of Their Daughters

Edited by
Andrea N. Richesin

HARLEQUIN®

What I Would Tell Her

ISBN-13: 978-0-373-89210-5
© 2010 by Andrea N. Richesin

Library of Congress Cataloging-in-Publication Data

What I would tell her : 28 Devoted Dads on Bringing Up, Holding on to and Letting Go of Their Daughters/ edited by Andrea N. Richesin.
p. cm.
ISBN 978-0-373-89210-5 (pbk.)
1. Fatherhood. 2. Fathers and daughters. I. Richesin, Andrea N.
HQ756.W468 2010
306.874'2--dc22

2009039407

www.eHarlequin.com

Printed in U.S.A.

"Often heartbreaking, sometimes harrowing and consistently hilarious. *What I Would Tell Her* tells the world about the savagely beautiful bond between fathers and daughters, and it does so without a drop of saccharin or sap. Spectacularly achieved, and fascinating from the very first page."
    —Jason Roberts, author of *A Sense of the World*

"Reading these 28 remarkable essays made me rejoice in that special bond that fathers and daughters share. . . . These essays will win over every father and all of their daughters."
    —Ann Hood, *New York Times* bestselling author of
    The Red Thread and *The Knitting Circle*

"By turns thoughtful, hilarious, soulful and wry, *What I Would Tell Her* offers a direct line into the heart and soul of the Y chromosome-possessor we call father. This book brought me to my knees."
    —Karen Karbo, author of *The Stuff of Life: A Daughter's Memoir*

"With the help of some great writers, Nicki Richesin has managed to do what I thought was impossible: accurately and fully describe that life-changing, magical bond that exists between father and daughter. These essays are sweet and provocative."
    —Ad Hudler, author of *Man of the House: A Novel*

"Whether your father-daughter business is holding on, letting go, rocking out, coaching, doting, or enduring the terrible, beautiful twinning of love and loss, there is something here for you."
    —Catherine Newman, author of *Waiting for Birdy*

"This collection could have taught King Lear a thing or two."
    —Robert Mailer Anderson, author of *Boonville*

"With great candor, these writers bravely expose their inner lives."
—Karen Joy Fowler, *New York Times* bestselling author of
Wit's End and *The Jane Austen Book Club*

"The essays here are touching, funny, moving and inspiring—
sometimes all at once."
—David Liss, author of *The Devil's Company* and
The Whiskey Rebels

"Andrea Richesin has assembled a terrific collection of essays by
men who write with great wonder, humor, and abiding love for
their daughters…. *What I Would Tell Her* is an indispensable addition
to the growing literature of fatherhood."
—Caroline Grant, editor of *Mama, PhD: Women Write about
Motherhood and Academic Life*

"Humor, tenderness, joy and sadness: all are in great abundance in
this marvelous collection. *What I Would Tell Her* is a book all fathers
and daughters should read."
—Ron Rash, author of *Serena*

"Moms get all the sweets writing about the real loves of our lives—
our children. But in Nicki Richesin's exquisite collection about
what fathers would tell their daughters, daddies lay bare their great
hearts."
—Jacquelyn Mitchard, *New York Times* bestselling author of
The Deep End of the Ocean and *No Time to Wave Goodbye*

"A beautiful collection of fathers' singing of and to their great
loves. Some essays are funny, some somber and intense, but what
unites them is emotional honesty….There is something to learn
here for every woman who has a father, and every man privileged
enough to play that role."
—Mat Johnson, author of *Hunting in Harlem* and *Drop*

"You can find the whole world in this one book. Twenty-eight powerhouse writers prove again and again the immutable power of a father's love and the eloquence that comes when a heart speaks. These pieces are by turns touching, hilarious, painful, tragic and ultimately uplifting—a true gift to the reader. This collection is not just entertaining. It's important, probably even transformative."
—Susan Wiggs, *New York Times* bestselling author of
The Summer Hideaway

"These writers—some of the best of our generation—have big stories to tell. They love their daughters; they protect their daughters; they let their daughters go. It's powerful material—written with tenderness, compassion and great insight."
—Ellen Sussman, author of *Dirty Words: A Literary
Encyclopedia of Sex* and *Bad Girls: 26 Writers Misbehave* and
On a Night Like This

"If you're expecting a syrupy, fairy-tale collection of father-daughter essays, this is not it. The writing here is so raw and pure."
—Rachel Sarah, author of *Single Mom Seeking* and founder of
a blog by the same name

"Bursting at its covers with love and wisdom, *What I Would Tell Her* should be required reading for fathers and daughters. No book has ever made me feel happier, and more fortunate, to be a dad."
—Will Allison, author of *What You Have Left*

"Reading *What I Would Tell Her* illuminates the love, loss, heartache, and hopes in stunning, sharp essays that are at turns comedic and touching. Most of all, these words are like the best conversations with my own dad: honest."
—Emily Franklin, author of *Too Many Cooks: Kitchen
Adventures with 1 Mom, 4 Kids, and 102 Recipes* and
The Girls' Almanac

For my father,
Don Richesin

It is always a matter, my darling,
Of life or death, as I had forgotten. I wish
What I wished you before, but harder.

—Richard Wilbur, "The Writer"

CONTENTS

INTRODUCTION

In the Swedish folktale "Singeli's Silver Slippers," a poor cobbler sews his daughter a pair of magical shoes to protect her from harm and lead her on many adventures. When it's time for her to go out in the world on her own, her father says, "These silver slippers will guide you in the right way. Into them I have put all my love."

The writers in *What I Would Tell Her* have invested a similar love, almost overpowering in its intensity. With a touching vulnerability, they write from their hearts about their hopes for their own daughters.

The beauty of this collection lies in the many different ways the contributors attempt to become like mythic heroes to their little girls, to protect them and guide them throughout their lives. They recognize how important it is to be a strong male role model. After all, how a little girl sees her father and the strength of their relationship will shape and inform her relationships with men for the rest of her life. Knowing that they are the first man she'll ever love, these fathers are devoted to nurturing them. I have noticed this with my own daughter, how much she looks to my husband for encouragement and how he reflects this back to her every day. Fathers are arguably the most important men in their daughters' lives.

After editing the heartfelt essays in *Because I Love Her: 34 Women Writers Reflect on the Mother-Daughter Bond,* I was frankly stunned by the outpouring of emotion in this collection. I suppose I initially expected a more stoic and practical, far less impassioned and confessional response from these fathers. As both a mother and daughter, I felt I deeply understood the innate connection between the two, but found I had much to learn about the depths of the father-daughter connection. At first, men don't always experience the same intuitive attachment like a mother's love and it may often take some time for this nurturing bond to develop. For all these reasons, I was happily surprised by the tender essays I received.

This remarkable anthology delves into the intense nature of the intimacy of these ties between father and daughter. The talented contributors write about their love for their daughters, the emotional conflicts they've overcome together and what they've learned from them.

They also demonstrate the role their parents played in informing how they rear their daughters. Some have chosen to embrace their background, while others have decided to create a whole new model for their families. They take us on a journey through the many stages of fatherhood: birth, toddlerhood, adolescence to sweet sixteen, graduation, becoming a grandparent and even the loss of a child.

As Steve Almond amusingly explains in "What Next, Papa?" "We all fall for our girls. We all worship them. We get to perfect the heroic version of ourselves that mates never grant us. Our love resides in a passionate physical connection that is not sexual, but grounded in the sensuality of childhood." Eric Goodman echoes a similar sentiment in his essay "Do I Dote?" He discovers a father's relationship with a grown-up daughter symbolizes "an idealized kind of love, with all the sweetness and caring remaining from childhood, but without all the real-world difficulties and concerns that color a relationship with a wife or lover." Goodman believes if he has made his daughter feel "loved, respected and admired," he will have "succeeded as a father, representing to her everything that a loving relationship with a man can be."

Protecting their daughters emerged as the most common theme in this collection. Akin to a warrior impulse, the writers often feel a strong need to defend their daughters. Dean Bakopoulos realizes as a father, there are many things he cannot fix. For him, parenthood is ripe with what he deems "small mournings," or "those brief moments of daily clarity when you realize that you are unable to protect your children from every danger, humiliation and woe that the world can offer." He recognizes his daughter is likely to experience all these things with and without his help, and sometimes despite his best efforts. He ventures that it's "possible that men do not fully realize the precarious sadness of the world until they watch their own children try to navigate their way through it." Bakopoulos wonders whether as fathers "we have long realized it, and now the shattering part is that we must watch a tiny creature, whom we love more than anything else in the world, realize it, as well."

His daughter's "guarantee against everything," David Teague straps the colicky three-month-old Annabel to his chest and walks the mean streets of Philly to keep her nighttime existential woes at bay. They witness a gang of hooligans brutally attacking an innocent man. In a moment of heroic determination, Teague hands Annabel to his wife and mysteriously mumbles, "I've got to see about something." No spoilers here, but in the end, he confesses if he saw the ne'er-do-wells again today, he would "crush them to powder, take that night back and give it to Annabel."

James Griffioen offers an alternative view to the clichéd idea of "shotgun dads" and the mythology of protecting daughters from teenage boys. Although he understands the emotions involved, he doesn't think his daughter needs to be protected from boys or her own feelings. His essay is more about "sexual" protection than actual physical protection (i.e., standing by the door during dates with the mythical shotgun). When he attends a "purity ball" in his wife's hometown and talks to other fathers about their fear of their daughters' sexuality, he decides he wants his daughter to develop a healthy attitude about sex. In his stunning conclusion, he offers his most astute observation that fathers must protect their daughters from themselves, asserting "it takes real strength to stand aside and let her navigate the darkness without you." In his essay "The Man on the Stairs" Robert Wilder also notes, "A father's love for his daughter is borne out of weakness and that's the way it should be, if he only lets it." Even though Wilder would like to defend his daughter, he realizes he must let her fight her own battles.

As part of this poignant journey of fatherhood, they must witness their little ones growing up. In his mind's eye Laird Hunt creates a film that doesn't exist. His little daughter is running away from him, past the monkey bars, until he catches a last glimpse of her "grown tall and strong shouldered, racing across…the grass field beyond the playground fence. Then she is gone." Fathers ache with bittersweet longing for their young daughters and, like Hunt's flickering film, the passing of their youth and innocence. When Steve Almond's daughter Josie proclaims, "I'm starting to grow up, Papa," he experiences "a thrilling, terrifying moment, feeling the weight of her, breathing in her hair, and it's all so fleeting, the chance to love her with such uncomplicated fervor, such uncensored declaration." He suspects "Josie has sniffed out the secret power of every childhood, which is that it ends little by little, that it's ending all the time, that each moment, whatever else it might contain in the way of joy and love and need, brings her a little closer to escape."

What begins as such a sweet, uncomplicated love can become fraught with frustration and misunderstandings as daughters grow up. An uncomfortable distance may grow out of this disconnect as father and daughter try to determine how to act around one another. Robert Dugoni is heartbroken when his eight-year-old daughter locks the bathroom door for the first time. He mourns the loss of his little girl, but wears a lipstick heart tattoo with her name in the middle on his arm to prove his devotion to her at the school sock hop.

Single fathers Trey Ellis, Richard Farrell and Michael Kearns have insecurities about being both mother and father to their little girls, but leave no doubt they are all this and more. They have forged a bond with their daughters not unlike a mother's wherein they, too, dispense advice and form an intimacy based on mutual respect and compassion. They've discovered a way to communicate and connect with their girls, even during especially difficult times like puberty. They find they, too, can braid hair and offer advice on how to deal with boys, while never losing sight of how to help their daughters not only survive but also flourish during these tough years of adolescence.

In their attempts to encourage them, fathers often feel frustrated by their ambitions for their daughters, but must learn to let go. David G.W. Scott recognizes when he needs "to arrest my ambition for her, and let her find her own." Although he had the best intentions, Swan Adamson finally realizes his expectations for his stepdaughter "didn't fit the reality of who she was, or thought she was, or was trying to be." Although Carl Lennertz felt the need to stake out his daughter's after-prom party, he eventually learns how to let go of her and take pride in knowing he has adequately prepared her. They've ultimately learned to accept that their daughters are on their own journeys and have faith in their judgment.

So much depends upon finding inner strength. Richard Nash is plagued by insecurities of not being enough, and the responsibility of living up to his daughter's expectations may seem terrifying at times. Yet he finds the courage from his daughter. Michael Kearns draws strength from his bond with his adopted daughter, Tia. Together they have formed an unlikely duo, sharing a mutual love so powerful it has helped Kearns survive living with HIV these past fourteen years. We feel the pain and immensity of these ties when Amitava Kumar's daughter, Ila, reaches out to her father through tears in the dark when he becomes frustrated with her. He yearns to fulfill his "secret desire to be the person that my daughter thinks I am." Robert Bausch experiences a strange mix of regret and pride when his determined and defiant six-year-old Sara stands up to him when he tries to punish her. These intense moments demonstrate, as Nash observes, that the tiny girls who come into their lives "expand dramatically the universe of what matters."

As with all familial relationships, there are also regrets. Robert Bausch never knew his daughter Suzi until she was nineteen. She contacts her father, they're reunited and she ultimately forgives him for abandoning her. Although he is still haunted by the loss of the years he missed with his daughter, she becomes a part of his new family. Suzi teaches him an important lesson, one that he writes to her in a birthday note, "Love is something to be done, not simply to be said. Loving is taking action."

Carrying on the legacy of his family, Rand Richards Cooper's daughter seems to him a little reincarnated version of her grandmother. When Cooper's brother-in-law and mother die tragically, he's diagnosed with skin cancer. In his "Late-Onset Fatherhood" he observes, "A child demands a future of you, but she also gives you one, changing your place in the procession—not only the ancestors lining up behind you, but now the descendants in front of you as well." Thomas Beller believes, "In becoming parents we meet our parents again. In some way, we meet them for the first time. And if you didn't really know one of your parents that well, then the dialog that springs up becomes not so much a reunion on different terms, but a whole new acquaintance."

And so, too, they must deal with death as Daniel Raeburn grieves over the loss of his daughter Irene and somehow must survive the hellish months afterward, when a compassionate albeit uncomprehending world cannot understand his and his wife's terrible despair. On their visit to Thomas Beller's father's grave, his daughter must recognize her father's father is no longer alive, which must mean her father will one day die, as well. Mike Adamick tries to reassure his little Emme when she discovers a dead baby bird on the street and insists on staying with it until the mother bird returns to it.

In quite a few instances, these fathers not only admire their daughters but have also learned from and seek to emulate them. Rob Spillman has the surreal experience of going from being a depressed, sullen teen who listened to a lot of punk music to now having a daughter who performs the same music in her rock band and has embraced it as empowering. When Isadora writes angry punk songs, he can't help but feel a fierce pride. While coaching his daughter Phoebe, David G.W. Scott becomes frustrated when she fails to dribble ahead of her teammates during a soccer game. When she points out that she must build her teammates' confidence rather than just try to score a goal, Scott recognizes, "Sometimes, the child is father to the man. Sometimes the daughter is coach to the father, and I think that if I'd missed that moment, not let Phoebe coach me, I might have undone years of work."

The fathers featured in this anthology don't need to offer magical slippers to their daughters. They would defend them to their deaths to protect them from wolves in sheep's clothing, false friends and enemies. With great hope and trust, they attempt to help them choose the bright paths and lead them to a future not of their making but of their daughters' own creation. My dad certainly did the same for me when he encouraged me to follow my bliss even when it meant leaving him and my family behind. As a young father, he sacrificed his youth by working long hours to pay for ballet slippers and cello and piano lessons. He believed in me even when I didn't. Dad encouraged me to travel the world to find what I was looking for. And I did. When I was just eleven years old, my parents put me on a plane to Sweden to live for a month abroad. I've never felt more blessed than I did being given this opportunity and knowing they had faith in me even as a little girl. I hope to embolden my daughter in the same way.

Love is the answer and the key to these mini-memoirs. Claude Stanush wisely notes that "Love isn't something you can demand, or even expect, of children. It has to be spontaneously given." His daughter Michele has proven her love for him by carrying on their strong family legacy of storytelling. In their mutual admiration as adults, daughters are no longer a possession to their fathers, but grown women they know as equals.

T. Colin Dodd tells his young daughter Ava, "Love is like magic. It won't let you quit until you're ready to quit." He imagined an intimate relationship with his daughter and together they have created it. All of these influential writers have envisioned such a future for their daughters. Through their steadfast support and constant encouragement, they ensure their daughters will grow strong and realize their dreams. They have no need of magical slippers, as they're already demonstrating to their daughters how to navigate their world. Yet after reading their powerful essays, I've learned the bond between a father and daughter is also a kind of magic.

Andrea N. Richesin
San Rafael, California
July 2009

What I Would Tell Her

FOR GRACE,
AS SHE GROWS INTO HER NAME
Chris Bohjalian

The Sunday morning you were christened, when your parents' friends and the weekly faithful in the congregation were filing into the church, an older woman held all ten pounds of you in her arms and commented upon your first and your middle name. "Grace Experience," she murmured softly, rocking you in her arms in the tiny antique white dress your mother had picked out for you. "Your parents were so wise when they named you. Grace is the gift we all receive at birth. Experience is that which we will earn every day of our lives."

Your mother and I were mightily impressed with her insight and later we would tell ourselves that we wished we had been half so clever when we had named you. We chose Grace because it is indeed a lovely name and because of a distant, elderly relative in Sweden who always seemed to embody the word. She was dignified and elegant and unfailingly good-natured. On a Christmas card she sent us toward the end of her life, she was sitting at the bottom of a slide in a playground in Stockholm. We chose Experience because it, too, was a family name, though this one went back to an ancestor we knew nothing about who had lived in Massachusetts in the seventeenth century. (Actually, that's not completely true. We knew one detail about this ancestral Experience: she had had a sibling named Free Love. So, consider yourself fortunate that you weren't born in San Francisco in 1968. You might indeed have wound up as Grace Free Love.) And here is something else, should you ever wonder

1

about your name. Be grateful you're a girl. Had you been born a boy, we were going to name you Atticus. The reference, of course, is to Atticus Finch, the widower lawyer with the profoundly accurate moral compass in Harper Lee's *To Kill a Mockingbird*. But imagine going through life with the name Atticus Bohjalian. The phonetics alone would have been debilitating.

In any case, when we combined Grace and Experience, we did so largely because we liked the rhythm and the sensual fluidity of the sibilance, not because we had contemplated the meaning of the two words together. It was all just good luck.

But so much of raising you has been good luck. Nurture matters, but it sure helps with a nature as kindhearted and empathetic as yours. We may have molded the clay a bit, but it was prize earth to begin with. I don't think a month has gone by when someone hasn't told me that you have lived up to your name.

Still, you have no idea how often your mother and I were faking it as parents and making it up as we went along. The reality is that a lot of child rearing is ad-libbing, but it has always seemed to your mother and me that we did more ad-libbing than most. As you know from photographs—though not from recollection—we took you with us on a forty-five-hundred-mile car trip when you were but five months old. Part of the journey was to Arches National Park in Moab, Utah. I tucked you into a Snugli and walked with you against my chest past red rock and sandstone arches, until we sat down near the edge of a cliff overlooking the iconic Delicate Arch…and your mother and I realized we were irresponsible lunatics. If you didn't roll off the side of the ledge to your death, you were going to wind up cooked by the searing heat or slowly dehydrated like an orange tree transplanted into the desert. Cautiously your mother and I retreated away from the ledge on our fannies, afraid even to stand up. Sometimes I think it's a miracle you made it to kindergarten.

And I know in those early years I never felt I had anywhere near the competence of my own parents, those people who seemed so sophisticated and erudite in the faded Kodachrome slides that molder in the attic. There is my mother—the grandmother you never knew—in a white sequined sheath as she leaves the front door of my own childhood home on her way to a New Year's Eve party. There is my father—the grandfather you view only as a frail old man who denies he is deaf and watches television with the volume set on Jet Engine—in a tuxedo, his hair a creosote black, a glass award of some sort cradled in both of his hands. They were in control. They were in charge. They could have been movie stars. They seemed to me to have been born middle-aged just as, I imagine, your mother and I have always seemed middle-aged to you.

In my mind, our family unit of three has always been a perfect fit with our three separate sensibilities. Before you were born, your mother and I had envisioned a family of four or five, and when your mother discovered she was pregnant, we fantasized in those first weeks that she might be carrying twins and in an instant we would have a family of four. The moment you were born, however, those very first seconds we held you in our arms, that idea melted away. We felt utterly complete as a family and your mother and I couldn't imagine how we could ever love another baby as much as we loved you. (In the coming weeks, the few times we contemplated another baby, we had only to glance at our kitchen to return to our senses. It always looked like an earthquake had rumbled through it. Your mother and I like order, and infants—even you at that age—are anything but orderly.)

Still, I hope you have been as content to be an only child—

an only daughter—as your mother and I have been happy to be the parents only of you. From an early age your mother and I brought you into our decision-making processes, even if your vote at seven or eight wasn't really going to be a tiebreaker. But we wanted you to be aware of what we were thinking, and we wanted to know how you were viewing the world.

Now, I like to believe that there isn't anything of consequence your mother and I haven't already told you. There are the platitudes, of course, about self-esteem and body image and boys. (Just for the record, an idea usually becomes a bromide because it makes sense. Just because something is trite doesn't mean it isn't true.) You should love your body and you should love yourself. No boy is worth compromising yourself for. And the best friends really are the ones who don't judge you and really will watch your back. I am heartened by the reality that already you have friends like that, young women who someday will be bridesmaids at your wedding and young men whose companionship hasn't a sexual agenda.

But I also realize how much is unsaid even in families such as ours that put a premium on dinners together and communication that is honest and precise. So, here goes.

I am painfully aware that I can be a disabling, almost disempowering control freak. It's one thing to solicit input; it's quite another to use it. Even though you are sixteen, I still want to solve all your problems, always, whether they are big or small, of your own making or bad luck that has fallen upon you. Think of how often I text or e-mail or call you since you have left for boarding school. As I recall, I was texting you what to eat for breakfast the morning of your first day of exams your first semester away from home. I used to run next door to the church Sunday mornings when I wanted you to sleep late and make sure that whoever was ringing the bell knew one pull was

4

enough: we didn't need to wake the dead at the nearby cemetery—or my sleeping daughter in the bedroom perhaps fifty yards away. One time, a Saturday afternoon when you were a toddler and taking your nap, I even did that at a wedding I wasn't a part of.

When I imagine my death—and in these macabre visitations it is usually a death that is slow and debilitating, since in this day and age that is the statistical likelihood—I am driving whoever is on death watch crazy with murmurs and weakly scribbled Post-it notes of advice for you that you really don't need:

"Don't wear four-inch heels around SoHo if you don't have to. You're just asking to derail a promising dance career."

"It's your room and your space. If you can find the shirt you want in those mountains of clothes, it doesn't matter if there's no path on the floor to your bed."

"Yes, food is love. Especially bruschetta made with good bread, finely chopped tomatoes, and extra virgin olive oil."

"There's nothing wrong with chick flicks. The term is sense-lessly derogatory and offensive."

"Get a rope ladder for your bedroom window. Fire happens."

"Wear a scarf around your neck when it's cold. You need always to protect that larklike voice of yours."

"Your laugh is charismatic. It's candy. It's chocolate. It makes everyone who hears it fall in love with you."

"You don't have to stay up till four in the morning. Really. There are things to do as early as midnight."

"Minimize your regrets—which means minimizing your tattoos."

When that time comes for me, the hardest part will be the fact that I am no longer there for you. And when that moment arrives, I imagine I will wonder if as parents your mother and I told you too much. I watch now how you worry. I know how anxious you can become. And while anxiety seems to be one of those things you inherited from your mother and me in your genetic hardwiring—the flip side, perhaps, to your magnificent cheekbones or the lovely almond shape of your face that comes with being your mother's daughter—I have speculated often over the years that you might have been better served if your parents had been a tad more circumspect.

So, when that day comes, when I am refusing to go quietly to that undiscovered country and am texting or scribbling what seems to be wisdom to me in my morphine-addled brain, I hope somehow I convey to you this: The sun seems to rise, even when one of your performances hasn't been perfect in your estimation or your boyfriend (or husband) has been thoughtless or your inherent kindness or decency has been abused. Perfection is not merely overrated; it's impossible to achieve.

Finally, about your name. Your last name. Your mother and I decided before you were born that if you were female, you would have her last name and not mine. Hence you are a Blewer and not a Bohjalian. Why? We wanted you to have a sense of female empowerment and a connection to the generations of interesting women who came before you on your mother's side of the family. Also, there was that issue of phonetics. Grace Experience Blewer simply sounded better than Grace Experience Bohjalian. And while most of the time I am comfortable with that decision, there have also been moments when I have felt a tinge of regret. That's because I am always so proud of you—so filled with amazement at who you have become and how you comport yourself in this world—that I want even strangers to know that you are my daughter. Certainly those moments occur when you are singing or dancing or acting, but they occur also when you are far from a stage or movie camera. Because you are not simply a singer or a dancer or an actor, and that has never been how your mother or I have judged you. It's not why we love you. We love you because you are an individual whose heart is immense and whose laugh is like birdsong.

Yes, you are going to make some decisions in your life that are spot-on brilliant and some that are train wrecks of spectacular proportions. There are going to be people you will meet in this world who will love you and people who are going to be jealous of the gifts that you bring to it. And sometimes people will let you down. Sometimes you will be rejected—at auditions and in life.

But, please, never lose sight of the wondrous and beatific ways that you have grown into your name.

WHAT NEXT, PAPA?
Steve Almond

My daughter Josephine is at the bottom of the stairs calling out "Papa! Papa!" My office is a converted attic, so it sounds like she's standing inside my ear. Or perhaps that's just fatherhood.

She begins rattling the gate.

The gate, if properly assembled and installed, would not rattle. But my wife and I are writers; we haven't properly assembled or installed a single thing in our home, ever. That our bodies were able to assemble and install a child remains an astonishment.

Josie continues to rattle.

"Papa needs to work," my wife calls out halfheartedly.

"Papa!" Josie shrieks. "I want Papa to come *down!* Papa! *Papa!*"

I now make the mistake I so frequently make. I appear at the top of the stairs. My thinking is that I can reason with Josie this time, I can impress upon her that Papa is working on a book—a boring book, okay, but a book nonetheless—and that I've reached that crucial juncture where something potentially unboring finally happens and so I need to concentrate, I need to bear down and enter my dark cave of revelation, and so I'm sorry, Love, but no, Papa can't come downstairs right now and swing you by your toes while bellowing clearly racist samurai gibberish.

I look down.

Here is where my plan falls apart, right at this point, where I look down and see Josie's face. And there's really no use in my describing her face, nor the ease with which it crushes my puny will. If you're not the father of a daughter, words won't even get you close. And if you are the father of a daughter, I'll leave you to envision your own daughter's face (and God bless you for that, brother). You already know how this story ends.

This all starts a long time ago.

As a child, I lobby my parents for a younger sister, whom I envision as a kind of daughter by proxy. We are a family of angry and insecure boys and I'm certain a daughter will tame us. A single gummy smile and the wolf pack will fall to pieces and lick her rosy cheeks. My parents say, "*No way José.*"

When, at seventeen, my girlfriend announces her possible pregnancy, I receive the news as fate. A daughter of my own. A little sooner than planned, sure, but isn't life crazy like that? I am going to be a teenage father! I am going to be a teenage father like you'd seen in some heartwarming TV movie, wounded and painfully noble and perfectly coiffed. I will take my baby girl to the mall and everyone will sigh as I feed her a bottle and burp her and rock her to sleep on my shoulder. Then I'll head off to Sears and shoplift her some new clothes.

But my girlfriend isn't pregnant.

I spend the next decade in a blizzard of erotic irresponsibility subconsciously designed to produce a daughter. It never happens. So I begin writing short stories filled with baby girls. The most inexcusable of them is written from the point of view of a doomed Russian farmer with four girls, all of whom worship their—*yes*—wounded and painfully noble father. He dies with one (or perhaps all four) in his arms.

It is clear by this time that I know nothing about girls and even less about women.

I remain convinced a daughter will arrive and make everything right in my soul. This conviction lasts another decade. Then, rather suddenly, the moment is upon me. I am holding Josephine Almond and staring down into the stunned gray extravagance of her eyes. Her brow furrows and her cheeks flush and her exquisitely tiny mouth opens to release a howl that can only be described as Wagnerian. This goes on for five minutes. I think, *Wow.* I think, *I should probably do something.* I think, *This is going to be a little more complicated than planned.*

At Kindermusik class, teacher Pam is saying, "Okay, everybody, we're going to sing about Little Feather now! Is everybody ready to sing about Little Feather? This will help with our listening and motor skills."

She starts singing about Little Feather, a boy who walks around the forest hearing various sounds, such as the owl sound (hoothoot) and the squirrel sound (scurryscurry), and finally walks into a bear cave, and rather than *freaking out,* he makes a bear sound (roarroar).

We're supposed to be sitting in a circle. But Josie makes a beeline for Pam and pulls away the Little Feather doll she's using for demonstration purposes and drags Little Feather around the room by his little legs. Then she starts bashing Little Feather's skull in with a mini-xylophone. The other moms stare at her in horror. Then they look at me, with that disingenuous "Oh, isn't your little sociopath adorable" look.

"Roar," says Josie. "I'm a bear!"

Little Feather makes no sound, because Little Feather is dead.

It's the eve of my first out-of-town trip. I'll be gone for three days. My wife and I have been mentioning this to Josie all week, trying to prepare her for an extended absence. "Papa has to go away for work," we say. "But then he'll come back!"

Right now, we're getting in a little roughhousing before I have to pack. I'm taking bites of her ribs, which I call "Josie burgers." She's laughing in her breathless, convulsive manner and pushing my head back, then squealing "Josie burgers!" so I'll dive in and take another bite.

We all fall for our girls like this. We all worship them. We get to perfect the heroic version of ourselves that mates never grant us. Our love resides in a passionate physical connection that is not sexual, but grounded in the sensuality of childhood, the smells and textures and tastes.

Suddenly, she grabs my cheeks with her hands. It's a weirdly dramatic gesture. She wants me to *listen*. She looks down, as if to gather herself, and when she looks up again, her eyes are sad planets. "Papa goes away," she says softly. "Papa works."

Josie is on day five of Nap Strike 2008. The flesh around her eyes has that red puffy look of impending meltdown.

"Do you want to read a story?" I say.

"No!" she says.

"Do you want Play-Doh?"

"No!"

"We could go downstairs."

"No!"

"Or we could take a walk."

"No!"

"How about if you have a time-out?"

"No!"

Bambien, I think. *Baby Ambien. Just strong enough to induce the sleep your baby deserves.* My wife came up with the name. All we need now is seed money, legal counsel and a small bank in the Caymans to handle the fortune.

It's the middle of the night and Josie is crying. I find her at the railing of her crib, wiping her nose. When I lift her out she breaks into a grin and says, "I want to get down! I want to see Mama!" She squirms free and runs into our bedroom.

Punked again.

But then I hear my wife let out a soft sound of distress.

"Honey," she calls out. "Honey, please come in here." I walk into our bedroom. The light shows that Josie's face is covered with a bright red substance. *That's funny,* I think. *I don't remember putting any cherry syrup in her crib.*

My wife glances at me. She's trying not to panic, which immediately makes me panic. I briefly, and sort of morbidly, marvel at my own negligence. I can hear a state worker saying, "So you didn't notice anything *unusual* about your daughter's face when you took her out of her crib? That's your testimony, Mr. Almond?"

My wife gets a wipe and cleans off Josie's face. There's no discernible wound. "It must be a nosebleed," I say. We read about nosebleeds for the next half an hour, while Josie bounces on the bed cheerfully. Injury is a minor villain in her production. Death doesn't even make the program.

I coax Josie back into her crib, and then I lie awake for the next hour. *It's over,* I think. *It was nothing. Don't be a dope. Stop worrying.*

We've just emerged from our nightly bath and I've put Josie on her changing table for our "dry the princess" ritual. She flips over and I pinch her tush until she gets the hiccups and agrees to be diapered. I stand her up to put on her footy pajamas and she leaps into my arms. I gently apply Vaseline to her nose and make farting noises on her belly. Then we make a bottle and I read her two stories and we do "hugsies" and "kissies" and I tuck her into bed and rub her back until she sighs.

"She is so your little girlfriend," my wife says when I walk back into our room.

"Hell yes, she is," I say, because what's the point in denying anything? I've said from the beginning that I'm delighted to have a child who eventually will want to sleep with me and kill her mother. Consider the alternative.

"Seriously," my wife says. "It's like you're dating."

"We are dating," I say. "What can I tell you? She's totally hot. She totally gets me. I thrive on the erotic confusion."

At night, when she's supposed to be sleeping, Josie holds court over the creatures in her crib. She recites bits of books she's been read and repeats back everything she's learned during the day. "I'm a little shy around Nils. Just a little shy. Oh, isn't that cute! Hey, baby brother's looking at you! Josie can share. It's hard to share." She sings songs in her piping alto and tells rambling symbolic stories. There's a whole mind on display, a mind not yet sealed off from the rest of the world, from us, from me. I stand outside the door and listen in the dark. I wait for her to say my name.

Josie has commandeered the giant cardboard box in which the Swedish eco-friendly diapers arrived. She is slowly destroying it from the inside out. I'm bored, as usual, and hoping to provoke this little scat routine we have. "Jos," I say, "are you a bookus minookus?"

No answer.

"Are you a tookus…or maybe you're a pa-pookus?"

Josie's head pops up and she casts me a withering glance. "I don't want Papa to speak. I want Papa to go away."

"That's not very nice," I say.

Josie's head sinks out of view. "Go away, Papa," she whispers. "Go into the kitchen."

"Fine," I say. "Fine. Papa's going to go away! But don't come running to Papa in two minutes, when you want to be swung around. Because Papa might not have time for that. Okay?"

Josie says nothing. I can hear her punching the box's glued panels apart.

"Have you noticed that our daughter's kind of an asshole?" I say to my wife later.

"She's two," my wife observes. "Wait until she's sixteen. She's going to crush you like a bug."

"She is not," I say. Then I go into the bathroom and use some private time to collect myself.

We're on the couch, reading about Curious George and the bike he receives from the frankly creepy Man in the Yellow Hat. We reach the part where George crashes the bike and mangles the front wheel and sits by the riverbank, crying. Josie says, as she always does, with a genuine pity that shocks me each time, "Oh, George is crying!"

She herself woke up this morning crying. When I went in to get her, I could feel immediately that she was feverish. Her diaper contained the sort of digestive horror that only a parent could face without gagging.

All of which meant that she'd finally, inevitably, caught the stomach flu that I'd gotten and given my wife the week before, a flu we had assumed was somehow related to the nasty cold we'd been trading the week before that.

Anyway, Jos has been dosed with medicine and cleaned up and now we're trying to keep her hydrated and distracted.

"George is crying," she says again. "Don't cry." She dabs at George's tears. "When I was a baby, I used to cry," she announces. "But now I'm a big girl."

"That's right," I say. "You *are* a big girl."

She pauses and lets out one of those sighs that, I think, arise in children from a particular effort of thought.

"I'm starting to grow up, Papa," she says suddenly.

And there's a moment, a strange, thrilling, terrifying moment, where the truth of this statement rears back and socks me in the heart. I'm sitting with my sick two-year-old daughter on my lap, staring at the blazing cuffs of her ears, feeling the weight of her, breathing in her hair, and it's all so fleeting, the chance to love her with such uncomplicated fervor, such uncensored declaration. This reaction is sappy and absurd, as are most of my reactions to the world. But the gravity of her statement makes me suspect Josie has sniffed out the secret power of every childhood, which is that it ends little by little, that it's ending all the time, that each moment, whatever else it might contain in the way of joy and love and need, brings her a little closer to escape.

So, all right. She's started her getaway. Soon I'll be seeing her off to school, then summer camp; then I'll be greeting her prom date with a make-believe-just-kidding shotgun; then she'll go off to college and major in something stupid and I'll go bald and tell her she can move wherever she wants, the world is her oyster, if she doesn't mind dynamiting her old man's heart.

We're living in a lucky age, in a lucky precinct, so I won't need to worry about her being sold into servitude or forced into a joyless marriage. The big mistakes are hers to make.

And if I'm doing a number on her as a father, as I no doubt am via my indulgences, my impatience, the smallness of my self-regard, well, then, she'll have to live with those. Nobody knows what the hell they're doing in this business so far as I can tell. We're all just nervous suitors, bowing before whichever princess is ours. We pledge our love in each little scene, then sweep them up and call it life. Josie won't remember one bit anyhow. The brain is forgiving like that. It keeps stuffing itself full of fresh disasters and wonders. It pops her up each morning and tells her to call out for her father, who appears drowsy with adoration. *What next?* her brain tells her to say. *What next, Papa?*

VESSELS
Daniel Raeburn

On our third date, Rebekah gave me one of her bowls. We sat at my kitchen table, her bowl between us, while she told me how she'd made it. She explained that a potter needs to throw the same pot over and over until the shape of the vessel becomes second nature, until she can form it so fluently that even her slipups grow spontaneous and confident. I turned Rebekah's bowl in my hands as she pointed out the accidents that had occurred during its creation. On the wheel, the lip of the pot had relaxed from a strict circle to a more comfortable roundness. Inside the kiln, the iron glaze on a neighboring pot had vaporized, ghosting its ruddy afterimage like a blush across the bowl's glossy cheek. These imperfections were what Rebecca cherished. Mistakes made the clay human.

Rebekah had innumerable freckles, small, weathered hands and dirty overalls. A year or so later, at that same kitchen table, I asked her to marry me. She said yes, and in no time she was pregnant. After a few months, just as she was growing heavy, our baby died. We never found out why. Miscarriages were usually for the best—that's what everyone said, and that's what we said, too.

In the spring of 2004, five months after the miscarriage, Rebekah was pregnant again. One hot summer morning, there was pain, blood and a grim drive beside a blue Lake Michigan to the emergency room, but this time our baby persevered. At twenty weeks, an ultrasound revealed that our survivor was a girl and in good health. As proof, the technicians gave us a black-and-white image of her suspended in limbo. She looked like an alien glimpsed through a telescope, a white dwarf forming in a distant galaxy.

Her name came to me in the night as I was falling asleep, her hands and feet drumming against Rebekah's belly and my palms. *Good night, Irene,* I thought, *I'll see you in my dreams.* I didn't know anything about this song other than the chorus, which haunted me just as a song is intended to. Irene Raeburn: Rebekah also liked the sound of it, and so the name stuck. I did see Irene in my dreams. She appeared as she had in the ultrasound, a cloud growing in the warm, humid air beneath our blankets.

After a Christmas party, when she was more than eight months along, Rebekah had to sit down. She felt dizzy and queasy, but she took a startled pleasure in caressing her visibly thrumming belly.

"Irene's kicking like crazy," she said. "She's never kicked this hard. Never."

"Any day now," I said, "any day." I wound my scarf around my neck and shrugged into my coat, offered Rebekah my hand.

Three days later Rebekah called me at home from our midwife's office. I raised the receiver to my ear, heard a silence that I sensed was Rebekah's and felt anguish tremble like electricity. I knew immediately that Irene was dead. When Rebekah at last uttered my name, the crack in her voice confirmed it.

A quiet African man piloted me in his yellow taxi toward our midwife's office. His radio emitted news of a tsunami that had just struck Asia, India, then Africa, killing so many thousands that the authorities would never be able to count all the dead. Lake Shore Drive slipped past. Chicago's concrete sky weighed on the frozen lake and the stone-and-steel downtown where

17

families from around the planet had gathered to photograph themselves shopping and ice-skating beneath trees whose bare stalks branched like capillaries for giant brains that had gone missing.

At the office the receptionist regarded me gravely, then showed me to where Rebekah was waiting. Rebekah's pants were unzipped. She'd been running from room to room, from test to test, carrying her parka and holding up her pants. She took me into her arms and held me as though I were her child.

Our midwife told us that we could cut Rebekah open, extract the body, and be done. A cesarean, cheap and fast. But she asked Rebekah to consider going through childbirth. Doing so would give her slightly better odds of success in any future pregnancy. Of course, she warned, a hormonally induced delivery would require a day or two or three of labor. Eventually, Rebekah said, "Okay." Her assent sounded minuscule, as though spoken by a girl.

We drove to the hospital and checked in to the maternity ward. Rebekah and I worried that we did not belong with the normal parents, but the head resident assured us that stillbirth was birth and that we were parents. "But what you're going through sucks," she said. "It just sucks."

Our room came with a candy-colored baby blanket and a matching beanie. I told the nurse who injected Rebekah with hormones that we wouldn't be needing the clothes. "They're for the photos," she said. I stared at her. "We won't be needing photos," I said. She removed the clothes, but after dark she returned them. She set them on a table in the far corner of the room and petted them, as though putting them down for the night. She whispered, "In case you change your mind."

In the middle of the night voices murmured through one wall, growing louder and more rushed until a baby cried out, clear and angry, accompanied by cheers. Rebekah rustled, then shifted. She was just a shadow. So was I.

In the morning, a social worker sat beside us. She had to verify that we were certain about the photographs. "I know this sounds weird," she said, "but parents in your situation who decline the photographs often return, begging us to please let them see a photo of their child. Don't you at least want the option to see photos—not now, but someday?"

"No," I said. Rebekah shook her head, and I signed papers promising not to sue anyone. The social worker asked if there was anything else we wanted to talk about, anything at all. I told her about the cry in the middle of the night. "That must have been hard," she said.

Rebekah didn't say anything. "Yeah," I said, "but it was also kind of life-affirming." It wasn't, but I knew that I'd have to see it as such—not now, but someday.

The social worker left her business card and a pamphlet she called "literature," which featured a teddy bear dressed in overalls. A butterfly had alighted upon the Teddy bear's nose, forcing him to cross his eyes and smile. "When Hello Means Goodbye," the title read. Inside was a collection of advice and verse that was written by other bereaved parents and untouched by affectation or talent. Rebekah dropped the booklet onto the nightstand, but I found succor in every artless word.

The booklet also presented a series of black-and-white photographs of a woman propped up in a hospital bed, holding an inert baby while her husband stood by. None of these stills dared to show the baby's face.

In the afternoon, we were visited by Rebekah's best friend and Rebekah's sister. When they arrived, I was sitting beside Rebekah's bed, wearing a new sweater and reading aloud from a magazine while we waited for the labor to intensify. We appeared perfectly normal. Realizing that there was nothing they could do, our loved ones cried.

Then they sat with us as we drank tea from paper cups. Our midwife put on a cardigan and joined us. Night was falling outside, but nobody stood to turn on a light. In the room, a spell was falling and none of us dared to dispel it.

We told our own birth stories. I stood to tell mine. My brother and I were delivered by a doctor who did not know, in the pre-ultrasound 1960s, that my mother was carrying twins. When he broke the news to my father, the doctor, a Japanese man, was ashamed. "So sorry," he said, bowing. "You have not one but two healthy boys." He bowed lower. "I only charge you for one."

As I bowed, all the women laughed.

Rebekah's labor grew heavy. Soon all she could do was breathe in and out. She sat still, physically in this world but attuning to the next one, the one that would deliver Irene. Our friend cried again as she said goodbye. Rebekah's sister said that she ought to be going and left. Then she returned. "I want to stay," she said. "I need you to stay," I said. She sat with me as Rebekah was increasingly possessed by her labor and by the strength she summoned to bear it.

Blood sloshed out of Rebekah and dripped onto the floor. The midwife pressed warm towels against Rebekah's genitals in an attempt to stop them from tearing. I took hold of one of Rebekah's legs, her sister took the other, and our midwife bent between, ready to catch the emerging corpse.

Someone once said that William Carlos Williams was sitting by the bed of one of his patients when she died. He turned to look out the window and saw a red wheelbarrow glazed with rainwater beside white chickens. I saw a salt-stained sidewalk under the funnel of a streetlamp, a beige plastic armrest beside a blue blanket, my left foot in a black boot slipping in my wife's red blood.

Irene was in the breech position and she came forth rump first. Our midwife said, "Push," and Rebekah pushed, and pushed again, pushed so mightily that at the apex of her effort the red hole in the center of Irene's exposed butt opened and a black turd slithered out.

Rebekah expelled Irene in a final burst, and I watched the prunelike corpse, embalmed in gore and ichor, flop into the hands of the midwife. The nurse snipped the bobbing umbilical cord and whisked the body out of sight.

I bent down to Rebekah and whispered into her ear that she'd committed the bravest act I had ever witnessed. Rebekah tried to make a noise or nod but she was numb. She closed her eyes. Then I turned to face our baby.

The nurse had set Irene's collapsed body under a heat lamp so that it would stay warm to the touch. She asked if I wanted to cut the remaining tendril of umbilical cord. I did. The cord felt alive and muscular; it was like cutting through someone's finger.

Irene was red, yellow, and blue, as limp as if she'd been thrown against a wall. Her nose looked as though it had been driven back into her head; it was a raw, upturned pug.

"A beautiful girl," the nurse said, tenderly nudging Irene's pudenda with her finger. "With perfect little girl parts." She traced the inverted V of Irene's nose. "That's because she was breech," she said. "Coming out backward, babies always get their noses bent out of shape."

Irene had mooned us, shat at us and now she'd gotten her nose bent out of shape. She even smelled like a sourpuss: slightly sulfurous and vinegary. She was a pickled imp, delivered at last from whatever it was that she had died fighting. I gathered my girl into my arms.

The nurse who'd induced Rebekah had tried to warn me. "The tone," she'd said. "After they've been dead for a few days, they don't have the tone. The tone is missing." What she meant was that my girl would feel lifeless. She had no blood pressure and so her face splayed flat in my hand, like a deliquescent tomato. I placed my thumbs above Irene's eyelids and eased them upward, intending to look into her eyes, but the milky, unfathomable slivers awed me and I stopped. The unknitted plates of her skull grated and clicked as I cupped my palm and rounded her face to its likeness, which I recognized. It was not like looking into a mirror. Facing a mirror, you see merely your own countenance; facing your child, you finally understand how everyone else has seen you.

When Rebekah opened her eyes, I handed her our child. She looked down at Irene's misshapen face. "Take her!" she cried. "Can you take her!" Rebekah's sister stepped in and scooped her up. I sat on the bed and ran my hands up and down Rebekah's hunched back as if to dampen her quaking. Her sister walked our baby around the room, rocking her and singing her assurances.

The afterbirth was causing problems. The placenta that Rebekah had been growing for eight months was supposed to slide out at the end of the umbilical cord like a veined lung, but it wasn't coming. It had somehow adhered itself to the uterus, possibly because of scarring from the summer's near miscarriage. Our midwife tugged on the dangling end of the umbilical cord. The cord snapped. "That's not supposed to happen," our midwife said. "I mean, it happens, but it's rare." She called in the supervising doctor.

The doctor inserted her right arm into Rebekah up to its

elbow. She braced herself and pulled. She exhaled, pulled harder. Rebekah's sister and I attempted to restrain Rebekah without slipping. I felt something inside her tear and the doctor slid back, holding a raw piece of the organ. She handed it to the nurse and reinserted her arm. She pulled until she again stood back, clutching another purple fistful. "I don't want for you to have to leave this room and check into surgery," she said. "Not now, not after all that you've been through." She reinserted her shaking arm and pulled. As I held on to Rebekah, her rigidity absorbed my own trembling. This time I did not look at anything.

Finally, the doctor stepped back, her bloodied arm hanging at her side. "I think that's it," she said. She asked the midwife and the nurse to please gather up the scraps of afterbirth and send them to the lab. Then a fever seized Rebekah, racked her, made her shiver so alarmingly that her sister and I gathered a mound of blankets and buried her beneath it. The nurse stuck more needles into her. Rebekah slipped into sleep, her eyelashes like a pair of parentheses that had each toppled to the side, releasing whatever secret they'd contained.

It was late now and dark and I was left alone with my family. Rebekah's face floated like a freckled moon above the blankets that swaddled her. I marveled at her, as if she were my child and I were seeing her for the first time. Across the room, Irene lay in the glow of the heat lamp.

The night nurse stepped in and told me that they were coming to take my baby away. Did I want to spend just a little more time with her?

"No," I said. "We've had our goodbyes."

In the middle of the night, I startled awake. A voice had sung Irene's song to me, but with a twist. "Good night, Irene," it sang. "I'll see you, but only in my dreams." *That's the chorus,* I thought.

Only in my dreams. Never in real life. By naming my daughter thoughtlessly, I had jinxed her. I had killed her.

I recalled the chorus radiating from a jukebox amid the smoky hubbub of a tavern, playing over the film credits scrolling down a blackened theater screen, howled by a friend from college, a rocker named Zollo. Zollo, who had chronic throat problems, had once set up a piano in the backyard at a party and croaked out "Good Night, Irene" as his final song. As he sang, I'd stood there with my beer and wondered, *Where have I heard this song before?*

Fifteen years in the future, that's where. I fell back asleep and dreamed of Rebekah sobbing. When I awoke in the dark, she was sobbing. I fell back asleep. At first light I awoke again and felt a split second of equanimity, of tranquility, before I remembered that none of it had been a dream.

We'd heard a lot from parents about the agony of lying awake at night, tormented by their children's cries. Instead, we were tortured by each other's.

Rebekah and I stepped into the shower, where I washed her body as gingerly as would a newlywed. The hospital served us milk and eggs. We drove home in heavy traffic beside the gray lake. I waited as Rebekah limped up the flights of stairs to our apartment. In front of our door was a box, standing like a sentinel. We knew what was in the box, but I carried it inside and opened it, anyway. Rebekah contemplated each hand-me-down jumper, each bib, each onesie, before folding it and tucking it into Irene's dresser, beside Irene's cradle and Irene's toys.

We climbed into bed and spooned together. Rebekah's breasts wept milk, so she bound them.

If Rebekah and I had lived two hundred years ago, when Illinois was still prairie, she would already have borne a dozen or more children. Those who survived would have lived to their mid-thirties, the age Rebekah is now, the age at which she, too, would probably have died, probably in childbirth. But at least she would have been allowed to bury Irene with her own two hands. She would have been able to advertise her mourning with a black veil or a rent garment, so that strangers would have known to oblige her: not to attempt to amuse her, or ask after her children. Strangers would know to oblige her. Nobody would have told her that stillbirth was a tragedy, or that she should try to make art about it, because every woman back then had babies who died.

The telephone began to ring. Only the older friends and relatives thought to send their wishes and prayers in writing. Everyone else wanted to talk. They wanted to feel for themselves what it was like for us to have glimpsed at once both the birth end and the death end of this wormhole we call life.

Rebekah's aunts insisted on visiting. They wanted to cheer us up. They were more nervous than we were; they greeted us with loud, determined voices and dramatic, almost frantic gestures. One yanked open a bag of nacho chips so violently that the chips burst forth and skittered across the kitchen floor. I followed the aunts into the living room.

The *living* room? What was that supposed to mean?

One aunt talked until the other picked up a sentence and ran with it, overrunning the silence I held to with increasing conspicuousness. I excused myself, said I had to make some phone calls. I went into my study and closed the door. The phone rang. It was my project manager at work. I told him that my daughter had been born dead and that he'd have to excuse me from everything, at least for now. All morning I answered calls from our other friends. Upon hearing the news, one collapsed. Her cries seemed to be my own, amplified through another vessel.

I assured her that Rebekah and I were doing okay and asked her not to worry about us. Consoling her took all my strength, but it was easier than being in that living room.

Another friend told me about his great-great-grandmother's diary. This woman had settled a home on the prairie, just like Laura Ingalls Wilder, whose work I'd procured for Irene's library. Reading the diary, my friend had been surprised by how common a certain sentence was: "'Baby died,'" he said. "'Baby died.'" Almost every year—the phrase was like a refrain.

As soon as Rebekah's aunts left, the fever that had seized her in the hospital returned. No more visitors, our midwife commanded. Strict bed rest. Rebekah's mother drove from Maine to help me watch over her daughter. On New Year's Eve, we sat on Rebekah's bed and served her steak and wine by candlelight. For several weeks, Rebekah's mother helped me with our shopping, cooking and cleaning. She sewed new slipcovers for our furniture.

A couple of weeks into it, Rebekah broke down. "I have to start doing things for myself," she cried. "I'm not a baby!"

She didn't want to go back to her old job. When she had recovered enough to walk around, she got dressed and rode a bus to the skyscrapers downtown, where she took a job managing an office whose employees knew nothing of her but her name.

The results of the autopsy came. Irene had died for no apparent reason.

We had to have one. We considered the fact that Irene had heard us argue. Perhaps our slam-bang shouting matches across the kitchen table had alerted our daughter at her gut level to be frightened of us.

Rebekah remembered having gotten drunk at a birthday party before discovering she was pregnant. She'd had high blood sugar and low blood sugar. Her thyroid gland had been out of whack.

Before Christmas, I'd heard an anecdote. Ernest Hemingway had once boasted that he could write a novel that was only six words long. Asked to prove it, he took a napkin and wrote, "For sale: baby shoes, never worn." At the time, I'd repeated this anecdote gravely but wryly.

I fixated on the song. Twice it had come to me in the night, as unmeditated as breathing, and I discovered why: the song is a traditional arrangement, meaning that no one knows where it came from; it exists in the air of our culture.

The very last words that I heard her say were, "Please sing me one more song."

> *Irene, good night*
> *Good night, Irene,*
> *I'll see you in my dreams.*
>
> *Last Saturday night I got married,*
> *Me and my wife settled down.*
> *Now me and my wife are parted,*
> *I'm gonna take another stroll downtown.*
>
> *Stop rambling, stop your gambling,*
> *Stop staying out late at night.*
> *Go home to your wife and family,*
> *Sit down by the fireside bright.*
>
> *I love Irene, God knows I do,*
> *Love her till the seas run dry?*
> *And if Irene turns her back on me, I'll take*
> *morphine and die.*

Huddie Ledbetter, better known as Leadbelly, is often given credit for writing this song, but he was merely the first to record it. According to legend, he heard it when he was in jail for attempted murder. When he got out, the song made him famous, and vice versa.

Rebekah and I tried to be strong for each other. But if I attempted a joke, she saw me laughing when our only child was dead. If she wanted to visit a friend, I saw her abandoning me to my grief. By trying to be strong, we hurt each other, and by trying to be normal, we grew numb.

On a rainy Saturday, Rebekah and I walked to the Museum of Science and Industry to see an exhibit of human bodies that had been preserved in plastic and laid open for our viewing astonishment. Rebekah stayed in the exhibit hall for twice as long as I. She made a side trip to see the museum's permanent collection of preserved babies. Fetuses, as people are always careful to say. On the walk home, Rebekah was calm, almost peaceful; it was as if those dead babies, folded in their jars, had reminded her that she was not alone.

After a month, we prepared for our first night out with other people—dinner at a friend's place. Our friend was eight months pregnant. She and her husband had moved into a big old house, and a celebration was in order. As we neared their driveway, running late, Rebekah started crying. "I can't do it," she said. "I can't."

I pulled over while traffic whizzed by. For more than a month I'd been inundated by family. Family! I needed to see my friends.

Rebekah needed to be alone. So I drove her home. The only words she spoke on the drive were to the effect that she didn't want to bring her curse to bear upon our friends. When I cast doubt on this superstition, Rebekah refused to elaborate. "I just really hate myself right now," she said.

I wanted to argue with her, but I didn't know how. I dropped her off at our door and drove back to our friend's house, where, surrounded by boxes and empty rooms, I picked at a casserole under inadequate lighting and talked about anything but.

After Valentine's Day, Rebekah and I returned to the hospital to attend a meeting of people who had "experienced perinatal loss"—miscarriages, stillbirths, accidents, babies with deformities so monstrous that the parents had elected to pull the plug.

Under humming fluorescent lights was a conference table with coffee and untouched cookies, ringed by twenty or so frightened faces, one of which was flashing indignant looks and leaking angry tears. The woman said that she'd lost her girl and now everyone wanted her to pretend that her girl had never existed. The rest of the room seconded her complaint. We finished each other's sentences. At last we were among people who could understand us. Society was on trial and we were the jury.

Everyone outside the room seemed to think that having another child would somehow erase the loss of this one, that death was some kind of math problem to be overcome by procreation. Everyone was supportive, but they were all secretly hoping that "it" would get better, that "things" would go back to normal, as if normal were an option, as if normal even existed. If one more person encouraged us to put it—it!—behind us, we might just lose it.

I asked the room, "What do you say when people ask you if you have kids? If I say yes, they're going to ask about them. If I say no, I'm lying."

Nobody knew how to answer my question.

At some point, a Mexican woman began to speak through her translator while her husband kneaded her hand. She had been carrying twin boys, she explained. For five months everything was fine. Then the ultrasound revealed that the heart of one of the twins had stopped beating. He had died, except he didn't die. His brother's heart came to his rescue by pumping enough blood for both of them. His brother kept him alive. But that baby was going to die, too, because his heart couldn't take the strain. So this woman flew to see a specialist who could extract the doomed brother so that his savior might live. But something went wrong. The translation wasn't clear, but in the operating room both of her boys wound up dead.

"My heart," the dad said in English, "it has been cut."

I cried, not because I'm a twin, and not because I felt for these parents, though I did. I cried because I was hearing a story that was worse than mine. I cried with relief. I was still lucky. We were still lucky. For the first time since Irene had died, I wasn't angry.

To claim Irene, I drove to a place that called itself a home. There I paid a man who called himself a mortician to hand over paperwork, along with what he called cremains. The ashes were stored in a cardboard box laminated with faux wood grain, like the vinyl paneling that adorns family recreation rooms and the flanks of station wagons. Inside the box was a gilded tin; inside the tin was a plastic bag closed at the top with a twist tie from which dangled a dog tag: Montrose Cemetery 27683.

At home, I removed the Baggie and threw out the box and the tin. I slipped the dog tag into an envelope along with the death certificate—there was by law no birth certificate—licked the envelope and sealed it. After a moment of deliberation, I filed the envelope under Medical Bills. After another moment of deliberation, I made a new file folder—Irene—slid the envelope in there, and filed it after Investments. Then I wept. That was my fatherhood.

Her ashes weren't like fire ashes. They were sandy, with tiny bits of bone not quite incinerated by the furnace, like the crumbled shells and coral that arc along the seashore, marking the line where the tide had retreated. There wasn't much: a handful or two, about what a family of four would shake out of their shoes after a Saturday at the beach.

Rebekah and I already knew which of her pots would hold the ashes. It was a squat vase that could hold only a single flower. Its small, circular foot swelled to a bulbous middle before contracting at the top to a nipple-like eye. The eye was so small you couldn't see inside it. You could put things in but they wouldn't easily come out. The urn resembled nothing so much as a top, spinning around on its point.

Rebekah had glazed it a glassy gray, like ice under an overcast sky. This glaze was webbed with nearly invisible cracks, like the fissures that knit the inside of an old and cherished tea mug. She had spun the pot on its foot and slashed brushfuls of a darker gray glaze around the shoulder of the pot, and this darker glaze had insinuated itself into the network of minute cracks, forming veined crystals that bloomed like snowflakes from bruised winter clouds, spiraling in toward the eye of the urn. A few burnt streaks of carbon still adhered to the sides. This clay had also passed through a furnace.

I sifted the ashes through a sieve into a mixing bowl. I rolled a sheet of paper into a cone, lodged the funnel into the pot's aperture, and poured in the fine ash. It hissed like sand from an hourglass. I took the larger, unsifted bits of Irene from the sieve and dropped them into the eye one piece at a time. When I came across a lump that was too large to fit, I put it aside. I resolved to begin a second pile of these larger pieces, one I would return to later and—what? Crush with a hammer? But at the end of my sorting, I was confronted by only the one lump. Upon studying it, I realized that it was a molten zipper pull. I debated keeping the relic, until Rebekah came home from work and reminded me that Irene had never been dressed in anything with a zipper. The zipper was from the body bag.

Although I will never forget seeing Irene, I have already forgotten what she looked like. I can no longer recall, exactly, her face. In the absence of photographs, all that remains is the image from her final ultrasound. I have returned again and again to this image and peered into it. The phantom gathering of features is so cloudy that my daughter could be anyone.

Postscript: On May 22, 2006, Rebekah gave birth to her and Dan's second daughter, Willa Raeburn.

ON INEXPLICABLE WEEPING
Dean Bakopoulos

It's Christmas Eve—snowy and windy, dangerously cold—and my daughter, Lydia, is running around in circles, laughing and shaking her head. She is three and a half. She is, against our better judgment, cranked up on the high-fructose corn syrup that laces candy canes and chocolate elves. And although the prospect of Santa Claus and reindeer on the roof and presents under the tree are all wonderfully exciting, she is anticipating something even more exhilarating: the limelight. In just a few minutes she will take the stage—wearing one of the many masks my wife, Amanda, an artist, has drawn and painted for this day—and become a donkey witnessing the birth of a savior.

We're at our small, progressive rural church, Plymouth United Church of Christ in Dodgeville, Wisconsin, just minutes before the start of the Christmas Eve service and the performance of *The Friendly Beasts* by the 2008–09 Sunday school class. And Lydia can hardly contain herself. She's dancing around, joking, twitching with nervous laughter. She looks, I think, just like me before I give a reading or lecture. Cool, laid-back on the surface—a happy clown—but nearly delirious with nerves on the inside. Her brother, Amos, just over a year old, watches her dance around backstage with something like terror and glee.

Unlike any of the other kids about to take the stage, Lydia knows her lines. She knows exactly what the donkey is supposed to sing. She's been practicing for weeks. She wants to own the stage. She's ready as anybody can ever be for anything.

And then, when the kids take the stage, all of the kids have the sort of deer-in-headlights look that dominates church youth programs, but not Lydia. She's focused. I'm working the camera in the front row of the church, and as I look on my daughter's face, I swear she's thinking: *Be the donkey. Be the donkey. Beeeee the donkeeeeey.*

The music starts. Lydia's the only kid singing the chorus, and then, just as the donkey verse is coming up, my wife gives Lydia the "get ready" cue and Lydia misinterprets the cue as "Now!" and she begins to sing her heart out. "I said the donkey," she sings (quite well, too, on pitch), "shaggy and brown."

But she's come in too early. And the six-year-old girl playing Mary thinks she's early, too, because nobody else is singing. It turns out that the pianist is playing the melody through once before the start of the first verse. And Mary turns to the donkey, my little girl, and gives her a harsh *shush*. Lydia goes silent. Her face falls. The adult choir members—the "backup" singers—take over and sing the donkey's lines and my daughter drops the donkey mask, absolutely crestfallen. She clamps shut. She says nothing, watches her big moment go by without her, and then, full of anger, she shushes Mary back, near tears, and comes off the stage in the middle of the number and crumples in my wife's arms.

I swear I can hear Lydia's tiny, perfect heart crack and shatter.

Later, in the Kiddie Keep room, my wife and I spend the rest of the Christmas Eve service listening to her wail. For about fifteen minutes she cries, thrashes around and expresses a desire to cut off Mary's hand. She's just seen *The Empire Strikes Back* (like the high-fructose corn syrup, it was another bad parental decision), and she's obsessed with Darth Vader's swift severing of Luke's limb; it's the perfect revenge. Lydia has an all-out meltdown. She's almost dry heaving with despair, and she shudders with each sob. And my wife and I, because we are artists ourselves and because we know the bitter burn of failure, let her get it all out.

I'm tempted to go back in the sanctuary, stop the Christmas Eve service and demand that my daughter get another chance. But even though I am a father, and there are many things that I can fix, I can't fix everything. I can't protect her from the bitter, ashy taste of failure, or its unwelcome cousins: dread, worry and regret.

By the end of the service, our family is back in the pew, lighting our candles to sing "Silent Night," and Lydia seems to be getting over the shushing incident and the fact that she didn't get to sing. She still is growling—literally growling like a cornered wolverine—at Mary and her family in the next pew, but soon enough she is running around the church basement with Mary, Joseph and all the friendly beasts for about an hour after church, buzzed on cake and cookies, delirious with the kind of breathless joy that children experience when running in a place where running is normally discouraged. But it's Christmas Eve. Nobody's going to tell these kids to settle down. In fact, I imagine at least a few of the adults would like to join in the screaming and chasing and leaping that's going on. All of us in need of a little steam release, so wound up we are with the chores of the holiday, the weight of familial obligations, economic uncertainty and the weariness of endless social effort.

Soon we are home again—the "Whole Four Family," as Lydia likes to say—in our little Victorian house, decorated with lights and wreaths and a gorgeous tree, and outside our yard is dusted with snow. *My life is a postcard,* I think, happy as I've been in a long time.

Lydia gets to open a few presents before bed. Amos has

already passed out for the night, and soon Lydia, who is still talking about the incident but in less violent, lamentable terms, falls asleep, snuggled up next to me as I watch the final thirty minutes of *It's A Wonderful Life*. Amanda is in the next room wrapping presents. I am in my long johns and a flannel bathrobe. But I am sipping on a glass of Irish whiskey on ice, and I am holding my daughter, and I am awash in my own tears. For the sake of decorum, and my wife in the next room, going about the business of Christmas Eve, I hold back what feels like a million desperate sobs.

After I finish my whiskey, I carry Lydia on up to her bed, tuck her in and go back downstairs to the kitchen. My wife is tying a ribbon on a package; soft Christmas music is playing. She looks at my face.

"What's wrong?" she says.

"She would've nailed the donkey if Mary hadn't shushed her," I say. "Did you see the look on her face?"

And I start to cry again.

"I know," Amanda says, "I know. It was my fault, too. I cued her too early."

Lumps in our throat, tears in our eyes, we finish wrapping presents.

Is this an overreaction? Well, of course it is. On Christmas morning, Lydia will wake up way more excited about Santa Claus and the presents and the stockings than she was about the donkey song. She will wake up smiling, restored. It's no catastrophe; it's not tragic. But there's still grief involved.

For me, parenthood is ripe with what I call "small mournings," those brief moments of daily clarity when you realize that you are unable to protect your children from every danger, humiliation and woe that the world can offer. In fact, because your children are human and you are, too, they are likely to experience all of those things with you, then later, without you, and sometimes, despite your best efforts, because of you.

And this is why I am now the sort of man who cries, all the time.

I can't lie and say that this is a totally new phenomenon for me. It's not as if I was a stoic, stiff-lipped soldier before. I'm Ukrainian and Greek, two cultures known for tolerating a bit of heavyhearted passion in their men. But since I've become a father, I've broken down in the middle of bits on *All Things Considered*. I've started weeping while listening to my town's only local radio station, Outlaw Country, and on hearing the sort of trite, cliché-ridden drivel that would have made me want to vomit just a few years ago. I've cried at the sight of my old dog running in the woods; I've wept at the baptism of other people's children. I've cried at the end of *A Charlie Brown Christmas*. The sight of those Peanuts kids turning toward heaven with their loo-loo-loo-loos is just too much for any grown man to behold.

I'm not sure if this is normal. Is it possible that men do not fully realize the precarious sadness of the world until they watch their own children try to navigate their way through it? Or is it that we have long realized it, and now the shattering part is that we must watch a tiny creature, whom we love more than anything else in the world, realize it, as well?

A few months after Lydia was born, our cat died. It was cancer and it was extremely sudden and she was only eight. I am not a cat person; but I was a *Willis* person. My devotion to the cat was limitless. Willis purred and squeaked when I heaped tuna on her cat food every morning to make it moister and more palatable. In the mornings when I wrote, she'd sit on the desk and wait for the sunrise and purr some more. My wife had gotten her as a kitten when we were first married; I declared loudly that Willis would not be allowed in our bedroom. That night Willis meowed outside the door, lonely, frightened, so I slept with her on the futon in the living room. I did this for a week, hoping to reassure her enough so that she'd learn to sleep alone. Eventually, my wife, Amanda, told me to let the cat in the bedroom so that *she* didn't have to sleep alone anymore. Willis entered the bedroom and never left. I developed asthma and hives.

After Willis died, I cried for two days straight; I could not believe my weeping. I'd be holding our beautiful four-month-old daughter in my arms. Lydia would be smiling and cooing and being as precious as she could possibly be, and her daddy was holding her, trying to smile back, but he was sobbing. The neighbors, good friends of ours, had a baby next day. I rejoiced for them, but I kept weeping. Small miracles—human miracles all around me—and I was mourning for this cat in a way I had never mourned for anything, not even other people.

This, I suppose, was the beginning of the Inexplicable Weeping.

A few days after we put Willis down, I left to do a reading in Missoula, Montana, where it was gray and raining and I spent a lot of time in my hotel room, missing my cat, or in one of the many bars, drinking two-dollar beers, looking for songs about cats on the tavern jukeboxes and feeling bad and small under the purple shadows of the mountains. I also missed Lydia. Since her birth, I had not been away from home for more than twenty-four hours, which means I had not slept through the night in four months. Lydia was, at least then, a good sleeper; her father was not. I woke every few hours in a panic, and I checked to see if she was still breathing. When I finally slept for seven hours straight my first night in Montana, I woke up depressed and lonely, rather than refreshed.

But back to the cat for a minute:

Willis was a well-protected cat. She was an indoor cat, because our street was a fairly busy urban street, a bus route, and the yards were small. There were many tougher, streetwise cats that roamed the neighborhood, as well, and I worried about her getting outside. In fact, I was maniacal about it. When we had houseguests, I would reiterate that Willis was not to be let out. When we had house sitters, Amanda and I left instructions so detailed that they resembled an FAQ from a corporate recall Web site.

For eight years, I fiercely defended Willis from any danger. And then Willis died. I had protected her and pampered her and had given her everything she ever wanted, and she was dead within a few days of her first symptoms. I watched her die. I was slammed. I couldn't protect her from anything in the end. There was suffering and I could not do anything to better it. As a new father, this was a troubling, and hollowing, realization. This contributed, I'm sure, to the days and days of weeping.

One of the most horrifying scenes in my literary memory comes from *Macbeth,* in Act IV, Scene iii, when Macduff is told that his wife and children have been killed in the shattering and ongoing cycle of violence that dominates the story. Macduff chokes out one of the saddest lines ever uttered on the stage: "What, all my pretty chickens and their dam at one fell swoop?"

Macduff, sobbing, is quickly reproached by Malcolm, who says, "Dispute it like a man!"

And Macduff snorts back, "I shall do so; but I must also feel it as a man."

I know that all fathers, and mothers, too, go to these dark places, when we imagine all the horrible fates that can befall our children. Not only do we worry about the sort of sense-less evil, war and violence that comes upon Macduff's family, but we also watch the news and imagine the worst: killer viruses, murderous weather and environmental destruction. I, on occasion, do lie awake at night worrying about these things, as well as other, more minor dangers, like sugar sensitivity, inadequate health insurance and the cost of college.

Worry is probably an unavoidable element of parenthood. And it's true: I come from a heroic and long line of worriers. I watch too much news. I often think in terms of the worst-case scenario.

But I don't think that's the reason why I sometimes get choked up in the grocery store and have to hide in a corner of the produce section for a minute. I don't think that's why I often come back from my morning walks with red eyes.

I think I puddle up when I realize that Lydia is growing up at an alarming rate and that each new day is filled with the life lessons and realizations that maturity brings with it. Sometimes people are mean for no reason. Sometimes you fail. Sometimes you have to get a shot and it hurts.

My family and I recently moved to Ames, Iowa, so I could join the faculty of the university there. We are now about four hours away from the small Wisconsin town where we lived.

But before the move I found myself unable to sleep at night, and yes, weeping, when I thought about Lydia packing up her room, which she didn't want to do. She loved her room. I cried when I thought about her saying farewell to her best friends, Hank and Franny, whom she loves with a passion that borders on obsession. I cried when I thought of all the people in this cozy town whom she'd come to know—Office Steve, or the hardware store owner, or the staff at Café Four—and whom she would be leaving. I cried for her when I thought about the playground, whose intricacies she'd just begun to master, or the city pool, where she was finally tall enough to touch the bottom.

I'm sure any parents who read this and have children who

are going through much more exhausting and substantial challenges—illness, disabilities, the death of the other parent—must find my weeping pathetic. They must long for life's hurdles to be as simple as the ones I've just lamented.

But my point is just that: none of the milestones I've described—from a botched role in the Christmas play to a move to a new town—are monumental or devastating to a three-year-old. My point is that parenthood, the birth of my first child, has not only brought me a great and unbelievable amount of joy, but it has also illuminated the world in a new way: as a place fraught with uncertainty and sorrow. As a place I can never control.

Dispute it like a man?

But I must also feel it like a man.

A few weeks after Lydia was born, a curious thing happened: our neighbors got chickens.

There was a new ordinance in the city of Madison that allowed people to keep up to six chickens in a coop in their backyard; in Madison, this was a big deal. People went chicken crazy, including our neighbors over the back fence. I am not a huge fan of chickens, but I did find it interesting (as did my bird dog, Milo) that we had chickens running around behind our house. (Later, I found it terrifying. After all, this was the year of the "bird flu" scare. I must have washed my hands [and baby Lydia's] a million times.)

One day, a hawk made his way into our neighborhood, probably while doing a flyby on the way to the lake and arboretum down the street. He circled in the sky over my neighbors' chickens for a long time, considering his options, and when my neighbors saw this, they decided they should keep their chickens locked up while they were at work, and not give them free range of the fenced yard during the day.

But a week later, I came outside and saw the chicken pecking around in the grass, despite the fact that my neighbors' seemed to be away from home.

I asked my neighbor about it that evening.

"Oh, yeah. That. Well, we've decided to let the chickens be chickens," she said. "And sometimes chickens get eaten by chicken hawks."

It was just small talk. Just two neighbors talking about their lives over the back fence. But it struck me as profound. *We decided to let the chickens be chickens.*

I have to remind myself of that simple statement again and again as a father. When I see my daughter, and now my younger son, embark on the business of living and its attendant disappointments and confusion, I have to pull myself back from the impulse to avoid all sorrow and to fix every mishap. I have to resist trying to control the universe. And all of that resistance, all of that buried impulse, I suppose, has to come out somewhere.

For me, I suppose, it comes out in the form of tears. I now often cry at the sight of chickens.

PUNK ROCK ROADIE DAD
Rob Spillman

Pity my daughter, for she is thirteen. When I was thirteen in 1978, I was a mess. But, to paraphrase the Velvet Underground, my life was saved by rock 'n' roll. The Ramones, the Sex Pistols and Talking Heads were in the air, but not at my school. At the Boys' Latin School of Baltimore, my popular classmates worshipped the gods of cockrock—Led Zeppelin, Aerosmith, Van Halen—while those not in the in crowd knelt at the altar of lesser rock deities like Rush, Styx, Bad Company and Ted Nugent.

Before Baltimore, I had grown up in Berlin, mostly with my single gay father, in the classical music world. My parents, both of whom were American classical musicians, separated when I was three. At eleven I moved to Baltimore with my mother and started attending the all-white Boys' Latin School. In Berlin I had been an outsider, but in a city full of outsiders, amidst a creative ex-pat community full of similar kids from around the world. At Boys' Latin, which I considered homophobic, racist, anti-intellectual, I was way way outside. I lived in the gritty, dangerous pregentrified Harborplace downtown and every morning I rode my bike to the edge of the city where the school loomed among the other mansions, my classmates' BMWs streaming by, some kids poking their heads out to yell "Germy" at me (clever, eh?).

With my allowance I bought a Tandy all-in-one stereo/eight-track/record player. At night I would listen to the radio, the volume turned way down so as to not disturb my mother, one floor below. One night, as I was inching down the dial, I happened on a college station playing "Psycho Killer" by Talking Heads. I was terrified, but also mesmerized. Blondie, the Ramones, the Velvet Underground, Television, Joy Division, the Sex Pistols—a whole new world followed. I couldn't quite put my finger on what it was that was speaking to me, but I knew it was different, that it was anti-everything-Boys'-Latin, not to mention my parents' classical music. Listening to the alien sounds beamed into my bedroom, I had the revelation that I wasn't alone—there were others out there, listening to this weird music of alienation, frustration, anger. There were others who did not fit in, and by listening to this music, I was suddenly not alone but part of a greater group of weirdos and outsiders.

My junior year I took extra classes so I could graduate a year early. Punk, new wave and underground music became my lifeline. Music was my motor, powered solely by negative energy—inside my music bubble I stewed, drank a lot, became a distance runner, pounding my body into the ground, then at night pounded my body some more in alcohol-fueled mosh pits.

In 1981 I was sixteen. I was a two-tone punk, my skinny lapels covered in pins. On weekends I would head out with the two other punks at Boys' Latin to the hard-core shows at the Marble Bar, a club in the basement of a downtown tenement hotel, every surface covered with black marble. TSOL, Black Flag, X, 999, the Circle Jerks—loud and fast, the music was an outer manifestation of my inner rage. "Live Fast, Die Young" by the Circle Jerks said it all. It was the end of the world. I didn't have a clue what I was going to do past age sixteen, and I didn't care. I wrapped myself in a sonic cocoon of narcissistic noise.

Flash forward nearly thirty years.

I'm back in clubs, this time onstage, lugging drums and

amps. Leather-clad dudes with long black hair who are half my age help me set up. Then my thirteen-year-old daughter takes her place behind the kit and starts wailing. The usually calm, composed teenager hits hard, her purple-tinged hair flying as she throws herself at the drums and cymbals, breaking sticks, yelling into the mic as her two bandmates jump up and down to the driving beat.

At three, the Ramones soothed Isadora. Mozart made her cry. She snubbed the piano in favor of the guitar. At age eight she wanted to go to Rock 'N' Roll Girl Camp in Portland, Oregon. Even though she'd be among the youngest campers, and despite her shyness, she wanted to go. Not only that, she didn't want to play guitar—"I can't make enough noise with it," she said—she wanted to play drums. The all-female faculty embraced her. Within a week she was part of a band and played in front of five hundred screaming fans.

When Izzy came home to Brooklyn, she and her good friend started a band. I'd never had the guts to play in a band. I had played the piano, dutifully grinding out scales with some aptitude but little passion, and I'd performed in numerous operas—I could sing and, like my parents, had perfect pitch—but to go up on a club stage and turn my inner turmoil outward, this I could never do.

John Lydon, formerly Johnny Rotten, fronted Public Image Limited, singing "Anger is an energy." For me anger was a negative energy.

Of course, rage and hate can often mask desire and jealousy. Did I, as Shakespeare wrote, protesteth too much? Did I want to be part of the Boys' Latin cliques? Did I want to be in with the stoner jocks who ruled the school? Did I want to look forward to four more years at some middlebrow mid-Atlantic college, where I would join them in a fraternity and date girls that looked like those boys' sisters?

No, a million times no, but with a little bit of yes.

Watching my daughter do what I never could was and continues to be a strange, humbling experience. I couldn't be prouder, but it does make me wish that I had been more like her. Picture my daughter covering Joy Division's "She's Lost Control" at age twelve. To me, this dour Manchester song was the end. To her it was only a beginning. To her the brooding feel of the song was empowering, a way to get control over complex emotions. Or the Ramones' "I Want To Be Sedated." Or the Clash's "Should I Stay or Should I Go?" Now she and the rest of her band, Care Bears on Fire, write all of their own songs, turning their fears, frustrations and hopes into musical statements.

My daughter articulated her intention to dance to her own drumbeat early on. When asked, at age five, if she wanted to join a soccer team, Izzy replied in all seriousness, "I will *never* wear a uniform."

I recognized this streak, and worried that her choice not to join would in time make her feel isolated and lonely, but it didn't. Not wanting to play didn't mean she wouldn't go and watch and cheer her friends on. Unlike me, she realized that you could say no to one aspect of life, without saying no to everything else. Life didn't have to be black-and-white.

Once, when she was in fifth grade, I was walking down the street in our neighborhood with Izzy and her mother when one of the school's alpha girls appeared in front of us. The girl saw her, put on a big smile and said hello. My daughter nodded to her and kept walking.

"Why didn't you stop and talk to her?" my wife asked. "Doesn't she want to be your friend?"

"No. She was just being nice because you were there," Izzy replied.

"But don't you care what she thinks of you?" her mom asked, clearly remembering her own days on the periphery of middle-school popularity.

"No. Not at all."

While our experiences with music are very different, the fact that she's an outsider at her school—has chosen to be an outsider—makes her very much like me. There is a common misconception when people learn about my daughter's band that she must be the popular kid in middle school. This assumption sends my daughter and her bandmates into screaming fits of laughter. Nothing could be further from the truth.

All middle schools have cliques of shiny, happy, superficial people who at the age of twelve or thirteen are at the apogee of their powers, those who have mastered the social rituals that would impress even a Tolstoy or Proust. After Izzy returned from playing four shows in three days at the South by Southwest music festival in Austin, Texas, the leader of the mean-girl clique at my daughter's school greeted her with, "Oh, my God, you missed the best manicure party ever. *Every*body was there."

If it were me, I wouldn't have replied, would have gone off and turned up the Velvet Underground and stewed. Isadora, on the other hand, takes the dumb girls and drops them into her songs—"Pleaser," "Five Minute Boyfriend," "Everybody Else." The inane, bovine joiners are immortalized in perfect angry pop/punk songs.

Watching Izzy navigate through the hellish waters of middle school, like Jason steering the *Argo* past the sirens' call of death, I can't help but feel a fierce pride. I'm envious of her self-confidence, but even more so of her strength and kindness toward her friends and her brother. I want to take credit, but she certainly doesn't emulate me. If anything, I emulate her.

COACHING PHOEBE
David G.W. Scott

I've set out eight pairs of orange plastic cones about three feet apart in a corner of a rough, makeshift soccer field where my daughter's middle school soccer team practices. I'm the coach. We've lost all but three games in the three years since I started the team. The ladies in the office want to get me a T-shirt that says "Winningest Coach in School History" which is technically true.

These are artsy kids, children of professors and musicians, and soccer is a tiny wedge of their daily pie. In fact, there are several who just want to run away from the ball, their faces a mix of fear and dodgeball delight. Other kids take everything literally, and when I tell them to play on the other side of the field, they stand on the far sideline and are hard to coax off it. They never remember their equipment, and when they do, some just don't know what to do with it—socks over shin guards or vice versa?

They're brilliant in other ways. The school is progressive and small. The soccer field backs up to a rental house in a stand of trees, where, during one practice, I had to tell the kids to keep their eyes on me—not the deer skull and antlers curing on a tree. What I mean to say is, it's not your typical athletics program.

I'm explaining what I want them to do, which is to dribble through as many "gates" as they can in thirty seconds. My daughter, Phoebe, is listening to me but looking at the gates, perhaps planning a route.

She's the shortest, slight and small for thirteen, but she's the most powerful soccer player on this coed team, dwarfing the other players in soccer ability. I started working with them three years ago, when Phoebe was in fifth grade. She's been the center midfielder—like a quarterback—for her entire career. Now, in eighth grade, she's a legend.

Phoebe is ready to cut a path through these cones, so I finish my instructions and I say, "Ready. Set. Go!" She's off. It's late October and we've just switched our clocks back, so the late afternoon sun is beautiful on her auburn hair. She moves like a soccer player, cutting the ball with the outside of her foot to set up her next turn, now rolling the ball with the sole of her cleats, her ponytail flashing at the back of her head. There is nothing more beautiful than this.

Around her, shrieks of dismay and delight careen around the field. A ball whizzes past my ear.

I grew up playing basketball. A country kid with a hoop bolted to a barn. I had visions of being a college basketball star (like my uncle) until I enrolled in a summer camp at Phillips Exeter Academy right before I entered high school. My coach there, who had put me in charge of our team, asked me how tall my father was.

"About five-eight," I said, smiling and breathing hard after completing a shooting drill. I was a fiery kid with lots of temper, but also lots of gumption and not much quit.

"Do you play any other sports?" he asked. I really think that he wanted what was best for me. But I was a basketball player, on the cusp of beginning my high school career. I was stunned. Then, devastated.

"Baseball, uh, soccer, too."

"Good. You should think about those. It's going to be tough for you. It's a tall man's game."

I spent the rest of the summer chucking the worn leather ball my uncle had given me at the backboard, punting it into the night sky. I watched the bats dart and duck and disappear into the blue-black New Hampshire night.

Soccer. It made sense for my body type. There was lots of running around, lots of open space. I could practice endless hours by myself in the yard and take shots against the barn wall. I ended up loving soccer. There is a simplicity to it that I find sweet. And there is a deep complexity, crazy depth of skill and an openness to creative interpretation that has kept me engaged in the game for thirty years.

I ended up being a good high school varsity player on a team that won the state championship my senior year. I played Division I college soccer at Villanova University, where I was a walk-on. I spent a season in the New York/New Jersey metropolitan league with the Union Lancers in the late 1980s and then a few seasons with the group that became the Greensboro (NC) Dynamo while in grad school. All this to say, I made it pretty far up the American soccer food chain.

And I kept my children out of it. The American sports mill grinds kids up, spits them out, turns them against the sports that are supposed to give them a lifetime of activity, recreation and health. Instead, crazed parents and coaches judge success by wins and losses and discard the kids who can't cut it. We end up losing kids—not to other sports—but to the blue pallor of indoor inactivity, i.e., gaming.

So I kept them out of sports for as long as I could. But really, I was dying to have them play. When Phoebe was five and my son Finn was three, we lived across from a grassy common, and we'd kick the ball around—no lines, no offsides, no real teams even, no formal coaching. I just played and they played with me. We played Keep Away, Monkey in the Middle and Knock Down the Cone! Sticks on the ground marked the goals. And Phoebe was fast and competitive with a natural affinity for the ball. When she did finally step onto the soccer field, she was almost a fully formed soccer player. She had a natural grace and balance, and combined that with speed and determination.

A defining moment came in a U10 (under ten) game. One of the other players booted a ball into her face. It lifted Phoebe off her feet and sent her flat on her back. She had the wind knocked out of her. She got up and kept playing until she got the ball back. She asked for a sub and collapsed crying into my arms. She cried for about seven seconds, wiped her face and said, "I want to go back in now." That's Phoebe.

I wanted to be the type of coach who would encourage players, make them have fun playing the game. I did not have many coaches like this. My high school coach would grab me by my jersey, pull me up to his face and call me gutless. He ended up killing himself after my sophomore year. Throughout college I struggled with a coach who couldn't find a regular place for me among his scholarship players. For many years after that I railed against mindless referees and their dim-witted linesmen. I became a hothead, was kicked out of one league altogether, was red-carded even as a coach for yelling at the ref.

And then I started my fifth-grade daughter at midfield in a middle school soccer match. I encouraged the kids who were terrified of the ball. I cheered when they made simple traps and passes. I found the positive in every aspect of a lopsided loss— and I never had more fun in my life.

There are only a few other soccer players in Phoebe's middle school of forty-five kids, but I let anyone who wants to play come out. I start by teaching them the absolute basics of passing and receiving the ball with the inside of the foot. I teach them that there are twenty-two players on the field and one ball. And that the goal is to move the ball as a team toward the opponent's goal using the feet, legs, chest and head, but never the arms or hands. I show them how to perform a throw-in. I teach them that the soccer lines are imaginary and extend upward to the sky.

Our first season—with Phoebe at center midfield—we lost every game and scored only one goal. We played teams filled with mostly eighth-grade boys. We played real soccer teams, and we were the cultural outreach program of our school. No, we didn't hand out admission packets at halftime, but I wanted the team to be a true extension of the mission of the school. I integrated the school's core virtues into every practice: respect, self-discipline, giving, perseverance, compassion and honesty. All of these applied to team sports and to this team.

At practices, I say, "Every good pass makes our whole team better."

After each game, I say, "This is one of the most important times of the game for me. We were just involved in a competitive game. I want you to tell each member of the other team 'Good game,' but you have to mean it!"

I tell the parents, "We're looking for competitive moments on the field. If we find ourselves in a competitive situation, say with the ball at our feet and we complete a pass to a teammate, then we've had a success. We'll let others judge the success of the match by looking at the scoreboard."

As an ultracompetitive person, I've been forced to find success with this team. I figured out that losing each and every game in our first two seasons did not constitute failure. In fact, the soccer program was one of the great successes of the school, according to the director, because it put the students in challenging positions where they had to reflect the values of the school.

But by Phoebe's eighth-grade season, I wanted her to have success the way the rest of the world defined it. I wanted her to win. I wanted to touch my lips to the golden cup and taste the sweetness of victory! This would prove to be a challenge. I blow the whistle and Phoebe drives her ball through one last gate.

"How many gates?" I ask one of the other girls.

"Four," she says, a little out of breath.

"What happened?"

"I kicked the ball into the hydrangea bush and didn't want to defoliate its branches."

"Ah, I understand," I say, moving on. We practice on the school's playground, not a true soccer pitch, so there are some unexpected situations. "Keep at it. Next! How many?"

"Six!" Tyler says, very proud.

"Awesome. That's a record for you, isn't it?"

"Yes, but no. Six is the number of Plecostomus in the aquarium. I couldn't find one of them today, but after my ball went under the building, I saw the tank sitting in the window and decided to count again. Six!"

"That's great. You didn't get any on you, right? I mean, a pleco-sphere isn't hazardous, is it?"

"No. It's a fish, Coach. A fish," Tyler says, clearly disgusted by my lack of fishy knowledge.

"Okay, back to soccer!"

I go down the line, saving Phoebe for near the end, but not for last, because that's too prideful. I know she's got more than the other kids.

"Phoebe?"

"Sixteen," she says quietly, a hint of grin curling at one side of her mouth.

"Okay," I instruct the group, "now top your own mark. Ready. Set. Go."

I need to make it clear that Phoebe is not just some sweaty jock who mindlessly pounds a ball all day. She is also an accomplished artist. Last summer, we were at wits' end as to what to do with her. It's too hot to play soccer during the humid Florida days. We had purchased a pottery wheel the year before and she'd made a bunch of cups and bowls with a friend of ours, but she'd been so busy with soccer and school that the gray clay was caked and dried. Her unglazed pieces littered her work shelves.

I searched online for summer camp, pottery and Tallahassee, and—surprise, surprise—found a summer pottery camp in town that was starting the next week. She took off! The teacher was accomplished—an artist and a businessman, doing gallery shows and selling his work nationally. Phoebe kept bringing home these amazing pieces. First a facejug. Then a raku-fired pot. Then she brought home a large bowl with a beautiful metallic glaze. The teacher talked about her combination of manual skill and artistic vision. It was her best summer experience.

I realize I'm jumping around a bit, but Phoebe's complicated like that. She's not some one-dimensional soccer droid. And I'm not a soccer-crazed dad bent on having his child fulfill his own unrealized dreams of stardom. But I am worried about that in myself. I constantly recognize moments where I am pinning goals on Phoebe and need to arrest my ambition for her, and let her find her own.

After practice, we drive home and talk about which players are improving, what type of drills we could do to get more organized on the field. It's really the sweetest time with Phoebe.

My sons are eleven, eight and almost two, and they all play soccer, too. Maybe it's that Phoebe is the oldest and the first to go through this. Maybe it's because I took over training her and her team three years ago, but we seem to have a deeper soccer connection than I have with the boys. This strikes me as odd. I just assumed I'd be connected with my sons through sports and that I'd search for ways to connect with Phoebe.

I think the truth may lie in the middle. Soccer is the conduit through which we connect. For both of us, soccer is creative, an outlet for us to express who we are with our bodies. Others do it with dance or music or swimming or gymnastics. I can see that Phoebe's personality comes out when she's on the field. I think mine does when I play.

Okay, time to come clean. I'm holding back. Coaching Phoebe is like a thrill ride at a cheap carnival. It's wild and herky-jerky and I love it because it's going to end. How long can I hang on? How can I will myself to enjoy the wildness of it, and *not* wish for the ease of its ending? Can I relish these lightning quick days? Will the memories of them be any solace once they are gone?

Those of you who have gone through it know all. But Phoebe is my oldest. She was born by cesarean section after thirty-six hours of labor in the hospital. When my wife went under the knife, I huddled by her head, talking to her, not able to bear to see her cut open. And not wanting to pass out. Then they lifted Phoebe above the blue curtain that separated me from the incision in my wife's abdomen. She was perfect. She was staring at me from the incubator, even as my tears were dripping out onto her.

"Don't cry on the baby," a nurse said to me, and then she squeezed opaque cream into Phoebe's eyes. I was in over my head. *Don't cry on the baby?* Did someone actually say that to me?

I vowed to cry on the babies. I vowed that I would be involved in the lives of my children, that it would be messy and I would let it be so.

I knew it would be wild. Life was going to pull at me, my children would demand things from me, but I was going to give them everything I had, everything I have.

And this brings me back to coaching Phoebe. In the first game of the season, we were playing a team that was beating us by five or six goals. I wasn't keeping track. I wanted Phoebe to have a good soccer moment, but also the traditional kind where you score goals and win games. I was caving on my idealism. Also, the coach of the other team was a younger guy who I played against in the local league. Dark and frightening thoughts were creeping into my head. At halftime, I told Phoebe that in order to beat these tall eighth-grade boys, she would need to pass the ball into the open space behind them and then run to the ball by herself, rather than trying to dribble past them. Early in the second half, she had the ball across midfield, and she passed it to a teammate.

"Phoebe!" I shouted, and then made a hand gesture, signaling her to pass the ball into space.

She waved me off.

I was irate. "Phoebe!" I held my hands out as if to say, what are you doing?

Again, she waved me off.

"Lars, go in for Phoebe."

Lars, unaccustomed to playing, removed his hands from the pockets of his cargo shorts. (He had forgotten his soccer shorts at home that day.)

"Where is she playing?" he asked, which was a logical question from a kid who wasn't really paying attention to a game that baffled him.

"Center midfield."

"Where is that?"

"In the middle of the field. You run all over the place. You just go get the ball."

"Okay." And Lars started to run onto the field.

"Lars! You have to wait until the ball goes out of bounds."

"Oh, right," he said.

A few seconds later Phoebe was standing next to me. She was very mad. "What are you doing?" she asked.

"You can't wave me off. I'm the coach."

"I know what I'm doing."

"You're not doing what I told you to do."

"Look," she said, "the score is five to nothing. It's the first game of the season. I don't care about scoring a goal. I have to get my teammates involved, make them feel confident so we can get better. Having me dribble around the defense doesn't make us any better. It doesn't make our team improve."

This is the part of coaching and teaching, oh heck, the part of life I don't like. The moment when you must eat crow immediately. That the error of your ways is so apparent, so obvious—even to you!—that the only action possible is to open wide and bite into it fully.

"You're right," I said. "I'm sorry. Go back in for Lars. He's playing left Plecostomus."

Sometimes, the child is father to the man. Sometimes the daughter is coach to the father, and I think that if I'd missed that moment, not let Phoebe coach me, I might have undone years of work.

As she stood at the sideline, waiting to reenter the game, I looked at her. She was poised, already involved and prepared to make her team better. She did not look at me. She did not look back. She would not have liked what she would have seen. Me, staring at her with awe and wonder, ready to cry into her upturned face. I imagine she might have said, "Don't cry on the baby."

Last night, our team played its archrival. Both teams had four or five real soccer players on the field, and those four or five (and the coaches) knew it. But it was a really fun game, lots of end-to-end action. We scored first (our first goal of the year!), and they came back to tie the score. My sixth-grade son, Finneas, scored a beautiful goal, and they tied it up again just a few minutes later. With about ten minutes left in the match, Phoebe got the ball at the left corner of the penalty area. She dribbled to her right. And she dribbled again.

"Shoot it, baby, shoot it," I said to the field. "Why isn't she shooting it?"

And then she did. A right-footed blast that tucked neatly in the top right corner of the goal. I was on my knees. I punched the soft ground with my fist. Everyone was yelling and screaming. A beautiful goal. She couldn't hear me. She was celebrating with her teammates. I didn't coach her. She did it all by herself.

EL CORAZÓN
James Griffioen

Despite the obvious handicap of receiving half her genes from me, my young daughter has turned out to be an attractive kid. Of course I think so: I'm her father. I am sure I would still feel this way if she had a face that could back a bulldog out of a meat truck. But any parental bias has been repeatedly flamed by random, well-intentioned strangers we encounter during our days together (I am a stay-at-home dad). "She is going to be trouble someday," they all say, almost always followed by the same punch line: "You'd better get a shotgun."

The general consensus among the people we encounter in elevators or grocery aisles is that someday I will need to maintain a small arsenal to keep a population of rabid male teenagers at bay. I picture myself behind the barrel of a Remington 870, a doe-eyed future version of my daughter behind me in short shorts with the tip of her pinky wedged in the corner of her mouth as hordes of dim-witted, neckless jocks try to break down our doors like zombies who definitely aren't after her brains.

When I was in high school, I once asked a nice redheaded girl from the cross-country team to accompany me to the winter formal. On the advice of two middle-aged homosexuals who ran the Rainbow Thrift Store downtown, I bought an ill-fitting waiter's tuxedo and made sure the cummerbund matched her dress; I bought her a corsage and clutched it nervously while approaching her front door. Her screened-in porch was dark except for the embers glowing intermittently at the end of a lit cigarette sagging in a man's mouth and illuminating his disapproving gaze a demonic orange. Her father just sat there while we waited for his daughter to finish getting ready, staring at me with that 12-gauge glare. I was seventeen and terrified of even talking to his daughter, and here he was, treating me like a Nordic berserker there to cut him with the blood eagle and haul his daughter off to Reykjavík. Couldn't he see that the shy, pimple-faced teenager his daughter was pinning a boutonniere to that evening had no designs on her other than maybe slow dancing to a slamming track? What was wrong with this guy?

Fast-forward a few months and I'm in some other girl's living room. It's the whole movie cliché: Her parents are out of town; a cassette is in the stereo. Judging by the fact that she's sitting on my lap with her face in my neck, I'm guessing she likes me. Why, then, am I so terrified? She fumbles around the button of my jeans, and I ease her hands away. "Not so fast," I say, fairly certain that I'd heard some girl in a movie say that once. I knew, from movies, that I was supposed to want her hand in there. But I also knew it would have repercussions. I was pretty sure regret would come with daylight, if not much sooner. Others would find out. I'd have to hold her hand at school. The more serious things became, the more serious the hurt would be when everything fell apart. And it would. "Slow down," I said. And she did.

Other scenes would follow, in basements, dorm rooms and the backseats of cars. I saw girls turn into creatures surely more terrifying to their fathers than a thousand lustful suitors: human beings who actually enjoyed the way their bodies made them feel. The girls who eased me into sexual awakening were almost always more Apollo than Daphne, more bullish than any Europa. In darkened rooms, most girls know they have the power to reduce even the most domineering boys to quivering, vulnerable supplicants.

This is the truth of basements and backseats; there is an unspoken understanding that you must learn all this on your own terms, this private, exotic knowledge of another: their breath and hands and the smell of their hair; the delicacy of the inner thigh; the strange delight and awkwardness of it all. It is as important as any other knowledge we learn. Years before we see it all for what it is, left to our own devices, in darkness we learn about each other with our hands.

My wife grew up in one the most religious and conservative communities in the United States. On a recent trip back to her hometown, I decided to use my daughter as a ploy to get inside one of those daddy-daughter purity dances advertised in the events section of the local paper. This one included a "purity circle" where the teenage daughters of several members of the congregation took a vow of purity until marriage and the men took an oath "to go to war" for their daughters' purity, to acknowledge themselves "as the authority and protector" of their daughters' virginity. I didn't go as a journalist. This was espionage. I wanted to actually hear these fathers talk about what it was that drove them to fight for their daughters' virginity with a ceremony at the local Holiday Inn.

It was like a school formal squeezed of anything fun by the iron fist of evangelical Christianity. Most of the older girls were wearing formal attire, while the younger ones wore "princess" dresses. There was a deejay and a balloon archway for photographs. The girls danced with their fathers at arm's length to songs about Christ's love. I sat down at a table with some other men with younger daughters, all of whom were running around playing with balloons. I was the only one at the table who didn't belong to their church, and they spent most of the conversation pressing me to attend the next day's service with my family. The church, they said, offered a weekly schedule of fun-filled activities that, as one man put it, ensures "your whole social circle is godly people."

When I explained that my reason for being there was fear about raising my daughter in an increasingly immoral society, the discussion quickly turned to The Problems with the World Today:

Some girl at the public high school sent a picture of herself—naked—to her boyfriend and he sent it around the entire school!

Some of the clothes they sell nowadays are so suggestive. Like baby prostitutes.

My brother sent me an e-mail about these lipstick parties. You heard of them?

It seems like kids just aren't allowed to be kids anymore.

Here were men of my own generation sitting around like a bunch of kvetching old farts witnessing the collapse of everything good about the good old days due to secularism's foul-smelling tsunami of moral degradation. This was a perspective encouraged by a church preaching signs of the End of Days. By the end of the conversation, I just wanted to give them each a hug and whisper in their ears, "The world has not survived this long in spite of lesser generations. It has survived because of them."

Then a man just a bit older than me piped up, a contractor with a goatee and a blue blazer that seemed uncomfortable at the elbows: "I remember what I was like as a teenager. I want to protect her from guys like me. I certainly wasn't pure of heart, mind or body when I did get married. I want something different for her." Despite the hypocrisy of it all, I got the sense that this man's feelings and intentions were genuine. He was not railing against ungodly enemies, oversexed barbarians at the gates. He just wanted to protect his daughter from himself.

In the end, the event seemed no different than any other ancient or primitive fetishization of virginity. Men who feared losing control now felt empowered. The message was repeated over and over that girls who act out sexually have not had good father figures. Girls with "daddy issues" become the women we do not want our daughters to be: the porn stars, the strippers, the whores. When a father plays a certain role in his daughter's life, he supplies all her emotional needs, and she need not seek the "wrong kind" of attention from other men. The wrong kind of attention becomes right, of course, only when she's ready to get married.

If this all seems creepy, like a bunch of evangelicals obliviously heeding a road map of Jung's half-cocked Electra theory, it wouldn't be far from the truth. I left thinking of Sophocles' *Electra* and the line delivered not by a father, but a vengeful brother: "It would anger me to see another try to take me from you." Not *you from me,* but *me from you.* I thought of my own daughter, and I knew that deep inside I shared the same fears as any father, but I knew also that the fear was actually of being supplanted by a stranger, of her giving him her heart and him hurting her in some way I couldn't protect her from. The boy on the porch is a scapegoat. What a daughter really needs protection from are a father's irrational fears.

"You'd better watch out," one of the men warned as my daughter ran past, a comet with a tail of helium balloons. "She's going to be trouble."

"I guess I'd better buy a shotgun," I replied.

"You don't already have one?" another asked. "I keep mine loaded with one round in the chamber."

Before my daughter was born, my wife fell in with a new group of women who would all be giving birth to their first children the next February. Like dorm assignments or cellmates, you have no choice in these matters. Just look around at the women with bellies roughly the size of your wife's and the nervous-looking men by their sides. Say hello to your new friends.

These women sat around talking about their biggest fears in a new vocabulary of words like "episiotomy" and "anal fissures." Off to the side, their men sat around talking about their biggest fear, namely that the birth of their child would cause them to miss the 2005 Super Bowl. These were men already acclimated to fantasy sports leagues and March Madness office pools, so naturally they created a pool for their firstborns' birth dates, with the "winner" being the guy who had to spend the Super Bowl massaging his wife's shoulders while they waited for the epidural to kick in. He'd get about two hundred dollars.

"I'm not even going to lie," one guy confessed. "If labor is going to be like thirty hours or whatever and the game is in the middle of that, I'm totally going to find a way to watch it."

At some point in these pregnancies, the date approached for the ultrasounds to determine the sex of all our fetuses. One of the other fathers said he just wanted to know if his was a girl so he would have the rest of the pregnancy to come to terms with it. One woman told my wife she knew her husband would be devastated if the prognosis was pink. There was something so Old Testament about it all. These men were Web developers and investment bankers, not Plantagenet kings or Chinese peasants. "Why?" I asked one guy almost sobbing into his vanilla latte after the ultrasound tech was 80 percent sure his was a girl. "Maybe the tech was wrong," I said, "and really your son just has a microscopic penis." This made him cry even harder. "What's the big deal?" I asked.

"Because one day she will be a teenager," he said in all seriousness. "And man, that's just going to kill me."

I wondered if after my own daughter was born, I would understand this anxiety. But as she's evolved from feeble infant to chattering preschooler, I find it pretty pointless to give much thought to her future sexuality. I find it kind of disturbing, actually. Are teenage girls so terrifying that we should fear them when they're embryos? Is beauty really so dangerous as to create anxiety in a father even when she is just a child?

There's obviously nothing wrong with men wanting to defend their daughters from legitimate threats. Dads *should* protect their daughters. It's part of the job description, like falling asleep in a hammock when you're supposed to mow the lawn and owning obscure power tools. But what about men (such as myself) raising sons as well as daughters? How do these ingrained attitudes about young men as uncontrollable sexual maniacs fit with the reality of raising one? There are no purity balls for young men, no oaths for mothers to battle for their sons' virginity. There is, of course, a long tradition of the double standard, the stud/slut dichotomy. Virginity is really only relevant when there's a hymen to shatter.

To a homophobic father, the only fate worse than having a daughter who's a slut is having a son who "chooses" to be a homosexual. As if raging hormones weren't enough to handle, some teenage boys must live up to their fathers' expectations by never showing what their fathers would consider signs of homosexuality, encouraging a weird, hypersexualized masculinity. If a father already expects every adolescent male to be sex-crazed and dangerous with respect to his daughter, isn't this a stereotype some brothers might see fit to live up to, especially if doing so proves heterosexuality to an anxious father?

Teens who have pledged abstinence until marriage often speak of their virginity as a gift, of their love as something that must be saved for the one man with whom they will spend the rest of their lives. They speak of sexual relationships that do not begin in marriage as giving pieces of their hearts away, leaving nothing for the man who will be their husband. What a sad misunderstanding of love this is, to treat it as a finite resource, non-renewable and impossible to replenish. This is an idea of love sold by some parents to their children, despite the truth that every parent learns upon the birth of a child: that just when you thought you couldn't possibly have more of it to give, your baby shows you how much your heart is capable of; and if you have more than one, you see how no matter how much you might have loved your first, there is within you a bottomless well from which you will find more.

I know that one day I will be white-knuckled, waiting for curfews. And I know I will give any potential suitors a good looking over. I feel the same urge to protect my daughter as any man would.

But I believe the hardest part of being a father isn't preventing a daughter from becoming a sexual creature, but allowing it to happen in as natural and healthy a way as possible. I'm not even sure when it comes to sex that what my daughter will need is best treated as protection. I don't plan to teach her that all boys and men are predators. That certainly is not my own experience. As the father of a son, I hope to teach both of them that all people owe each other respect, and to watch out for *anyone* unwilling to grant that.

To expect a daughter to save sex—or even love—for the person she will one day marry would be to deny her the chance to learn what both of those things really mean. As a father, I only hope to use my relationship with my wife to model for my children the kind of relationship filled with respect and equality that I hope they'll one day find themselves. In the end, it is an act of weakness, not strength, to demand chastity from a daughter. It takes strength to stand aside and let her navigate the darkness without you.

My daughter has a curious obsession with the human heart. When she was only three, she would ask me to draw hearts when we were out chalking the sidewalks, and she'd reject figurative valentine-style hearts in favor of realistic ventricled blue-and-red lumps with severed aortic arches and pulmonary veins and auricles sticking out of blue atriums. "*That's* a heart," she'd say, having learned of *el corazón* from the lotería card we purchased at the Mexican grocery store.

Sometimes I think children get freaked out by things only after we expose them to our own prejudices; I pinch my wife extra hard when we're at the meat counter of the Mexican grocery and she starts gagging at the piles of spotted cow's tongues or beef hearts as my daughter's nose is pressed against the glass. One day we watched videos of working hearts on the computer and the creeping sense of doom came over me. This is what I have been avoiding since 9th-grade science, this reminder of that weird glistening universe that exists within us all, that pulsating network of wet alien tubes and tanks and tissues. The surgeons in the video chatted casually above the gaping chest cavity, and my kid watched, not the least bit bothered or frightened by it. I tried not to let her see me wince or turn away. *Why should she be scared of this?* I asked myself. What is it that makes us frightened of what's under our skin, if not the grim reality that our souls are tethered to dirt by those crude mechanics? "Do I have a heart like that?" she finally asked me.

"Of course you do," I answered. "You have a very strong heart. It's the size of your fist," I said, wrapping her little fist inside my own, squeezing it over and over against her chest while whispering "pu-dum, pu-dum, pu-dum" against the cool skin of her temple. I try to picture that heart inside her, so strong and fast and young.

She laughed and put her ear to my chest and listened. "I can hear your heart, Pops," she says. "It's a strong one, too."

A few weeks later I sat in a doctor's office, waiting for my wife-mandated thirtieth-year physical. I hadn't seen a doctor in a decade; he slipped the stethoscope onto my back, my chest. "Your heart sounds great," he said, echoing my daughter's diagnosis. I felt relieved, walking out through the cardiovascular ward looking at the faces of those with less optimistic prognoses. "As you are now, so once were we," their grim faces seemed to say. Out on the boulevard, I looked at all those bodies moving around in the afternoon sun, all those hearts nestled somewhere inside cages of bone among slithering viscera.

There was a time or two in the many years that my wife and I dated when we tried to break things off. There were hours of total darkness. There were thoughts, and more than thoughts, that maybe some other person might make us happier. There were times when ambition and geography threatened what we'd found in each other. Once she left to spend a year in Beijing and we tried to break up, and to say this broke my heart is not quite right. I remember doing a lot of running then. I would sprint up a mile-long stretch of hill, trying to get my heart to burst, but I could not run hard or fast enough. At the top I would double over, sometimes collapsing to my knees, picturing nothing but my heart at its brink inside my chest, nearly broken but somehow stronger because of this unnecessary exertion.

Another time we broke up, I was so despondent I went to see a counselor, a former professor who spoke gently about why seventeenth-century ascetic artists painted Christ with his heart on the outside of his chest. He said this symbolized not only his infinite, unguarded love for all humanity but also his vulnerability, particularly in those depictions of him nailed to the cross with his arms outstretched, his heart completely exposed, lance-pierced, but still burning with love. Vulnerability, he said, has its own sort of power. It lets you love even when you have every reason not to, to keep your heart on fire even when you have every excuse to let it go cold.

"Do I have a strong heart?" my daughter still sometimes asks me. I tell her it is a very strong heart. Her question sends me spinning, thinking not only of that tiny mortal organ inside her chest, *el corazón,* but her figurative heart: the heart of pop songs and bad teenage poetry, the one that will lead her through life's greatest joys and disappointments. I felt so helpless knowing that as sure as it has a rhythm separate from my own, there will come a day that it will suffer, and there will be nothing for me to do but hold her bigger fist in my hand again and squeeze it, and if she'll listen, I'll tell her how strong it still is, that it is never really torn or broken, but merely wounded and exposed, and that even in that state of terrible vulnerability, the most important thing to do is never let it grow cold.

THE MAN ON THE STAIRS
Robert Wilder

I am sitting at a round cafeteria table, two white circles like eyes on my brown tray: a plate of chicken enchiladas with Spanish rice and a bowl of salad drenched in ranch dressing. Thin flatware on a flimsy napkin. The middle school science teacher—who the kids say resembles Brad Pitt—is at my right elbow and the Latin teacher is at my left. I'm only half listening to the chatter about last night's vice presidential debate and academic matters. Instead I am staring at the entrance of the gymnasium, two steel doors propped open with thick textbooks, waiting for my daughter Poppy's head to pop through.

Poppy steps out slowly, her auburn bangs catching the shards of light that shoot across the room. Hair in ponytail, she clutches her green domed lunch box like a poorly designed shield. Her eyes scan and search, mouth flat, preparing for downturn in market. I can't take it, this painful waiting. My eyes well. I look away at the student microwave, the glass dripping with explosive inner liquids.

I started working at this school when Poppy was three months old. I was hired to teach seventh-grade English, but the girls' soccer coach needed an assistant, so I agreed to help when I could swing it. It was still summer 1996. I drove Poppy in my three-cylinder Daihatsu Charade, unclicked her from the base of her car seat, and carried her behind the goal, placing her back to the sun. Taking a baby to a high school girls' soccer practice is like bringing chocolate to a fast: players would stop dead in the middle of their passing drills and race to Poppy, tickle her feet, ask to hold her and coo like I'd seen actresses do in the movies. When I helped with the boys' team, Poppy was just an errant piece of athletic equipment that didn't need or deserve any further examination. Teenage girls, however, ate my daughter up.

Having just finished graduate school, I seemed to be growing roots. I had a half-time job teaching seventh-grade English in the day while the other half had me putting down plates at a local restaurant called Fabio's at night. I could now claim both a wife and a daughter on my tax return. A girl. My mother died when I was freshly seventeen and left me with my dad and three brothers in a flatulent house of men. I had always sought the comfort and friendship of women (often mixing those two up with tragic results), but now I had this girl. "Like forever," as my students would say. My wife, Lala, grew up in a house of women: three sisters and her mom. While we were dating and well into our marriage, we'd often hold tutorials on the other gender: why boys don't care so much about dirty silverware or washcloths, how girls sometimes just need you to listen to them without advice or comment. For hours. Our little "he said about guys; she said about girls" was mostly informational and often comical but didn't prepare me the way I'd hoped it might.

On the soccer pitch, I was cradling Poppy in the crook of my left arm like a football in a diaper, all while directing players in a short-sided game with my right. The longtime field hockey coach strode up to me, I mean us (now I was an us), her own daughter sweating in the scrimmage between the white lines. She didn't touch Poppy, as others did, just blinked at me from behind foggy eyeglasses.

"Just wait till Poppy comes to Prep." She nodded like a reluctant psychic.

"I'll be dead by then," I joked, and although I didn't think I'd really be underground, I couldn't imagine what having a child at my place of employment would feel like—the wheels of Poppy's overloaded backpack whirring in the English office hallway at 3:23, secretly viewing her diminutive figure on the volleyball court from the bleachers above, the ache, the joy, the worry. I was thirty when I held her like a wriggling pigskin at a soccer practice. I knew I wanted to write short fiction, hopefully someday a novel. I yearned to be a good father but only had a sliver of an understanding of what that meant other than changing diapers and taking this baby with me to fetch the mail or visit her mother vending with the transients at the flea market. No idea that this notion of bringing her along with me meant that we would someday share a campus for six years of our lives. If we both make it through, she'll be eighteen when she strolls the quad in a white dress, carrying three elongated lilies. I'll be forty-eight.

The English office where I work is maybe eight feet by ten feet and I occupy the west end. Plastered on the wall behind my computer are sketches my children have made over the thirteen years I have been at this school. The most recent additions are a series of Marvel superheroes my son London has created and the oldest are from when Poppy was barely old enough to clutch a Crayola. The drawing nearest my face is a portrait of me—red skull, a W of hair floating above a smiling although misshapen head. Two long sticks for legs and one swoosh intersecting them are my handless arms. A yellow sun burns next to where my neck would be if I had one, while on the other side are two orange spheres with lines penetrating them like balloons, lollipops or, as a biology teacher once enlightened me, spermatozoa. While Poppy was in preschool, she started signing her name as a series of those lollipops, three or four or five in a row. Lala and I slowly saw her lose those images as they evolved (or devolved) into a series of letters: *p-o-p-p-y*. Those lollipops were just undeveloped *P*s waiting to crawl out of Poppy's primordial muck. But the thing is: we liked her muck. We loved her muck. Many parents would feel proud to see their chubby-faced daughter write her name for the first time, but Lala and I felt a great loss. You cannot go back to times before you could write or read a sign. "Society never advances," Emerson writes in *Self-Reliance,* a text I try to win over on scowling teens every year. "It recedes as fast on one side as it gains on the other." I don't think good old Ralph was thinking about a tiny girl with a diastema learning to scrawl her name. But I am.

(P.S. At tennis camp this summer, a counselor told London that his spelling of *beast*—*b-e-s-t*—was wrong and had him change it. I wanted to sucker punch the sandbagger.)

I am sitting in an indoor arena, on the redbrick observation deck. There is a green director's chair to my right and a half fridge behind me with bottles of water stacked inside it like logs. On top an old plastic biscotti container is filled with plain and peanut M&M'S; next to it rests a memo pad and pencil and two books I have never read: *Directory of Equitation and Carriage Driving* (in German and English) and the *United States Dressage Foundation Directory.* In the arena, my former student Anya, who is now a junior at Stanford, is walking on the soft brown dirt. Dressed in black, she is directing Poppy, who is atop a Mexican pony named Peter. I try to envision what Poppy will be like when she's Anya's age—in college somewhere (probably not Stanford); I try to transform her by ten years, make her taller and less self-conscious. But I can't even get her to the age of my own students—seventeen—struggling over Hawthorne's "The Birthmark" and letting me know about that struggle in painful detail. No matter how I try, I still see those copper bangs, eyebrows that need no plucking or waxing, lips red enough for people to think the color originates from a tube. I wish her to be taller if nothing else just so she can get the bridle over Peter's head and the bit into his mouth without help from Larry, the gracious barn manager. *What would it be like to have Anya as a daughter?* I wonder as she stomps in her clogs, pushing Poppy to watch her carriage, her hands and other subtle gestures I can't see or understand. I imagine Poppy away from home, calling me about her postwar literature class, trying absinthe, driving a car (not as nice as Anya's Audi), my daughter behind the wheel of a moving vehicle, playing songs she may not have even discovered yet. I can catch a glimpse of that older Poppy, face a bit longer, giggling after a friend in the front seat does something silly with her hands. Poppy tilts her head back and laughs, then places her eyes back on the curving road ahead.

Peter's hind end lunges into the air as if he's been stung by a bee. I rise, the magazine sliding from my lap. Time slows considerably. The horse (no longer a being with gender to me) leaps off the ground, its back end first, then its front. I glare at Anya, hoping (praying? do I pray?) she can swoop Poppy off the black saddle somehow—the wooden slatted wall and two large bay windows growing closer to the horse and what seems like a human scarf flying about its neck. Poppy is bouncing up and down, side to side, trying to hold on to the beast's crest or withers, so hard to tell. I am now on the second step leading to the arena. My knees are shaking, knocking together in a cartoonish way. I want to run onto the dirt but what would I do? Punch the horse? I cannot help my daughter. I cannot scoop her up from the high school bleachers before she takes another tumble as I did eleven years ago. I cannot pull her out of the Bicentennial Pool near our home after she's gone under the blue.

Cannot steer her away from the snapping dogs or thorny patches of goathead on the cracked sidewalks we frequent together.

My fingers are shaking now and the tiny reservoirs behind my eyes fill with irrelevant tears. *This is what it means to be a father of a daughter,* I think as Poppy pushes herself off the shit-crazy pony and rolls away. Anya does something with her arms but the horse ignores her, bucking and jumping even though no one is requesting a flying change or a simple one, a canter or trot. I am so glad Lala is not here to see this but I miss her nonetheless. Even my own father wouldn't understand—he had all boys, each one hardening him a bit more after burying his wife. Poppy lies far away from me and I am only slightly higher in elevation. That arena, the oval space and golden light with bits of hay and dander floating in it, is hers, not mine. Even the danger that is married to the joy of moving quickly atop a galloping horse has nothing to do with this man on the stairs. I am merely a spectator, a visitor standing dumbly in the wrong shoes behind an old wooden gate.

Some parents never watch their daughters ride again after a fall. They sit in their cars in dirt parking lots, reading popular paperbacks or chatting on the phone with girlfriends about mothers they know who let their kids stay up until 4:30 a.m. or eat Twinkies for breakfast. I still observe with a mix of pride, terror and love that seems right for a guy like me with a daughter like Poppy. And it's worth those moments afterward when she leads Peter by his reins into the cool shadows of the barn and I smell the mix of manure, wood chips, hay, and sweet grain. I ask Poppy how Peter was and she says, "He was so good," patting his neck hard enough for me to hear. That's how she must have felt while being tossed around—terror, pride (of being able to hold on) and love for this creature shown through immediate forgiveness and understanding. "He thought I was asking him to do something he hated," she tells me. "Poor thing misunderstood. All one big misunderstanding."

I'm sitting on the floor. Sunday night. The yellow wall is to my back as I listen to how I cannot possibly understand what it's like to be her. How, after homework in science, math, Latin, New Mexico history and English, after riding three times this week, it is unfair to ask her to hike with the family, play memory with her brother or clean the house. How we never really listen to her.

I explain in my caring teacher voice (firm but supportive) that no one likes to vacuum, and I know she has a lot of homework, and we appreciate her diligence, and of course she wants a cell phone and it must be hard being one of the three in her class who doesn't own one. And of course she wants to see an R-rated movie starring Angelina Jolie with her friend Sarah. We let her decide when to do her homework and clean, giving her some autonomy, and when she needs a phone, she'll get one. And it's fine by us if she wants to choose another movie to go to with Sarah.

Then she delivers the rude, sarcastic comment that she probably (read: definitely) gets from me. I tell her so (without mentioning the origin) and close the door. Her surfer chick sign rattles like a big Brooklyn raspberry.

Later, after her mother has gone in twice and I've slipped the dishes into their corrals, brushed her brother's teeth (what's left of them) and put on his Hank the Cowdog tape and kissed and cuddled him like you do to a seven-year-old boy who still has all of his sweetness left, I knock. There is my daughter in the shape of a backward C, crying into a hillock of stuffed animals. She tells me what she's already told her mother—she feels anger that she cannot control, rage at us and she doesn't know why. And here's the clincher—a boy at school has been calling her names (*lesbian* and *bitch,* ones reserved solely for females). I have been that boy, I can be that boy, throwing barbs to see if they'll hook into skin and make the object of my attention turn and attend to me. Poppy doesn't understand what made him change from a quiet, awfully shy guy in sixth grade to this cruel creature in seventh. I tell her why he does it and how she should steer him away from the pack, look him straight in the eye and demand he cut it out, ask him what happened to him. As I'm doling out advice, I think how easy it would be for me to find this kid, among the unsuspecting parents and teachers, and squeeze his arm firmly enough to let him know I'm not messing around, whisper in his ear the kind of words that scare a student.

Even though I consider this more my school than any seventh grader's (which is wrong), this is her battle, not mine, and real love forces me to let her, paraphrasing that great twentieth-century philosopher Popeye, "stands it until she can't stands no more." And it will take strength from me not to track him on campus. I know Poppy is not perfect; she can be boastful and tease with the best of them. But instead of watching her get bucked on a horse from above on the observation deck, I am sitting below her and her mom, two women, one twelve and the other forty-five, all eyes full of tears. My first instinct is to run but then I go into gear, wanting to fix everything for these two women, fix it all for them and leave the pain for me. I lost a woman when I was young and I don't like to see mine suffer. But suffer they will. Someday that toothless boy sleeping in the room behind the wall to my back will need the same amount of attention, but he will require something different. A boy's needs are not the same as a girl's and a father's love for a daughter is not the same as his love for his son. A father's love for his daughter is borne out of weakness and that's the way it should be, if he only lets it.

CONFESSIONS OF A FAUX PA
Swan Adamson

He's her dad. I'm her faux pa.

I have accepted that she is not of my blood or biology. And because she is not "mine," I have never overstepped the boundary line that separates a child from her stepfather.

But I've wanted to. For most of the thirty years that I've known her, I've wanted to barge in and take over her upbringing. I pull back because I have no rights to do so.

Even "stepfather" is little more than a courtesy title. We've been together for thirty years, but my partner and I can't marry, because we're both men. Adopting his child has never been a legal option, because from age five to eighteen, she was mostly raised by her mother and saw her father (and me) only at appointed intervals. Now, when our thirty-five-year-old daughter introduces me as her "stepdad," I feel ridiculously grateful because I know what a small role I played in her upbringing.

A shadow hovering on the sidelines of a child's life—that's what being a stepparent is. (A shadow of a shadow if you happen to be a gay stepparent.) I wonder sometimes if it's more diffi-cult *not* being the parent. For anyone who's honest, observant and intuitive to the needs of children, the role of stepparent can be enormously challenging and emotionally frustrating. You can see exactly what's going on and what desperately needs to be addressed, but you can't do a damn thing about it.

Except argue with your partner.

And have long, exhausting conversations with your conscience.

Because, after all, of that insidious way guilt works, you know you are responsible for breaking up the child's home and introducing chaos and uncertainty into her vulnerable little life. You are the boogeyman who ripped away her security blanket and showed her the sharp fangs of your smile. You're the thief who stole her daddy away from her mommy.

How can you wriggle free from those strangling, Laocoönian serpents of guilt? You know that the union that was supposed to guide and support the child was a mirage. You know that her parents' marriage was doomed and that nothing could have saved it. You know that the fracture lines in that family structure were already there. But in the end, those are all rationalizations. Because you also know that *you* were the one who delivered the graceless coup de grâce—huffing and puffing until you blew a little girl's house down. You were the agent of change...the kind of change that no child ever wants.

You, being of guilt-ridden Scandinavian-Catholic stock that always assumes the worst, assume that the child will hate you. Or at least that she will regard you with resentment and suspicion. As she weaves you into the tapestry of her life, you can be certain that you, the gay stepfather, will be turned into a toad-tongued gargoyle instead of the charming prince your deep-seated amour propre would have you be.

I'm not breaking any new ground when I say we parent as we were parented. And I'm not breaking any vows of silence when I say that my stepdaughter's upbringing left a great deal to be desired. (She would agree.) I fumed and fretted but ultimately could do nothing to change it.

All I could do was "be there," a smiling ghost at her father's side, in the unlikely event that she ever came to me for help or guidance. Which she never did. My role, as I saw it, was to be welcoming and nurturing to a little girl who would have much preferred to be with her father and mother—together. She dutifully hugged me when requested to do so, but her heart was never in it. It always felt more like the kind of "performance hug" children learn in order to placate elders who insist on displays of affection.

It was something of a shock to discover that the person I'd fallen in love with had a child. But, as an ex-Boy Scout, I was primed to take on any situation and try to make the best of it. I did what I could. I was more than courteous. When her dad picked her up on weekends, I let her sit in the front seat, next to him. I wanted her to feel special, like she was the focus of his life. I didn't want her to think that I had usurped her father's affections. I was an awfully nice person, but I knew that little six-year-old girl had plenty of reasons to dislike me.

This is one of the hazards, I suppose, of being a fiction writer: you are forever seeing what is and imagining what isn't. You are in the moment but you are also analyzing the moment; you are with the person but are also observing the person; you are absorbing the situation but you are also shaping it into a potential story. And the story waiting for this little girl had me worried from the get-go. Perhaps it was because I didn't come from a "broken home" myself, and could only imagine what it would be like for a child to stand helplessly by as her parents separated and her world collapsed. Also, I'd been raised in a large family by a mother who absolutely loved kids, and my mom's caring concern for children had rubbed off on me. I wanted the best for my partner's daughter.

But by the 1970s that idealized model of strong, wise, selfless parenthood I'd grown up with in the *Leave It to Beaver* era was seen as cornily naive, stiflingly oppressive and a barrier to self-actualization. My partner, who had spent almost forty years trying to be heterosexual, developed an unshakeable determination to cast off the person he wasn't and find out who he was. That meant moving from Portland, the scene of his false life, to New York, where I had already moved.

What about his daughter?

Starting when she was eight years old—my stomach turns over thinking about this now—she began to fly out to New York, by herself, to spend a week with us every four months. The coast-to-coast flights back then required a change in Chicago, and though we were always assured that a flight attendant would escort her to her La Guardia–bound plane, it was a nerve-wracking experience for all of us. She was a real trouper about it, but internalized her anxiety so much that it resulted in mysterious stomach ailments, one of which was so severe that her dad had to take her to the emergency room. He would fly back to Portland at regular intervals between these visits to see her. But the day-to-day, year-in-year-out nitty-gritty of parenting was left to her mother. And it's there, of course, in the environment of the everyday, that life lessons are learned, life experience imparted and life patterns established.

It gradually became apparent to me that, in Portland, my stepdaughter was basically being left to raise herself. She was an only child, with a mother who was clueless about discipline, a father who was unwilling to set any kind of limits from afar, and me. It wasn't that she was naughty; it was that she had no guidance. Children do not know what is best for themselves or how to negotiate and regulate their lives: those are things they internalize through observation and example.

Her fearful mother never said no, and her guilt-ridden father always said yes, so she grew up thinking that whatever she did was all right and unchallengeable. Educationally, she was at the mercy of mediocre public schools (as I had been), which didn't challenge or inspire her. Spiritually, she was in limbo. Neither parent had any truck with "God" or dared to impart any moral or ethical wisdom of their own. Her understanding of money— where it came from, how it worked (or didn't), how it was earned—was being shaped by the welfare model adopted by her mother. And culturally, until I took matters into my own hands, she hadn't progressed beyond the banalities of network television.

When I went back to Portland and saw the environment she was living in, my middle-class heart nearly broke. It all looked so shabby. Her dad paid for child support so the basic necessities were covered, but her mother hated to work and didn't regard it as particularly important, so the duplex where they now lived had a makeshift, made-up, downwardly mobile look to it. I knew I could do nothing to change this living environment. As a writer, I was barely making ends meet. My partner was trying to run his own architectural firm, which ate up all his money. And anyway, the issue here wasn't really about money—it was about parenting. Which to me is as much about imparting commonsense wisdom as it is about providing a decent home.

Maybe as a lifelong gay person I saw the situation more clearly, or more judgmentally. It's always puzzled me how heterosexuals can accuse homos of destabilizing the family unit when they are the ones who are producing and neglecting their offspring.

I was the one who was consumed by endless, futile worry about how their child—I still didn't allow myself to think of her as *our* child—was going to mature into responsible adulthood with so little guidance and so few expectations. I had absolutely no right to demand any changes in her mother's "lifestyle" or outlook, and though I harbored a fantasy of having the child come to live with us in New York, I knew she would never agree to being uprooted from her mother in Portland and living with us in our cramped apartment on the Upper West Side, where she'd have to sleep on the sofa.

Nine years old, ten years old—things continued the way they had. We developed our own New York rituals. The night she arrived, we would always have dinner at Empire Szechuan on Ninety-seventh Street and Broadway. Her dad would take her to Saks and buy her a stylish outfit. I would arrange for us to go to a Broadway show or the Metropolitan Opera or a museum. Or a movie or out to Jones Beach or up to the top of the World Trade Center. She would visit her dad in his office on West Twenty-fourth Street or go for walks with me in Central Park. My goal was to broaden her horizons and make her love New York and the opportunities it presented. She met our friends, both gay and straight, in their apartments and where they worked. Nobody talked down to her. Everyone loved her because she was lovable and because no one else in career-oriented New York had children. Ours was an entirely adult world, completely different from her life in Portland.

I have some indelible memories from those adolescent New York visits. One day, out in our back garden, wearing her new outfit from Saks, she showed us how to tap-dance. Another day, during a rainstorm of monsoon proportions, we realized that the garden drain was blocked and the water was rising so fast that it would flood the apartment. We pulled on our swimming suits, dashed into the drenching storm, and bailed bucketsful of water away from the door, drenched and laughing hysterically. One morning she wanted an English muffin, so I pulled out our old, unused toaster, dropped in a muffin, and pressed down the handle. A moment later, an army of cockroaches flew out of the toaster, fleeing imminent immolation. I gasped in surprise; she screamed in horror; we grabbed whatever utensils came to hand and futilely beat at the insects racing across the kitchen counter.

Eleven years old, twelve years old—her visits continued with no major problems. I allowed myself to be lulled into complacency. But then, one shocking day when she was thirteen, she arrived with half of her beautiful black hair shaved off, the other half dyed a gruesome shade of green, and a peace symbol painted on her bare skull. She was sullen, sulky, uncommunicative. She'd taken up smoking. Something was obviously wrong but she wouldn't talk about it, and her father was unwilling to admit that she might need some help. It was more than puberty. I sensed a kind of brooding, self-destructive anger brewing inside her. I took her to see *The Miracle Worker* but I had a feeling it was going to take more than a miracle to get her safely through her teenage years.

This was when I started to argue with my partner about what was happening to her. I wanted him or her mother to get serious about setting limits. I was angry and disappointed with their ineffectual responses but had no authority or ability to change what I saw as my stepdaughter's descent into very dangerous waters.

To this day I don't know the full story of her Portland life between thirteen and sixteen. Obviously she was acting out the anger and unhappiness of her life. Every nonlesson or bad lesson was on display. She made decisions—always bad decisions—and presented them as faits accomplis. There was no constructive interference or intervention from either parent. They both seemed to be afraid of her.

Bits of information were given to me, passed on from her mother to her father and then, sometimes, doled out to me. Just enough to make the well-behaved, middle-class, overachieving control freak in me livid.

"She's going to quit school."

"She's decided to be a model."

"She's playing Dungeons and Dragons all the time with her friends."

"She's going to AA meetings."

Each new revelation sent me into paroxysms of fury and fresh, futile fights with my partner. His smart, beautiful daughter was in danger! This was a call for help. Couldn't he see that? Her entire future was being derailed. Were both parents going to stand idly by as she was sucked into a world of drugs, alcohol, fantasy mind games and pornography? Because that was what was out there, just waiting to prey on gullible, aimless, immature teens.

But what was the solution? Move back to Portland? Life outside of Manhattan had become unthinkable.

My hesitant little pep talks to her, infrequent and ineffectual, counted for nothing. She'd retreat into a deflective silence. No one was allowed to challenge her decisions or demand a change in her behavior. Her anger—which I don't think she's ever fully examined or exorcised—was like a slap in the face for years of dithering indifference. How dare any of us offer advice now? *It was too late.*

Was it too late?

In some ways, yes. In other ways, no.

We did move back to Portland, but that didn't alter her general outlook on life or prevent her from making (what I considered to be) one bad decision after another. My problem, I realized, was that my expectations didn't fit the reality of who she was, or thought she was, or was trying to be. The parental neglect had left her dangling in a void. She had to create herself, as we all do, but she didn't have the right tools to make sound judgments. She didn't want "safe"; she didn't want intellectual rigor; she wanted excitement and drama. She was always, at her core, a "good girl," but she seemed unable to think clearly about the possible consequences of her actions. When she decided to do something, no matter how extreme or outrageous, she convinced herself that it was the right thing to do. There was no backing down from the dare she'd given herself. Nothing could dissuade her.

She often bit off more than she could chew, and was forced to back away from decisions and obligations she had talked herself into and then realized she did not want to complete or fulfill (such as joining the army or marrying at nineteen). But she kept moving ahead at her own pace and toward her own goals. She finished her GED and went on to earn a degree from a community college. Today, after more life dramas than I have room to recount here, she is a bright, capable woman who holds a highly responsible position as an accountant, is the mother of a wonderfully bright eight-year-old daughter and is happily married.

She has created a life for herself the hard way and on her own terms.

A few years ago I created a life for her, too. I wrote a novel about my daughter and about our peculiar family dynamic. The novel almost wrote itself. And it came out as comedy. My publisher didn't like the original title—*The Dads*—and asked for an alternative. So I changed it to *My Three Husbands.* Our daughter had had only two husbands by that time, but the title came true in 2008.

I tried not to censor myself as I wrote it. I tried to imagine myself as her, dealing with what she had dealt with. I wrote in a fictionalized version of "her" voice. It was unlike anything I'd ever written before, and it was both exhilarating and terrifying.

Even though it's fiction, I like to think that it captured a bit of her life. And mine, too.

DO I DOTE?
Eric Goodman

Nearly twenty years ago, I published an article titled "Daddy's Girls and the Fathers Who Adore Them" in *McCall's* profiling three father-daughter pairs: Seneca and myself; a high school student and her father; and Lloyd Bridges, the star of the television show I was writing for, who had two famous actor sons and a third child, Lucinda, the daughter upon whom he doted.

McCall's sent a photographer to our rented house, and in my mind's eye (it's also displayed on our present living room wall), I can see one of the photographs snapped that morning. A smiling three-year-old in a red-and-white sundress sitting on her daddy's lap, having a storybook read to her. If that photograph were taken today, it would show one of us with considerably less hair, a fact Seneca never tires of teasing me about. I can recollect the long-ago moment the photograph records as if it were taken yesterday, and Seneca says she can, too; she remembers being excited getting dressed that morning because the Photographer! was coming.

At the time, and here is the point I have been trying to get to, I knew next to nothing about parenting a girl. I'm one of three boys, and for reasons that make little statistical sense, nearly all of my childhood friends also came from daughterless families. Because I attended an all-boys high school, not only little girls but girlhood in general represented an unexplored continent on which I had landed at age thirty-three, heart in hand. What I've learned over these past twenty-plus years is that if there's anything sweeter than a little girl's love for her daddy or, for that matter, a grown-up girl's love for her father, I don't know what it is, except, possibly, a father's love for that daughter.

Do I dote? Yes, I do.

I should mention that Seneca was a lovely child and has grown into a beautiful woman, with large dark eyes, thick dark hair in profusion, light brown skin and post-racial features that are assumed to be Eurasian in Southeast Asia, or Mediterranean in Europe, but which in fact represent a blend of Mexican, Native American, French, Irish and Spanish antecedents. I can boast, shamelessly, about her good looks because I'm not genetically responsible for them. We adopted Seneca the day she was born, and since her older brother (also adopted) had by the age of five or six (the moment that *McCall's* photo was taken) claimed his mom as *his,* Seneca, at least in those early days, was mostly *mine.*

So how did I respond, knowing little about little girls, to having this exquisite, smart, sweet-tempered child hanging off and on me (I did the middle-of-the-night floor-walking and bottle feedings for both our kids), proclaiming, "Daddy, *my daddy!*"

By deciding, with my wife, that the way to raise a girl, especially a pretty one, was to act as if her gender and appearance didn't matter. We'd drop Seneca at preschool, assuring her it was her job to return home with her clothes dirty. We'd hike most weekends, and I'd do my best not to carry her even when she begged to be picked up, praising Sen as the best three-, then four-, then five-year-old hiker in California. Later, because I love sports and because Seneca was strong and well-coordinated for her age, we signed her up for T-ball and soccer, and for several seasons in middle school, I coached her soccer team, along with another team dad.

Those were fun father-daughter years. We spent a great deal of time together, joined not only by our love for each other but by our love for the sport and the shared enterprise. Seneca reached her adult height (somewhere shy of five-five) quite early, and for several years she was larger and stronger than her peers. And she was tough, no girly-girl Seneca—opposing players got out of the way of her shot and her elbows—and something of a star on the team. I'd been an enthusiastic high school athlete, talented enough to play several sports, but never the standout she was at that time in her life. And how sweet it was to watch Sen dribble through the opposing team and boom one home, though she preferred playing defense even then, preferred not to put herself in the spotlight—and it was the first minor discord between us.

She's always been kind of shy, less forward than her brother, who takes up a great deal of psychic space. At that time Sen had a new reason to be shy. Her body developed before any of her friends'. By the end of fifth grade she had disappeared into extra-large sweatshirts and didn't reemerge until partway through eighth grade, pursuing the unassailable logic that if no one saw her shape except in muted outline, no one would suspect what had happened.

In hindsight, my response to Seneca's early physical/sexual development was laughable, yet paradigmatic of both the way parents learn from their children and the way writers cannibalize the lives of everyone around them. Rather than freaking out that my daughter was no longer a "little girl," I published a long research article on the changing age of menarche, starting with the observation that my daughter and her soccer teammates were getting their first periods at ten and eleven, while a hundred years earlier, in my grandmother's generation, the average age had been sixteen.

Around that time Sen began to call me Boppy, which she continues to this day, especially when she's trying to wheedle something from me. Also around that time, before she started eighth grade, we moved from Cincinnati, where we'd lived since she was five, to a small town nearby, where she was one of the few brown-skinned kids as well as one of the only Jews. Things went pretty wrong for a while. She was angry about changing schools and took to slamming doors and banging in and out of rooms.

Physically, other girls were catching up to her. She was no longer the tallest, the fastest, the strongest, and I was no longer her coach. During high school, she'd go from being a star to a regular player, with a coach who was not only a jerk but psychologically cruel. Instead of being a source of joy, in part because it was something we'd done together, soccer became a locus of shame. During one several-week period in which the coach (with whom, unfortunately, I shared a first name) refused to let her play or even to speak to her, she sat in mortified exile at the end of the bench.

Seneca stuck out her "punishment" partly for herself, but in great part, I fear, not to disappoint me. Though I might have said at the time, "Sen, if you want to quit the team, if you're not getting anything out of it, that's okay with me," those words never passed my lips. Instead, in arguments with my wife I maintained Seneca would feel bad about herself if she quit; that it would be better for her in the long run to stick it out; and surely the asshole coach would soon see the error of his ways. I maintained that position long enough—though in truth the coach never much changed or saw anything—that by the time I did start saying it was okay with me if she wanted to leave the team, she knew it wasn't true. She remained on the team through the end of high school in large part, I see now, because she loved me, because it had been our thing, and she didn't want to disappoint me.

Who's to say what was right? The high price of loving someone is being influenced by what they want, and there's no doubt my daughter loves me. She has grown into a young woman with an admirable character, who meets her responsibilities and gets her work done on time, and perhaps she learned some of that by playing competitive sports and by sticking it out when she ceased to be a star. I hope so, because she has chronically sore knees from soccer injuries, and pretty much from the time she graduated high school, she's refused even to look at a soccer ball.

That eighth-grade year, when we moved her and many things changed and not for the better, was also the year Seneca started to date. If I'd been less of an ignoramus about girls and girlhood, I might have known what to expect. In fact, given the pressures she was under—body changes, raging hormones and, most important, moving from a relatively liberal urban school community to a small, narrow-minded town—what happened was predictable. Still, I was unprepared for my darling daughter, the athletic daddy's girl, the younger, pliant and easy child in our family, entering her defiant, bad-boy boyfriend phase.

Here's what she was facing. Not only was Sen, who was one of the few nonwhite or Jewish kids in the eighth grade, beginning to hear herself referred to as a Mex-Jew or Christ-killer, her older brother was the only openly gay kid in the adjacent high school and she also received regular threats directed at the "faggot." It probably showed good sense and innate survival skills for Sen to respond as she did. Still, I was shocked and a bit horrified when Sen began bringing home her bad-boy boyfriend—whom I'll call C. Although he was intelligent enough, C was, by the second half of eighth grade, clearly a stoner, with a posse of similarly inclined best buds: stoners, slackers, skateboarders. In other words, bad news.

My wife and I told ourselves that if we were too negative about C, that would only alienate Seneca and bind her to him. That if we'd only grin and bear it, she would soon lose interest. But Seneca has a notoriously loyal and loving heart. And in the bizarre social world in which she found herself, C and his bad-boy friends offered real and necessary protection. This was a world in which, for some of the more ignorant kids, psycho-sexual logic was sometimes expressed like this: *Your brother's a faggot, which means you're a dyke, which makes your boyfriend a faggot, too.*

So we tolerated C because he made her feel safe and because, maybe, he really helped her be safe. From there, it was one short step to inviting him for dinner. The first time we all sat down together, we served, at her request, red meat, which we didn't eat at home all that often. She said it was C's favorite and would make him feel at ease (for years, we'd been embarrassing our kids by serving their friends the weird healthy foods we usually ate).

I wanted it to go well, I did. Whatever doubts I might have had about C, this was the first time we'd invited our daughter's first boyfriend for a meal and despite what I might have felt about him—was he trying to get into her pants yet?—I wanted it to go well for her sake. So I prepared and served a lovely roast beef because that was what my darling daughter wanted, and do I dote? Yes, I do. There we were at the table, all of us on our best behavior. I placed two large slices of roast beef on C's plate to demonstrate how welcome he was, and after a moment, the four of us began to eat. C speared one of the large slices with his fork and, without cutting it up, raised it from his plate toward his lips. While he ate, taking bites from the slice without ever putting it down, eating around the fork until what was left would fit in his mouth, I glanced at Seneca, who was watching C eat with some of the same horror I was feeling, compounded with shame because when she met my eyes, she knew what I was thinking: *What a baboon.* And I knew what she was thinking: *I know, I know, I know.*

C and Seneca's bad-boy boyfriend phase have, thankfully, vanished in the rear view of life, although they went out for nearly three years. She has a loyal and loving heart. Once she has given it, she finds it hard to take back. While that can be a mixed blessing, I like to think it reflects well on how close we are. She knows, with certainty, that I love her unconditionally. She knows she can ask me pretty much for anything and that, if it is within my power to provide it, I will. She knows that I am torn between wanting to do things for her and pushing her out into the world on her own, and I know, because she is such a good person, that she tries not to ask for too much.

I also *know,* or at least believe, that when a father and daughter have been close and loving since she was young, their relationship can't help but be a sort of model, unconscious or otherwise, of the sort she is looking for with a partner as she moves into her own life. It's not so much that she's looking for a man who is like her father, although I can't help but be flattered that once or twice in the days since breaking up with C, Seneca has confided to my wife that "so-and-so (the boy she is dating) is just like Dad" in some way.

While that has never seemed to be literally the case, it seems to me that what Seneca must mean is that so-and-so makes her feel as her father does: loved, respected and admired. In short, adored. At least that's what I hope it means, because then it means I will have succeeded as a father, representing to her everything that a loving relationship with a man can be.

And what does a father's relationship with a grown-up daughter represent? An idealized kind of love, with all the sweetness and caring remaining from childhood, but without all the real world difficulties and concerns that color a relationship with a wife or lover. Or so it seems to me. For as I sit here writing this, my daughter, twenty-two, brilliant, kind and lovely, is traveling in a country where a war has broken out. As I try to imagine what I would feel or how I would go on if something should happen to her, I can't. I simply can't imagine it at all.

LATE-ONSET FATHERHOOD
Rand Richards Cooper

I'm an older dad.

Which TV ad promises that good things come to those who wait? Well, my wife, Molly, and I waited. First we waited to get married. Then we waited to make up our minds about having children. And once we did make up our minds, we waited again, thanks to a three-year sojourn in Infertilityland—conception, which I had been raised to believe could happen by mere proximity of my lust to a female, turning out to be achievable only through repeated applications of high-tech fertility engineering. All these waits added up, and now I'm a fifty-one-year-old with a three-year-old daughter, Larkin, leading me, sometimes dragging me, by the hand through what I have taken to calling "late-onset fatherhood."

Long before Larkin was born, I wondered what late-onset fatherhood would be like. There was the comedy of being out of sync with other people and their lives. Your friends are attending their kids' college graduations while you attend parenting classes—like the one Molly and I went to four months before Larkin's birth, where I was the elder statesman in a group of twentysomething dads-to-be, all of us with plastic baby dolls hiked over our shoulders, burnishing our burping techniques. "Can you believe," I said to Molly afterward, "that these *kids* will be our fellow parents?"

I worried about the physical part of it. My landing in middle age had been bumpy. I had high cholesterol and borderline

95

blood pressure, painful bunions and a slightly enlarged and bosky prostate (the doctor's alarming word). My eyesight was in undeniable decline, so that I squinted even with my glasses on. And my body was paying for my stubborn basketball habit—ankle sprains, back spasms and finally, the mother of all sports injuries, a torn ACL. "Now," said the surgeon, "you can either alter your lifestyle to fit your knee or alter your knee to fit your lifestyle." His diagnosis raised the questions: What happens when you toss a twenty-four-hour-a-day responsibility, that bomb of a baby, into a middle-aged life? How would I get up and down off the floor five thousand times in the coming years, when doing so even once was a fairly major production?

Along with the physical challenges came metaphysical ones. Late-onset fatherhood means having a brand-new baby at a time when illness and death are already making inroads into the ranks of people you love. New life, midlife and end of life converge, making you feel the presence of ultimate things more acutely than you would at, say, thirty. In my case events hammered this truth home with cruel emphasis. Just as Molly and I were deciding to have a child, Molly's brother was diagnosed with inoperable lung cancer. Wes was a big, strong forty-two-year-old, an outdoorsman and house painter, and he fought hard. Gruesomely, his cancer treatments paralleled our forays into fertility medicine; on the first day Molly received my centrifuged and concentrated sperm via an intrauterine insemination, Wes sat in a hospital two hours away, being infused with toxic chemicals, another of the seemingly endless rounds of chemo he underwent. In Molly's family Wes was the wild character, a garrulous storyteller with a rowdy sense of humor; unmarried, he loved children and seemed born to be an uncle. For Molly our effort to conceive now became a race, driven by her urgent desire to have a child while her brother still lived. We didn't make it. When Wes died, in August 2005, Molly was four months pregnant.

And then, almost right away, we found ourselves in another awful race. Earlier that summer, my mother, Mary Ann Hook Cooper, had broken her arm, a spiral fracture of her humerus incurred while she was doing nothing more dramatic than reaching for a dropped fork. She was seventy-eight, and the doctors assumed that osteoporosis was the culprit. But the break refused to heal, and an X-ray revealed why: the bone had been weakened by cancer, a metastasis from a primary lung tumor. This was something my sisters and I had long dreaded. Our mother had been a heavy smoker for decades.

For Molly and me, these were months spent buffeted by wild emotions: her grief over Wes and my sorrowful worries about my mother, then our joyous amazement at the life taking shape inside Molly, that shadowy figure on the ultrasound, those ever-more-emphatic movements in her belly. By Christmas Molly was eight months pregnant. We celebrated at my mother's house. Because her broken arm had never healed, she'd been unable to wrap presents, so she'd bought decorative gift bags instead, artfully arranging the presents beneath colorful tissue paper. Bald from chemo, a Santa Claus cap substituted for the knitted one she'd taken to wearing, my mother was her usual effervescent self, telling riotous stories, pouring wine and passing out stocking stuffers, orchestrating our meal literally one-handed. She marveled over Molly's belly. "This is going to be a happy, healthy, beautiful baby!" she said. "I just *know* it."

It was a humbling display of courage—not only grace under pressure, but humor, laughter and generosity, too. Molly and I were silent on the hour-long drive home, mulling over things so painfully and beautifully obvious, they didn't need to be said aloud.

What does it mean for a particular day to be the happiest day of your life? For me it meant knowing it even as I was experiencing it; it meant feeling alive in every cell of my body—breathing happiness, sweating it freely through my pores. It meant laughter and tears melting together into some strange new centaur emotion as I stood there, video camera in hand, on the sunny January afternoon when our daughter, Larkin Fehr Cooper, uttered her first squawk. Hospital policy forbade videotaping the actual birth, but within sixty seconds of Larkin's emergence I was filming away. The tape begins with a nurse pulling a pink-and-green knitted cap over our daughter's glistening head. Then there's a lovely and amazing shot of the very first moment Larkin opens her eyes, cradled in Molly's arms. The camera wobbles because the cameraman cannot contain himself. The baby yawps; Molly smiles and weeps; I blubber. After the grinning stoicism shown by all the husbands in the birthing videos we watched in baby class, I turn out to be a six-two tower of Jell-O.

There's so much I remember from our three days in the maternity ward. Taking in the view out our window of the skyline at sundown, the whole city bathed in gold. Lying on a cot that first night as Molly slept, Larkin sprawled on my chest, making aimless little jerking movements. Filing her impossibly tiny nails with an emery board, wishing I had fine tools and a jeweler's loupe. The three-day "rooming-in" experience foments an intense togetherness: time stops, the world with all its news and duties recedes, and in your cocoon the three of you experience an exhilarating tenderness that takes the familiar old emotions and mixes them in powerful new concoctions. "I feel like we're being reprogrammed," I said to Molly. And in a sense we were. Adding a new person to the world, you become a slightly new person.

When I left the cocoon to fetch the car from the parking garage and pick up Molly and Larkin, it was the first time I'd been outside in almost three days. From our sixth-floor window I'd assumed that the clear blue sky betokened cold midwinter weather. In fact, the world had been enjoying a record-breaking warmth, May weather in January. All around me people were doing season-inappropriate things. Young guys romped in shorts; friends tossed a Frisbee; a very ill woman in a wheelchair sat basking in the sun. I walked across the lawn amid all this loud, warm, surprising color and vitality. Glancing back through the glass doors to the lobby, I could see Molly sitting with a cart loaded with all our stuff and vases of flowers and a balloon tied to a duffel bag…and our baby. The two of them waiting for me to drive around and bring them out into the shining world. Here it came again, that strange, sobbing laughter, welling up inside me. I felt our vulnerability in all its awful beauty, a heightening of the stakes, but also a strange and subtle kind of relief. From now on, it was not just about me anymore. *Now,* I thought, *I will be able to die one day.*

My mother, meanwhile, was dying now. In the end, her life and my daughter's life overlapped by exactly six months. Some of that time my mother lived at home, my sisters and I making frequent drives across the state to help.

Molly and I brought Larkin to see her for the first time. On the sofa in the living room she settled down to hold her new granddaughter. "Shift her around this way," she said, "so I can use my good arm." We sat and talked. Larkin slept, and Molly and I couldn't rouse her.

"Let her go," my mother said. "There will be plenty of time to get to know each other."

But not enough, not nearly enough. My mother's doctors kept trading in prognoses for less optimistic ones, dismantling the edifice of our hope, brick by brick. Sometimes I would come home from these visits weeping, and turn to Molly and Larkin for relief. The fact that Larkin so clearly resembled my family, and particularly my mother's side—her big forehead, the long and curvaceous upper lip that makes the Hooks look like they were born smiling—made things both sweeter and more sorrowful. We played silly games. I danced with her, humming the theme song from *The Munsters;* I grabbed her ankles and pedaled her legs bicycle-style while chanting the villainous melody that plays in *The Wizard of Oz* as the mean Miss Gulch pedals away with Toto in the basket.

As a baby, whenever Larkin had a meltdown, the one thing that reliably calmed her was a framed poster in our TV room. It was a big painting of dalmatians, a trio of dogs that merged surreally into a desert landscape, their spots blending with the dappled background. "Look at the dalmatians!" we'd say, as Larkin stared, eyes wide. In my family, dalmatians went back not only to my childhood, but to my mother's, and it consoled me to find that my daughter was captivated by them. Again and again I found myself grabbing at these strands of family history. My mother had grown up enjoying enormous German farm dinners in Ohio, and one night I visited her, bringing a dinner of weisswurst and sauerkraut. She was ecstatic. "All that's missing is the pickled tongue!" she enthused.

But her situation was worsening. There came the day when her stout insistence on sticking to the familiar turf of her own home yielded suddenly; she had fallen hard in the kitchen, and her voice on the phone shook with panic. "Rand, call them." I did, and the ambulance came and took her. There was a hospital stay, a brief return home, then a second hospitalization and finally a room at a nursing home, Beechwood—a converted mansion on a sloping lawn graced by two majestic copper beech trees and, from my mother's window, a view of the playground at a day-care center next door.

Molly and I visited, bringing our wriggling infant with us. My mother loved having us prop Larkin up at the far end of her bed and watching her topple over among the soft blankets and pillows.

"She's like a little rag doll!" she'd say, chuckling. "Prop her up again—I want to see her tumble over!"

Her laughter persisted, stubbornly, and right to the end she kept her ability to delight in beautiful things. Facing death, she still savored life. Molly and I brought fresh raspberries we had picked at a fruit farm, big, red, succulent fruits. We took Mom outside and sat in the sun. I watched her fingers, numbed by neuropathy, fumbling through the berries. She managed to eat a couple, lifting them to her mouth with agonizing slowness.

"They're fabulous," she murmured. "Fabulous."

And then, as if all that had happened wasn't enough, in the middle of my mother's dying, the gods smacked us again. It came out of nowhere: the phone ringing as I rode the exercise bike at home, the caller ID identifying my dermatologist's office. The previous week I'd had a mole taken off my back. Nothing to worry about, the doctor had said; I wouldn't hear from her unless "something unexpected" came back from the lab. Now my stomach lurched. Why was she calling?

"I have some unwelcome news," she said when I picked up. Much to her surprise, the mole she'd removed was a melanoma—the deadliest form of skin cancer. She'd had the lab run it through a second time, just to confirm.

"You'll want to take care of this pretty quickly," she said.

Her understatement chilled me, and I hung up, dizzy with fear and disbelief. More cancer? Melanoma was a notoriously tricky malignancy. It could spread quickly and lethally. At the root of my fear was a terrible thought. *Cancer is killing my mother, and now it's going to kill me, too.*

Molly and I endured several days of panic and dread. Phone calls to several physician friends and to my father, a retired surgeon, yielded some reassurance. Get to the melanoma early, I learned, and the cure rate is high. These hopeful thoughts helped keep me afloat, and I clung to them. But then suddenly I'd lose hold and float back into the swirl of dread, my thoughts cycling madly. I have to live. I can't check out now. Not with this little baby.

I visited my mother at Beechwood. She was alone in her room, and I sat on the edge of her bed and told her my news. She listened carefully.

"In the worst-case scenario," she asked, "how long do you have?"

The directness of her question caught me off balance, and I understood what blunt calculations she had gotten used to making. "Well," I sputtered, "in the *absolute* worst case, I guess I already have some terrible metastasis that will come out in the scan next week. But I'm hoping that's not going to happen."

She nodded. "Honey, I'm so sorry. This must be terrible for you and Molly."

She moved her hand toward me, and I took it in mine. Suddenly I found myself weeping. I hadn't wanted to do that— I'd made a pledge over many weeks and months never to break down in front of her.

"Go ahead," she said. "I'm your mother."

I sobbed it all out to her: my fears about cancer, about dying and leaving Larkin without a father. We sat for a few silent moments.

"Do you pray?" my mother asked.

I shook my head. "Not really."

"Well, then, I'm going to pray double. Because that's something I can do. I'm going to pray tonight for you and Molly and Larkin."

We sat for a long time, saying nothing. I held her hand—red and swollen, her fingernails grotesquely blackened by the chemo treatments. We looked out the window, through the woods to the playground at the day-care center next door, crowded with children of an age my mother would never see Larkin reach.

"Listen to me, Rand," she said. "If I get worse, I don't want any more measures taken. When I go, I just want to go. Do you understand?"

"I do," I said.

It was the last real conversation my mother and I would have. In the following days she worsened drastically, slipping in and out of lucidity, and died the following week. My sisters were with her when she died. I wasn't. But I had said my goodbye to her the day before—kissed her lovely forehead, and whispered to her words I hoped she could hear. *I love you, Mom, and I will tell your stories and bring up our little girl in your spirit and with your style as my guide. And I promise I will never forget.*

As for me, a two-and-a-half-hour surgery relieved me of a chunk of my lower back, along with lymph nodes north and south. The doctors sliced and diced the lymph nodes and found nothing nasty in them. They PET-scanned my body from head to toe. To pass the interminable hours before learning the result, Molly and I took Larkin up the block to Elizabeth Park, a vast rose garden on the grounds of a former estate. We spread out a blanket and listened to music as I drank beer after beer, trying to jump-start some badly needed courage. Because of the radioactive tracer injected into my veins, I'd been advised not to hold the baby for three hours. I joked feebly, "Daddy is glow in the dark, That's why he can't play with the Lark!" and kept a steady bead on my watch, waiting for 6:00 p.m. and the all clear to hug my laughing, oblivious daughter.

To our large relief, the scan results were negative, and two years later I'm still here. My oncologist tells me that my melanoma has an 85 percent cure rate. I can live with that—at least, I hope so.

But my mother is gone. Aching knees aside, my only deep regret about late-onset fatherhood is that Larkin will know the woman Molly and I call "Magical M.A." only through our recollections. And though I am a professional storyteller, I'll be lucky if I can convey one-fifth of the kindness, humor, eccentricity and courage of my mother. But I'll try. I'll sing what I can remember of the odd songs she cherished, curiosities she picked up over the decades and sang with glee. *In a bar on the Piccola Marina, life called to Mrs. Wentworth-Brewster.* "Oh the cannibal king with the big nose ring/ Fell in love with the lovely maiden ..." I'll tell Larkin how generous Magical M.A. was, not just with her money, but with her time, with her self. How whatever she did, big or small—cooking a meal, writing a card, caring for a stray cat out in the middle of winter—she never failed to give away a piece of herself in the process. How in conversation she never talked absently or perfunctorily, but was always *there*.

I'll tell about someone who never mocked others or tore them down (except in traffic: "You big fat *turd!*"), who loved hearing people's crazy dreams and grandiose hopes, who had an artist's eye for beauty. Someone who understood, with no pretension at all, the importance of style: that style is vision, and ultimately also courage—a way of seeing yourself in the world and then comporting yourself accordingly.

And someday I'll present her the copy of *The Little Prince* that M.A. gave us for Christmas, three weeks before Larkin was born. My mother was in the middle of chemo then, but her handwriting was still firm as she wrote out a message to the grandchild whose gender (and thus name) no one knew yet. "I love you so much," she wrote, "whoever you are. Love + Hugs Always, M.A."

I'm haunted by this message—words that seem to send a greeting of love from beyond the grave, even as they convey the great gift my mother had, during her life, for cherishing others as they are and never trying to remake them as someone else. I love you whoever you are.

It raises the question, whom do I want Larkin to be? Watching her, I've frequently thought that she's Mom, reincarnated. The way her body moves, leaning forward when she walks. The determined smile when she's concentrating on something. As Larkin hits three, the personality emerging in her is a mix of bright friendliness with covert steely stoicism, emotional perceptiveness, and an implacable desire to do things her own way. She smiles a lot, but she's stubborn as all hell. Hello, Mary Ann.

As a work-at-home guy who is also the family cook, I had more points of contact with my mother than most men do. We would chat two or three times a week, about books, dogs, recipes, dinner parties, whatever. In the same way, I spend a lot of time with Larkin, doing everything and nothing. In the afternoon we go shopping, we visit parks and playgrounds, spend an hour in the children's room at the library or go "'sploring" around the neighborhood. I love the hilarity of life with a toddler: the daily unveiling of new words and expressions, the crazy attitudes, the mimicry. When Larkin demands the afternoon's third reading of *Angelina's Birthday,* and I try to set a limit—"Just one more time, okay?"—she rolls her eyes and groans, "Yes, Dada, whatever you say." She traipses through the kitchen, convinced (correctly, even though we've told her that they're all gone) that we have hidden the M&M's somewhere, and she vows to ferret them out.

"I search *everywhere!*" she shouts.

Some of my favorite moments are the very quiet ones. On a spring evening, I am putting her to bed when I hear an excited intake of breath. "Look, Dada!" she says. "Look at the star!" She points toward the window, blocked by a room-darkening blind. It's still light outside—light enough for a tiny pinprick hole in the blind, one I've never noticed before, to create a perceptible twinkle. "It's a *beautiful* star," Larkin says in a hushed voice.

"It is," I say, and kiss her good-night.

What is this new parent's rapture that is part sorrow, part ecstasy? For the late-onset dad, it's all about the time, the time, the time. "We're playing in the third quarter," a friend of mine observed when we both turned fifty. "What's your game plan?" My game plan has one fundamental feature: spend as much time as I can with my daughter. I'll watch as Larkin ransacks her bookshelf, sending books plummeting to the floor and clapping her hands in glee, and it is as if I physically feel the passage of life itself, flowing from generations past, through me and into the future. My mother, who tottered toward death; my infant daughter, tottering to her feet; and me, right smack in the middle. We humans tend to believe we move through time, but really, time moves through us; and becoming a parent lets you feel it happening. Only after Larkin was born did I realize how meager my sense of the future had been. A child demands a future of you, but she also gives you one, changing your place in the procession—not only the ancestors lining up behind you, but now the descendants in front of you as well.

At the end of time, for us as individuals, anyway, lies personal extinction and the great unknown beyond. Perhaps because death has figured so prominently in our family these last three years, Larkin already understands something about it. Early on she was fascinated by the song "My Grandfather's Clock," with its refrain of "when the old man died." Then came the demise of her first snowman in our backyard. "Frosty *melted,*" she said, pointing at the spot where he stood. Such observations form a precursor to understanding that people, too, melt away, leaving us with memories and an aching awareness of loss. Larkin seems attuned to death-sadness. Several times when I've been preoccupied, she looked at me and asked, "Are you sad because Magical M.A. died?" On the anniversary of my mother's death, when I was in fact grieving, and told Larkin so, she sat on my lap, cradled my face gently in her hands, and consoled me. "That's all right, Daddy—Magical M.A. will come back to you sometime. Don't worry, you'll see her again!"

A few weeks after my mother's death, friends and family gathered to scatter her ashes into the waters of Long Island Sound. That morning, as I poured the ashes from the funeral-home box into a purple raku urn she had loved, out tumbled a small shard of white bone. Aghast, I set it aside, not knowing what to do with it.

Early the next morning, I put a spade in the trunk of the car and made the short drive to Elizabeth Park. It was a place my mother, a prolific gardener herself, had enjoyed visiting. She had picnicked here with Molly and me; and it was here, one fall day in 2004, I had told her that we were trying to have a baby. Now the park was deserted at 6:00 a.m., and I walked to the spot by the rose garden where Molly and Larkin and I had spent that horrible, wonderful afternoon in July, waiting for the results of my scan. In the nearest rose bed I dug a hole and buried the shard of my mother there.

Larkin loves Elizabeth Park, which she calls "the duck park," for the pond and its busy population of gabbling mallards. Wednesday nights in summer the three of us head over for concerts, bringing a picnic and dancing on the lawn in a mass mosh pit where parents and kids throng and bop. We buy ice cream from the ice-cream stand; we watch the tennis players and lawn bowlers. All summer there are weddings in the rose garden, and we stand among onlookers as beaming couples proceed beneath the rose arbors.

Larkin loves the roses. She runs willy-nilly among the rows of beds, stopping here and there. "Look at this one!" she'll exclaim. "This one is *perfect!*" I haven't told her about the little piece of her grandmother that is buried there. It's way too scary and weird a thought for her to handle at this point. But eventually, once she emerges from her fear of monsters and ghosts, I will tell her; and it will give her one more reason to cherish her duck park.

The places that matter most to us in our lives—the people, too—are the ones that help us put beauty and sorrow together, the love with the loss. And the laughter, too. Larkin is named in part for the poet Philip Larkin, whose best-known poem offers a mordant, tongue-in-cheek take on the family dynamic:

> *They fuck you up, your mum and dad.*
> *They may not mean to, but they do.*
> *They fill you with the faults they had*
> *And add some extra, just for you.*

My mother yukked it up over those lines, approving their sardonic wisdom. No doubt I will pass along my faults to Larkin—and, I hope, some of the gifts M.A. had in abundance. Meanwhile, I am grateful for how the father-daughter bond continually refreshes the mother-son bond; this familiar melody, sounded on a new instrument now, playing down the genera-tions to send me smiling through my tears.

I'm reminded of lines from another, sadder Philip Larkin poem, "Reference Back":

> *Truly, though our element is time,*
> *We are not suited to the long perspectives*
> *Open at each instant in our lives.*
> *They link us to our losses…*

I understand the gloom. The losses mount; and who doesn't feel a shudder, confronting Time the Vandal? Yet when I take the measure of my late-onset fatherhood, the poem seems too pessimistic a take on the balance sheet of our lives. Middle-aged—halfway, in all likelihood, from mystery to mystery—I feel linked not merely to losses, but to gains. Time passes onward, and the days with my daughter pile up like treasure. Yes, it is outrageous to ponder all that will be taken; but isn't it even more outrageous that it was given in the first place?

A KIND OF MIRACLE
Robert Bausch

My oldest daughter, Suzi, came back into my life when she was seventeen. She wrote a letter to me and sent it to George Mason University, where I was teaching. This was twenty-three years ago. When I saw her letter, I went into a bit of a panic. I was divorced from my first wife (with whom I had two daughters) and was married to my current wife, Denny. We had a two-year-old son. I was starting a new family and beginning to forget the eruptions of the divorce. My daughters were adjusting to our new circumstances and beginning to love and cherish their little brother. I wasn't ready for Suzi's letter.

When I was going through the divorce, my therapist said, "Can you tell me one thing you are sure you want right now?" I told her I wanted to contact my first daughter.

Suzi would have been twelve or thirteen then. I'd never seen her, but I knew where she was. Her mother had married a man who taught at Virginia Commonwealth University and had moved to Richmond—only ninety miles south of where I was living at the time.

The therapist said, "She is at a vulnerable age right now. She may not know you exist. You could cause real harm to her current family. It's better if she contacts you."

I knew she was right. So I did nothing and the years went by. My life adjusted. My two daughters—Sara and Julie—from my first wife came to love Denny. My first wife remarried. My son, David, was born. We were all getting back to normal. So

Suzi's letter, which came out of nowhere, struck me as a kind of portent of trouble and pain. I showed the letter to my twin brother, Richard. "What am I going to do?" I said.

He said, "Celebrate!"

I hadn't thought of that. Of course! Here was the girl I ran from and forgot, telling me in her letter that she just wanted to make contact. She said she "did not want to intrude in my life." She told me she was a senior in high school. She also said, "Congratulations on all your achievements." She'd read my novels.

I sat down that night with a yellow legal pad and wrote a fifty-three-page letter. I told her all my favorite books, movies, foods. About my other two daughters and my son. About Denny. My divorce, and everything I could remember about my own family: my brothers and sisters, my mother and father. I told her of the death of my older sister and her husband when their Ford Thunderbird smashed into a tree. How my father and mother raised their four children. I wrote until morning and mailed it before breakfast.

Then I waited. And waited. A month went by. Another. I told Denny, "I think I might have scared her away."

Denny said, "You should at least write her another letter and make sure she got the first one."

So I wrote her a note that said, "I know I might have overdone it a bit with my letter to you, and I understand completely if you want to back away; I have no rights in this at all, but I'd at least like to know if you got my letter."

She wrote back. "What letter? I never got a letter. I thought you just decided you didn't want to respond."

Neither of us knows, or will ever know, what happened to that first fat letter. Perhaps it's a good thing. We could not rush things as I wanted to. We ended up taking our time, something

Suzi thought was a good idea. We exchanged letters for more than two years, without actually meeting, and in that time I got a chance to ask most of the same questions and provide answers to many of hers.

When she was ready for it, we finally did meet, at a restaurant in Alexandria, Virginia. We knew each other in a way, but I was still apprehensive. I wondered if I would recognize her. She wondered what my voice would sound like, and if she would see in my eyes some measure of my response to her. She was nineteen. I was forty-three. She was already a young woman, and except for a few genetic miracles, I had nothing to do with who she was or the kind of woman she had become. She looked like me, had the same temperament, the same intolerance of shoddy thinking, the same impatience with inanimate things that don't work or frustrate our intentions. Denny said she was exactly like me, right down to the bouts of anxiety and acid reflux.

But we did not really know each other, yet. I had all these things I wanted to learn from her. What had her life been like? What did she love? I wanted to go biking with her. I'd fished with my other two daughters, fished and hunted with my son— I wondered if she would want to do these things. I wanted to give her the whole world as soon as possible.

I realized what I needed more than anything was to catch up, to somehow live the life we never had together. Her mother's pregnancy was an accident. I was very young, but one thing I knew for sure: it would be a mistake to get married under those circumstances. So her mother went on without me. I moved back to Virginia; her mother stayed on in Illinois.

In one of my letters to Suzi I wrote, "We're on this train and I like where it's going. At some point I know you may need to go back to the baggage department and root around in there and see what you can see, and I'm willing to do that when you're ready." It was a bad metaphor that I hoped would let her know that I was aware of the issues that might exist between us: I had forsaken her. I had loved two other daughters and my son as completely as I could; I celebrated them, even to her—I talked about what it was like when they were little and I lived in the same house and I got to rock them to sleep, to read *Goodnight Moon* to them, things I'd never done for her.

She was never concerned about that. What she wanted, she made quite clear, was family now. This was her family and she reveled in learning it, entering it. She was welcomed with open arms by everyone. My father was amazed at how much she looked like my mother, who was already gone and never saw her. I think she looks a little like my sister Barbara, who was killed in that Thunderbird and never saw her, either. She is so much a part of the family now, everyone has forgotten that she has not always been with us.

Having Suzi come into this big family so late in her life and mine was a kind of miracle that allowed me to think very hard about what I should say to her. How could I say my love to her now? She helped me come to it without guilt, which was a great gift. And I learned from her: She is a genius with relationships. She has thought so long and so many fatherless years about the kind of relationships she wanted in her life, about the family she wanted to have and belong to. From the minute I came to know her, I relied on her for advice in other relationships. When I had trouble with one of my other daughters or my son—trouble seeing things from their point of view—it was Suzi who could help me see.

I tell people now that I raised three daughters. But I really wasn't there for any of them in any real sense. I divorced Sara and Julie's mom when Sara was eight and Julie was five. I did not want to be a weekend father, so I spent as much time with them as I could—two days a week, every other weekend and all of August—but it was not a daily thing. I didn't live in the same house anymore. What your children learn from you has to be directly proportional to how much time you spend with them. I did the best I could, but when I say I "raised" three daughters, it seems very much like an exaggeration to me.

I don't know what my relationship would be with my girls if I had been around every day. I remember once, a year or so before the divorce, being so angry that Sara couldn't or wouldn't put her toys away, I went in her room, picked everything up, carried it outside and threw it into the back of my pickup. "I'm throwing this junk away," I yelled. Sara was six. I was loud and big and should have scared the hell out of her. I went into my bedroom, where I could see the front of the house through the window, and I saw her march out the front door, walk to the truck, take her toys out in armfuls and carry them back into the house. The look on her face was priceless. She was determined and fearless. I had tears streaming down my face, and I said to my wife, "Look at that little brat. I'm so proud of her right now."

I admired Sara that day. She showed courage and defiance— two things I believe are absolutely necessary for a good life. And she wasn't seven years old yet. It is that kind of courage that sent my other daughter, Julie, to L.A. by herself, to seek an acting career. I asked her if she had a backup plan. As all parents do, I worried about her if the business crushed her as it crushes so many. She said, "If I have a backup plan, then I'll plan to fall back. I have one plan, Daddy." She is just as determined, just as defiant as her sister. And both of them have come to love and admire Suzi.

But Sara and Julie and I have that long past, that baggage. We went through the divorce, which was very hard, and we went through that distant father thing—where eventually, friends and high school activities encroached on time with Dad. And we fought over that. My daughters actually sued me to reduce visitation time—they had lives they wanted to live and I was too blind to that fact. Suzi helped me see how wrong I was to demand so much of their time once they reached a certain age. In short, I had to let go a little.

We finally came to each other as friends and developed our relationships individually with something other than father and daughter as the operative force. We came to see each other as people. But Suzi's whole childhood was missing from my memory, and it still haunted me to remember those nights when Sara was a baby and I would hold her and sing a lullaby, and hope with all my joyous, sad heart that someone was holding my other little girl and singing to her.

On Suzi's twenty-first birthday I wanted to address all that missed time with her, so I wrote her this poem:

> *I was riding home from work last night,*
> *Listening to one of your tapes and*
> *"My Love Is Alive," made me want to dance.*
>
> *I've never known the true title of that song,*
> *Or the name of the artist, but I always loved it. The tape,*
> *As it turns out, is full of songs like that.*
> *Songs I've always loved, and that I've never known.*
>
> *Perhaps this thought has hit you too? That for*
> *A long time I did not know the sound of your song,*
> *Or a single note of your music. You were an imagined*
> *Girl, whose life went on secretly inside every day.*

You see now what I'm getting at? I always loved
You. And listening to that music, your music,
On the way home last night, I remembered once again
As if I had lived it, what time never gave me.

And I felt lucky and happy, and like your father.
I can write this to you on the occasion of your
Twenty-first birthday, because loving you now,
And having you to love me back, is like having
You all those years and I hope all the years after.

When she read this, she cried and then wrapped her arms around my neck and held on for a while. It really did feel as though all that we might have been to each other over the long years of her growing up had somehow come to pass, anyway. It could not have done so if she had not decided to give up recriminations and the past altogether. She has never mentioned any of that baggage, except to tease me once in a while when she wants something. Once I suggested all the children were too old for stockings on Christmas, and she said, "Well, in Suzi years, I've still got eleven years to go."

The other thing we gave Suzi on her twenty-first birthday was just as important to her. Denny and I wanted to try to give her what we'd been giving the other girls and David all along. We tried to put into words what we had given the other children in our daily lives with them. In a birthday note to her both Denny and I composed a list of what we believed were the most important things we could say to her. The first thing on the list was that "love is something to be done, not simply to be said. Love is taking action." Also she should remember that death is a possibility every day, and that each morning when she wakes up, she should try to make the day count. We reminded her that a person is a being apart from his or her mistakes, that insecurity is a fact of existence—we are *all* insecure. In fact, security might be a numbing and life-deadening experience and is probably not desirable. We told her to absorb all she could from experience; at each stage she passes through, to live intensely; to make choices that will allow her to better love those she does love, including herself; to find ways to do what she loves; to be open to new experience—to reserve judgment; and that she should learn the art of forgiveness. And finally Denny wrote that if she ever felt like preaching to anyone, "put it in a card like this one." I like to think now that we've come all the way to what we will be to each other. I have that kind of relationship with all my daughters and I have such admiration now for all of them. They are doing just what they want with their lives. All three graduated from college.

Sara lives in New York now and works in a job she is very good at—doing research for a think tank. She just negotiated a two-million-dollar contract. She is smart, insouciant and in love with the bustle of the city. She already knows it like the back of her hand.

Julie is still in L.A., struggling to make it. She waits tables and attends classes and goes to auditions. She has one film in the can that has yet to be released and she's had a small billed part in *Criminal Minds*. She has earned her Screen Actors Guild card and will stay with it until she has a chance to show her incredible talent for acting and singing.

Suzi has devoted her life to her own family. She now has a four-year-old son and a one-year-old daughter. When her son was just a little fellow, barely able to walk, she sent me this e-mail:

> Today we were so busy—groceries and errands....
> And this evening, when I was trying to wrap
> everything up and get ready for rest, Nathan was

wound up and following me and tripping over
himself and me and anything else near him. He was
frustrated at everything and fussy—and for a few
seconds I could feel it getting on my nerves. I just
wanted him to BALANCE, for God's sake, for two
minutes. And then...I just sat on the floor with him
and he ran over into my arms with a big smile on
his face and we wrestled and laughed—and just like
that, there were no bills to pay, no groceries
melting in bags on the kitchen floor, nothing to do
but enjoy that absolutely wonderful human being,
who is what he is separate of me entirely already.
It's amazing. It's a miracle is what it is....

I am a grandfather. And Suzi takes all her time to teach her
little ones things she has learned, and that she has always known.

KALEIDOSCOPE
Laird Hunt

"What's that?"
"A kaleidoscope."
"A leidoscope?"
"Yes. You look through it. Look through it."
"Look through it?"
"Yes."

Somewhere in the depths of my daughter's earliest years, she called me to come over and stand at bath side. Once I was correctly positioned with my back straight and my arms pressed against my sides, she told me to state my problem.

"My problem?" I said.

"State your problem," she said.

"Well, I'm feeling pretty good," I said.

"That's not your problem," she said.

"You're right," I said.

We looked at each other. Her long, pleasantly scrawny torso was glistening in the steaming air. There was a dollop of whipped bubbles on her shoulder. The ends of her hair were wet and stuck together.

"State it," she said.

"I'm a little tired," I said.

"That's not your problem."

"I have some deadlines coming up."

She shook her head. She could be devastatingly earnest. I knew groping about wasn't going to get the job done, but still all I could come up with, after lamely pointing at a green rhino floating beside her, was the patently untrue and damningly uninspired, "I wanted to play with that toy and I didn't get to."

This was not dignified with a response. I tried a few other things. Nothing hit the mark. What *was* my problem? Anxiety? Avoidance behavior? A tendency to disconnect? Too many snacks too often? No sweeping vision for the future? I should have asked her because, as it occurred, the moment when I might have done so quickly passed and we were on to the next part of the proposition.

"All right," she said. "Bend over and shake that problem out of your head."

"What?" I said.

She repeated her instructions.

I bent over. I shook. Both of us peered at the floor in front of my feet.

My daughter and I have spent a good deal of time sizing each other up. When she was born, after they had hauled her around the room to take the standard measurements, clear her lungs of fluid, listen to her heart, shine light in her eyes, check her ears, etc., they swaddled her, stuck a hat on her head and handed her to me where I sat beside her exhausted mother, who was undergoing the sort of painful postpartum procedure that obviates any much-longed-for cuddling.

"Hello, my daughter," I said.

She had been gazing off to the side. Stunned by the strangeness of the world. Brand-new citizen starting to take her own measurements. Agog but clearly more than a little adrift. When I spoke to her, she tensed and her eyes seemed to focus. I had been speaking to her daily while she had done all that agreeable, dim-light, low-gravity floating for weeks. Earlier in the summer she had been with her mother in the front row below a large loudspeaker when I had given a reading. Mine was a voice she knew. I would have liked to have said other things, but I was terribly choked up and didn't dare try to speak. So we just considered each other. My eyes glistening, her whole new face alight. She looked like someone I knew, not someone I was going to get to know, and it was as if for those few moments her whole life had already happened and we were sitting together, contentedly taking stock. Every now and again she would let out a kind of cross between a squeak and a growl.

Hello, hello, my daughter, I thought.

Presently came the days when my valiant wife had to call in the cavalry and it fell to me to soothe my daughter or put her to sleep by holding her on my shoulder and doing short, sharp knee bends in front of the bathroom mirror with the lights low and the ventilation fan on. I did this over and over. For months. As I did knee bends, I sang. I spoke. I recited poems. "Jabberwocky" by Lewis Carroll was a favorite. I switched the gender of the young hero. Sent my daughter's avatar out to slay the fearsome Jabberwock, chortled in my joy at her triumphant return. During these sessions, said daughter mainly chewed at my shoulder, burbled pleasantly or screamed bloody murder, and never, ever, went quickly.

In his great lecture on the concept of lightness, Italo Calvino proposes that in many cases sideward movement, peripheral vision or otherwise unexpected angles of inquiry offer the most direct approach to the subject being considered. I am quite convinced that during those months when I not only did knee bends to put my daughter to sleep, but also held her on my shoulder during her naps—while she looked over my shoulder and I looked at the reflection of her back in the mirror or at my computer screen or out the window at the little, windgrazed maple tree—we were looking straight at each other.

Here, memory proposes another image of merely apparent ocular obliquity: when my daughter was around two, we started playing a version of hide-and-go-seek that I found far superior to the more conventional way we now play the game. In this proto version, my daughter would announce to me where she was going to hide and then hide there, often somewhere in plain sight. The game was then for me, having briefly absented myself, to enter the room and pretend not to see her. My eyes swept over and under and even through her as she stood, arms pressed to her sides, doing everything she could to keep from bursting into giggles. Sometimes our eyes met as I scanned the room. This didn't mean I had *seen* her yet. According to the rules of the game, she was effectively invisible and would remain so until, after some unspecified interval, the jig, as they say, was up and I would come roaring over and tickle her. When it was my turn to hide, as my daughter walked around the room pretending with great restraint not to know where I was, I did not have to work very hard to feel myself grow invisible and was always surprised and slightly outraged to have to give this state up when without warning she would gleefully turn toward me and say, "Papa, *there* you are!"

Her regard, at these moments, was so intense that I felt agreeably pummeled, not unlike the way I did when she would gleefully use me as a jungle gym or jump up and down on my stomach or run across the room and smash into me. Even if these moments of fierce appraisal would find their end in a none-too-flattering remark about how hairy my hands were or how knobby my shoulders were, they were still exhilarating and more than once I asked her if she thought we should go another round. It was perhaps not surprising then that when she had gone running out of the room to seek out other pursuits, I would go about my subsequent business feeling reduced.

This sense of reduction had a pleasantly nostalgic aspect, whose source it took me some time to pinpoint. It wasn't until I was looking for something in the garage and my eyes fell on a half-buried midnight-blue baby carrier that I understood where it was coming from. I had once spent almost as much time as I had doing knee bends with my daughter in the bathroom wearing her—face out on my chest (as one does with that variety of carrier)—around town and far beyond: through airport terminals, the boulevards of Barcelona, the trails around Boulder and the streets of New York. In my opinion, far too many people in our fine republic are studiously, even aggressively immune to the visual charms of small babies, but put doggy-ear hats on those babies' heads and doggy-paw gloves on their hands and wear them around on your chest on a Halloween night in New York's East Village—as I did when my daughter was three months old—and even the most hardened melt.

"Damn, are you a doll!"

"Whoa, little doggie!"

"Look out, here she comes!" It would be hard to overstate the delight my wife and I took in being, effectively, reduced to nothing more than cute-baby conveyance, for my part, and cute-baby escort, for hers. There is enormous, deep-seated joy and, let's face it, no small measure of relief to be felt in vanishing in the face of your offspring.

Eager to somehow articulate what I was feeling, what I was imagining, what I was dreaming during this period, I scribbled down the following one day as my infant daughter slept.

My daughter of the long legs.
My daughter of the ruby lips.
My daughter of the mad laugh.
My daughter of the bright, bendy arms.

Of the lovely birthmark.

Ever desirous of chocolate.

Rapacious present gobbler.

Grumpiest little girl I know.

My daughter of night tears.

Little galloping dreamer.

Chair stander.

Brazen tumbler.

Crazy dresser.

Bad sleeper.

My daughter of delight.

When I read it to her a couple of years later, she scrunched up her eyes, grinned, frowned, squirmed and said, "You're so silly, Papa."

Maybe that's my problem.

The first thing I read aloud to my daughter, when she was four or five days old, was long passages from the English translation of Georges Perec's first novel, *Things*. We had her rigged up in a kind of jiggly chair, one that bounced and vibrated and seemed to keep her fairly relaxed. If memory serves, one of the passages I read to her concerned the nitty-gritty of farm implements, a kind of madcap avalanche of rural ephemera. I read and read and she cried or she didn't and the chair beneath her buzzed on.

"What do you think?" I asked her.

She gave no answer. This struck me as unusually wise.

A few days later we moved on to experimental poetry: a volume entitled *Political Cactus Poems* by Jonathan Skinner. Gertrude Stein's *Tender Buttons* came soon afterward. I contemplated the necessarily still largely inchoate flow of sound and image through her brain and read to her from *Ulysses*.

There is perhaps more literature than is necessary about the impact early stimulus (or lack thereof) has on the brains of infants. Nevertheless, I have often wondered what such early exposure to the twisting and looping sound patterns of exploratory fiction and poetry has had/will have on her. I suppose I like to imagine that the stories we now regularly make up and act out together—in which she and her friends scale chocolate mountains, cartwheel past trolls guarding bridges, stop to talk at length about their enemies and teachers, etc., and which, as they unfurl, are constantly, at her lead, commented on and critiqued by us in true postmodern fashion—are a byproduct of this exposure, but I may be fooling myself. Almost certainly I am fooling myself.

Lewis Hyde, author of *The Gift,* writes that "mystery refreshes." My daughter's first word, uttered repeatedly when she was six months old, was *apple*. Now, at three and a half, she uses words like *stable* and *promising* and *unusual* with startling resourcefulness:

> *"Papa, would you like to admire my unusual pose?"*
> *"In your opinion is this [block] tower stable?"*

Last week, after I had begun to gather these thoughts, I saw my daughter standing in front of the mirror in the back room. After a moment, she stood with her hands pressed against her sides and ordered her reflection to state its problem. Then, without waiting or needing to hear what it had to say, she bent over and shook whatever it was out of her hair. Whereupon, perhaps relieved, perhaps already thinking about something else, she straightened up and began to giggle. Which made me giggle, too.

"Why are you laughing, Papa?" she said.
"I don't know," I said.

Although now I note that there is an exponential, almost overwhelming quality to the daily growth of the mystery that this little human being trails behind her, one that I would be hard-pressed to ascribe to the Chopin and Mozart we have dutifully played her, and all the tricky books we have read. One that makes me, rather frequently, laugh aloud.

Mystery refreshes. When I was ten or eleven, I came across an unmarked cassette tape my father had made one weekend afternoon when I was three and my sister was five as we strolled through the botanical gardens in Singapore. On the tape, we pause at a fountain, and after some comments from my father and sister, my young self remarks, with great earnestness, "The water, it is going." That tape was later mistakenly (or not) recorded over. No great tragedy, but I am interested in how frequently, over the years, I have thought of it. I like to think I can still, sort of, hear that little voice making its pleasantly off-kilter, devastatingly accurate comment. It reminds me of someone.

In the past few weeks, I have been making movies of my daughter at the playground where she is more than halfway through her first year of school. While she and her new friends cut disconcertingly bright and unfailingly noisy vectors across the wood chips that cover the ground, I sit on the edge of the sandbox or lean against the twisty slide, creating amateur image and soundscape that we later sit down together with her mother and consider. Sometimes I film my daughter dancing in the living room, or painting at her little easel by the lemon tree in the back. In another, she is sitting at the dining room table, "reading" a home-decor magazine.

The three of us love watching these movies together, and do

so frequently, but I know I am not making them for that reason. Nor am I making them so that my wife and I, in our dotage, can look back misty-eyed at our clever darling aged three point five (though that will be nice). I am making them, principally, so that years from now my daughter, long since off on her own grand adventures, can show them to some young person(s) of her own and say, "You see, I was once like you."

To which that young person(s) might well respond, as my daughter likely would were I to put this proposition to her today, "No, you weren't."

Knowing this doesn't make me want to stop making these little movies or having these little thoughts. Still, perhaps it makes sense that the movie my mind turns to most is one that doesn't exist. In it, my daughter is racing away from me, her little arms churning, her blue-jean-covered legs pounding the wood chips. She races and races until she has disappeared behind the great red tube slide and the big-kid monkey bars. As this unfilmed and unfilmable scenario continues to unfurl itself in my mind, I catch a glimpse of my daughter, grown tall and strong shouldered, racing across the basketball courts and the grass field beyond the playground fence, then she is gone.

For fun, yesterday I reread the poem reproduced some pages before to my daughter, who had been running around the house, woofing like a dog and meowing like a cat, and she stopped, mid-meow, looked me in the eye and said, "I thought I told you not to be silly, Papa."

"I'm working on it," I told her.

"Yeah, you have to work on it," she said.

"Woof, woof," I said.

"Papa!"

BLOODLESS BUT NOT LOVELESS
Michael Kearns

"To a father growing old nothing is dearer than a daughter."
—Euripides

"IS YOUR DAUGHTER
THE LOVE OF YOUR LIFE?"

With the sound of water emanating from the splashing shower, I can barely decipher the lush language of Shakespeare, but listening intently outside her bathroom door, I'm fairly certain it is Juliet, in a lather about the nurse's untimeliness.

It is the voice of Tia, my fourteen-year-old daughter, who is preparing to audition for admission to LACHSA (Los Angeles County High School for the Arts). The words ricochet off of the walls like "swift Cupid's wings" and land squarely in my heart. Three realities hit: she will (1) graduate from high school, (2) leave home and (3) eventually find her Romeo.

Love of acting—and, by natural extension, Shakespeare—is not the only joy that I share with Tia. We both love oxymorons, Marilyn Monroe, Peter Pan, Ireland, the Beatles, photography, "Politically Incorrect Days," Cat Stevens, blue cheese burgers, cloud formations, *Breakfast at Tiffany's,* Noel Coward, *Breakfast on Pluto,* and Martin Luther King.

The list of things we mutually don't like is led by social injustice, including racism and homophobia. I am a single, white gay dad and Tia is my adopted black daughter. We were introduced when she was five months old, after she spent her first month in an incubator and the following four months in an unhealthy foster care situation (no abuse but no real attention, either).

I was forty-four when Tia entered the world, the same age my father was when I was born in Missouri. And while the circumstances of our births are differentiated by far more than the miles from Los Angeles to St. Louis, we dwell in limitless similarities.

Except for our blood.

For all of Tia's life, I have routinely had my blood drawn because of the disease that I carry with me; the needle pricks and the sight of my blood moving from my vein into a test tube are a relentless reminder, like a nagging alarm clock you can't shut off, that I am not immortal. I will die. I will one day be separated from my daughter.

"It is your job as a parent to let go," I remember the director of Tia's preschool saying at one of the first parent gatherings I'd ever attended. I was likely the only gay one there that night; this was 1998, when gay dads were still an anomaly (and gay, single, HIV-poz dads were virtually unheard of). "Your responsibility is to prepare your children to live their life separate from you," she stressed.

Huh? I spent how many hours? how many dollars? how many nerve endings? over how many years ? completing this adoption and I'm told that it's my job to let go? Yep, on a daily basis, with the utterance of each new word, with the manifestation of ideas, with the pulling away when all you want is the comfort of their touch. And that was all before she started kindergarten.

Even back then, I began noticing how alike we were. "You could put Tia in a room full of one hundred other kids of the same age," I would tell people, "watch their behavior for five minutes or so, and you'd be able to correctly identify my daughter even if you only knew me slightly."

Nature or nurture? That question has been consuming professionals for decades upon decades, perhaps even more compulsively now that adoption is out of the closet.

While we are pretty certain that *nature* means "genetic" or "blood-related," defining *nurture* is a bit more complex and has been expanded in order to include the influences on development arising from prenatal, parental, extended family and peer experiences.

But I am more questioning about the "prenatal development" since Tia's drug-addicted mother received no prenatal medical care and delivered my daughter at seven months' gestation. While I'm not suggesting that Tia is immune to the situation of her birth, she did, during her first few years, defy the odds. Not only did she "catch up" by her third birthday, her physical and cognitive growth spurted where the charts indicated she was supposed to be.

Yet I'm not naive to issues that might impact her in the future, including health factors that might be determined by her blood. And, yes, it's likely that there will be visceral fallout at some point in her future, perhaps decades from now, related to her mother. I get it.

"Is your daughter the love of your life?"

She sits at the computer, delving into the Kearns family history. She identifies Lannes Kearns, my father's father, and his wife, Katherine.

"Her name is spelled wrong," Tia says, knowing that her middle name, Katherine (not with a *C* but with a *K*), was

130

chosen to honor my grandmother. It was my saintly grand-mother who lavished me with immortal sweetness.

Even though her DNA would not attest to Kearns blood, my teenage daughter takes being a Kearns very seriously and she is determined to identify her European roots. Blood be damned; she chooses Kearns as the heritage of her narrative and that casts Lannes Kearns as her great-grandfather.

Tia wasn't given much more than a first name by the mother who abandoned her in the hospital. The man who impregnated her mother is unknown. This was proven when, during the contentious adoption process, "the family" presented a slew of possible "fathers" as ploys to gain last-minute custody during the final coda of a nearly three-year-long Grand Guignol–like opera.

"Why," everyone asked, "did they try to gain custody after virtually ignoring her for three years?" "Because you're gay?" was the most frequently asked question, followed by "Because you're HIV positive?" On the laundry list of their Reasons Why I Shouldn't Be Tia's Dad, my whiteness trumped anything having to do with what I did in bed.

A judge who was known for his stringent verdicts to keep blood relatives under the same roof finally rejected all the bogus claims presented by so-called friends and relatives and awarded me full custody. I've consistently kept the door ajar for communication, and there have been polite, albeit short and sweet, meetings with Tia's blood family. She is less interested than I am in being open to forging a closeness between them.

"You are my family," she says. She reminds me of the many individuals—gay, straight, young, old, black, white, rich, poor—who have helped me raise her since she and I embarked on this journey together.

"They are from Ireland," she reports from her room, where

she sits at the computer. "Both of Lannes's parents were born in Ireland!" Tia and I had already confirmed our deep roots to Ireland when we boarded a "Kearns Bus" while visiting Dublin. We also found more than one Kearns laid to rest in the luxuriant Glasnevin Cemetery. Her claiming possession of Kearns blood does not reflect lack of intelligence; she is not a Kearns in name only; she has made a definitive decision to take ownership of our surname.

Is there an inherent accompanying choice to deny her blood roots? Perhaps. Does it matter (at fourteen years old)? I don't believe that Tia is denouncing her blackness. I do believe that she's choosing to identify with the Kearns family rather than her blood family—something I didn't encourage or even suggest. But why would I, or should I, interfere? We all compulsively write and rewrite our histories, adding and subtracting this and/or that detail for multitudinous reasons—from getting a coveted job to keeping ourselves from going totally insane.

"Is your daughter the love of your life?"

On the day of 9/11, I remember the pangs of uneasiness when I dropped Tia off at Foundations School Community, a progressive K–9 school in the San Fernando Valley. Already in first grade, she was fiercely independent. But I wasn't, and like most every parent on the planet that specific morning, I held my kid a little tighter before leaving her in the care of her teachers. *Let go,* an embedded voice in my head reminded me.

Feeling useless as I walked away, I spotted a Red Cross building directly across the street from Foundations—had I never noticed it before? *I'll donate blood,* I thought to myself. As I headed for the building, marked with the bright signature red cross, it dawned on me. *My blood is bad. I can't give blood. I am going to die of AIDS,* I told myself. *How soon? Let go,* I said to myself. *You must let go of her.*

Some part of me hoped that the 9/11 bloodshed would provide context for me to introduce the notion of loss, if not death. It didn't.

So I waited until Tia was nine and then attempted to explain to her that my blood was "different"—a word we'd come to apply positively when describing many things about me and our family structure. While trying to avoid that other *D* word (disease), I read to her from a children's book created for the occasion, *My Dad Has HIV.* She seemed unfettered by this news, as if it was no more complicated than saying I had a stubbed toe.

If you were looking for clues as to how she took the news on a subconscious level, she insisted on wearing my shirts—from T-shirts to dress shirts, washed or unwashed—to school. My amateur psych evaluation is that she found comfort in keeping me nearby throughout the day—in other words, not letting go. Instead of my apron strings, she was holding on to my shirt-tails.

We seemed to be in synch on the letting go dilemma.

The momentous event of Tia's first period happened when we were out of town, attending the 2005 San Diego Gay & Lesbian Film Festival, where a movie I was involved with was being screened. Although we'd read all the right books (on the shelf next to *My Dad Has HIV* was that other tale about blood) and discussed bodily functions at length, she was understand-ably embarrassed and more than a bit freaked out. So much so that she avoided telling me until the day after she started—even though I wasn't insensitive to the fact that there had been a marked mood shift.

Would she have told a mommy immediately? Maybe, maybe

not. I spoke to various female friends who remember keeping their first period a secret from their mothers. My response to the news was measured, trying not to let her know that it wasn't the act of menstruating that made me apprehensive; it was the very concept of her growing up—far too quickly—that affected me.

Unlike her daddy, who is a veteran, Tia has a fear of having her blood drawn. In fact, she's a bit phobic and a scene inevitably ensues at the doctor's office whenever she has to undergo required blood tests, which are "a parent's responsibility," I remind her through clenched teeth. As the years melt, one into another, I feel needed during these moments of upset and I notice that, in some odd way, it is often the role of blood that unwittingly unites us.

I'm not suggesting that our life together is without peril. Are you kidding? There are the predictable parent-child dramas enacted on a daily basis in households worldwide, and ours is no different—no more and no less special, no matter the cultural and social distinctions—than any parent-child configuration.

The day that Tia is scheduled to find out whether or not she's accepted to LACHSA, I am shooting a film on location in Northern California's wine country. I play the owner of a vineyard—a single, widowed dad of a daughter who has just been accepted to college and is set to embark on her life away from home. Dying of cancer, he delivers a toast, brimming with emotion, at her going-away celebration. Using wine as a metaphor for life, this dad is celebrating the life and accomplishments of his daughter but he is also saying goodbye to her.

I fail to pinpoint this parallel motif until Tia and I talk on the phone a few hours before I'm scheduled to shoot the scene.

In anticipation of calling her, I check the messages on our home phone to see if there's news about whether or not her rendition of the Juliet monologue got her into LACHSA. When I find out that she has indeed been accepted, I hurriedly dial her cell phone. She cries when I tell her the news and that makes me cry, separated by so much space but bound by miles of shared excitement.

A few hours later, I am hitting my mark, portraying this dad whose daughter will be leaving him—or will he be leaving her?—knowing that he must let go either way. It's been a long day of shooting and everyone is tired—the crew, the extras, who are assembled for this critical party scene, and the principals.

This is the only time in my long career that I have ever asked the director for "a little time" before beginning the scene. I have to summon the feelings that the character and I share and do it simply, elegantly and authentically. When "Action" is called, feeling the feelings but not indulging in them becomes a tightrope act. Life and art meld and, honey, I deliver.

"Is your daughter the love of your life?" Asked by a man that I'm on a first date with, the question feels icky—too intimate and a bit confrontational yet unquestionably astute. The dinner has been romantic and he's sexy as hell, but I decide it's a trick question and I initially veer to the defensive track.

Even if the truth jeopardizes the frisson of the moment, I ultimately admit that it's true: of the myriad friends and relatives and lovers, past and present, Tia is unequivocally the love of my life.

He seemed to understand and then admitted that he was envious.

He doesn't stop there. "Do you think her love has kept you alive?"

This is another FAQ in my life. Do I think that Tia has been key to my enduring survival against some tough health conditions? Yes and no.

She is a daily exaltation, a jolt of giddy endorphins. However, the art of parenting is physically and psychologically wearing. No parent I know is automatically immune to occasional irresistible acts of self-destruction. And I know many people who die in spite of the radiance of human connection.

During the past fourteen years, my HIV history has not been without blips; some of them have materialized more severely internally than externally; what you see is not always a reflection of the indignities of my insides. When my body doesn't behave the way I'd like it to, I don't blame Tia's influence, so it's sometimes unwise to do the opposite. My health is not her responsibility. There are times when the body has a mind of its own and disconnects from what may otherwise be healing.

Yet I do believe that the illumination of Tia's constant presence has opened me to life's miscellaneous mysteriousness, likely a prescription for longer life.

Sitting across from me at the table in a neighborhood hangout, she is wearing a T-shirt with brown and white horizontal stripes. The pool of white surrounding her brilliant brown eyes appears to be uncannily coordinated with the top she's wearing. My daughter is ravishing, inside and out.

Our having been teamed together is the reason I believe in magic, in things unseen. Why? The moment I held her tiny body in my hands, she was my daughter. Fate? Perhaps. Our connection is deep and unbreakable; it may be bloodless but there is something equally powerful coursing through our veins.

I don't have to tell you what it is. When she was much younger, I used to tell her, "A string goes from your heart to my heart so that we are always connected." Now I think of it more as an artery, pumping life into both of us.

TO BE READ BY AVA ON HER
EIGHTEENTH BIRTHDAY
Trey Ellis

For some reason I feel compelled to spill all of my secrets. My second novel is a roman à clef based on my actual diaries as a young adult. Then, after my wife moved out, leaving me to raise my then three-and-a-half-year-old girl and her half-year-old little brother, I decided to write a book of creative non-fiction laying bare the most painful events of my nuclear family's young life. I began the book, *Bedtime Stories,* when Ava was in the second grade so there was no chance of her reading it. Now that she's going into sixth, I'm petrified that I'll come home and see her nose in the (sometimes steamy) pages.

Novelist Meg Wolitzer, daughter of novelist Hilma Wolitzer, wrote about this writer/parent dilemma in *Salon* a few years ago. When a boy in her high school discovered that Meg's mother had written a scene about a blow job in her latest book, it instantly became the scandal of the school. My memoir is not only infinitely dirtier but relives my mother's suicide when I was sixteen and my dad's death of AIDS complications when I was twenty-two. While I tried my best not to make Ava's mother my story's villain, the question hangs there, nevertheless, between every line and piece of punctuation: why did a woman walk out on raising her babies?

Amanda, my amazing girlfriend, is convinced that Ava will sometime soon open the book. I'm not so sure. Ava's heart is as finely tuned as a Stradivarius. I think she intuits that, at just ten now, she's still way too young to understand her father's complicated, R-rated life. Kids are amazingly adept at self-preservation. Just because they *could* hear their parents going at it if they pressed their ear up against the bedroom wall doesn't mean they necessarily want to.

Still, if I were writing the same book now, I know I'd have greatly abridged the story of my recovery from divorce, and learning to raise two little ones alone.

What I'm writing here is an explanation, an addendum, to what I wrote in the book—this time tailor-made for the most amazing little girl on the planet. May these words help her, and anyone else who's reading over her shoulder, understand my philosophy on raising a daughter.

Of course, all dads love their daughters, but a single dad's bond is more complicated than that. I've been Ava's daddy and in some sense her mommy, too, for the past seven years. I remember once when Ava was in kindergarten, the moms in her class decided to get together for margaritas and they invited me along as an honorary member (by the way, I declined). When Ava's brother, Chet, first started to speak, he'd often call me "Mommy-Daddy." I reveled in the challenge of single parenting, smug in my holy martyrdom. I guess it runs in the family. From the time I was sixteen, I was raised by just my dad after my mother killed herself. Then, six year later, I nursed my dad through his short and losing battle with HIV. So by the time I was twenty-two, I'd decided that we Ellises are good at surmounting the seemingly insurmountable. If we were destined to be tragic heroes, I dedicated myself to being the best tragic hero ever. The most noble single dad in all of single-dad-dom.

Somewhere along the line I think I'd forgotten that raising kids was a marathon and not a dash. I'd foolishly believed that conscientious parenting was zero to five and with that good base the kids were set for life. They're in school now—my job is done, I tried to make myself believe. They'll go nuts as teenagers and then regain a bit of sanity sometime around their sopho-more year in college.

The reality is that in a month Ava will graduate from middle school and I don't know if I've ever felt less prepared.

I should've known I was heading for trouble three years ago, when Ava was eight. The wife of one of my best friends asked me how, when the time came, I would explain to Ava puberty and menstruation. Back then I thought I'd just consult what I always consult when I want to know more about something, but then I realized that looking up "training bra" and "men-struation" on Google was not only ineffective but seemed like a great way to get Chris Hanson from *To Catch a Predator* breaking down my door.

So my friend's wife urged me, when the time was right, to buy the book *The Care and Keeping of You* from the American Girl Library. Being addicted to the nearly instant gratification of Amazon's one-click, and even though my daughter was only in the second grade, I immediately ordered it. Two days later I unzipped the cardboard envelope, pried off the shrink-wrap and the book fell open to a two-page spread of a cartoon vagina.

I instantly closed the book and haven't touched it since. It wasn't a total waste, however. Just last month I discovered that Ava had rediscovered it, but of course when I gingerly tried to quiz her on its contents, she only offered her name, rank and serial number. I was hurt. I realize that most daughters couldn't talk about such things with most dads, but c'mon. *Me?* The guy who makes her lunches for field trips? The guy who volunteers to run the Hot Wheels racing booth at the school fair? The guy who sits down for an hour every Sunday and conditions and de-tangles her magnificent hair?

Ava's hair. A young black woman's hair. Volumes have been

written on those voluminous manes. I pride myself on my prowess wrestling with my little girl's locks yet for her middle school graduation she wants braids. "You can do it, Daddy," she told me. Flattered as I was, I'm afraid she'd end up looking she'd been electrocuted. I'm working on getting her mom up here from her home in Atlanta, not just to be there to watch her daughter march, but the day before to do her hair.

To better understand my relationship with Ava, I think it's important to know a little bit about my mother. As I wrote in *Bedtime Stories,* "My mom was a feminist squared, so growing up in the seventies, I didn't have a choice but to believe that a woman's place was in the House and in the Senate, and in my mom's case, Yale Law School. She graduated magna cum laude from Howard, with all but her dissertation for her Ph.D in psychology from the University of Michigan, where she also taught; then when I was a teenager and Mom was thirty-three years old, she enrolled in the best and hardest law school in the country. So I was singularly unprepared to find myself raising a four-year-old girl who was passionate about cooking, baking, her nails, edible makeup and anything having to do with princesses. I am terrified that she is going to grow up and become a Republican."

Ava is less girly now and not at all Republican. In fact, just today, when I crazily suggested that she bring some spray conditioner to school because her rock-star hair sometimes looks dried out and frizzy by the end of the day, she said, "Dad, I'm not one of those girls." Impossibly, I loved her even more.

I also wrote in my book about how we as dads have to keep loving our daughters through the difficult tween and teen years, easing them gently from loving us to getting ready to love boys. Chris Rock, also a parent of little girls, says our job as dads is to *keep them off the pole;* that is, raise them so that they don't grow up to become strippers. The film *American Beauty* crystallized this dilemma for me. Near the very end of the film Kevin Spacey stares at a picture of his once happy family. It had been taken only a few years before but the smiling little girl in the picture clutching her father's neck bears almost no resemblance to the Goth teen dad-hater we see in the film.

"In fact almost every woman whom I have ever dated has also had a troubled, contentious, aggressive relationship with her own father. Perhaps for me it's a prerequisite. In my lowest points, when everything around me seems to be disintegrating, I terrify myself with the thought that my own little girl will one day stop loving me. After all, there was a time when her mother looked at me the way Ava looks at me now."

"On my deathbed, whenever that will be, the degree to which my kids still love me will be the only criteria by which I will judge the worth of my journey."

I didn't realize how much stronger my bond was with Ava than the one between, I think, most dads and their daughters, until I met Amanda. Amanda sometimes calls Ava my other girl-friend. Ava isn't classically jealous—she's been less jealous than her brother around Amanda in general, but I do get the sense that not only am I her "best friend," as she tells me daily while she squeezes her whole body against my arm, but I'm also "her man." It's unbelievably cute to watch her just now as she begins to separate. She became addicted, instantly, to the *Twilight* books and it was so lovely to see in her the precise moment that she felt romantic love for another man. She is *Twilight*'s Bella Swan and Edward the vampire is taking her away from me. She actually told me, "Don't worry, Daddy."

Like Bella Swan my Ava is as beautiful as they come. Like her mother. Her personality is more like mine, retiring, soft-spoken, but her beauty is loud. It's always the first thing that anyone ever says about her. It's so hard to figure what she will make of love, of mating. With my loving, long-term relationship with Amanda (we plan on marrying), I hope to model for Ava a counterargument to the failed relationship that hatched her.

The more that I think about it, when she's ready, perhaps reading the book will answer some questions for her. Or at the very least it should open up between us a series of interesting adult conversations.

HEADSTRONG, HEADLONG
Richard Nash

I'm conscious of the fact that to begin an essay on the father-daughter bond (bind?) with "It was about five-thirty in the morning…" would suggest I was about to tell the story of her birth. But her story, for me, begins about two weeks before her birth (almost a month before my wife's due date), and I'm going to start it at five-thirty even though it really begins about twenty-eight hours earlier still.

I was in the courtyard of an elaborate hotel, having been drinking largely mooched red wine and beer since about ten the night before, and smoking mooched cigarettes because I'd quit smoking (till then, with complete success) that past June.

It was the world's biggest book fair that brought me there a month before my wife's due date. (It had been at the end of the world's third biggest book fair that I had quit smoking.) Most people hate going—the 150-minute drunken naps masquerading as one's nightly sleep, the overpriced alcohol, the sterile fluorescent trade-show floor, the twenty meetings a day (every half hour)—but I loved it. It had become self-defining, after a fashion: I performed this specific role in this specific profession because I was one of maybe ten thousand people on the planet who actually thrived in this environment. So I was supposed to be at the Frankfurt Book Fair because it was, well, my destiny to be at the Frankfurt Book Fair; such were the grandiose notions of the pre-paternal Richard.

Just as I thought it might be my destiny to have a girl. I'd been more or less preparing for this since my parents adopted a girl when I was ten years old. When the nuns showed up at the house, introduced as "friends of the family" (everyone in Ireland, where I'm from, had priests and nuns in the family, and "friends of the family"; this was just the way), and asked my brother and me if we wanted a little sister, we said, "No!" We wanted brothers, nine of them, so we could have a football team, soccer being our then favorite pastime. My parents were horrified but were reassured later by the nuns, who were of course inspecting the family for suitability for adoption, that our reaction was ideal—we wanted siblings to play with. We were not of the "then our parents will love us less" mind-set. That's all they needed to know.

There is nothing a bookish, maladroit, "self-conscious in all the wrong ways" boy can benefit from more than a tiny girl who comes into his life and expands dramatically the universe of what matters. Feeling your own mouth drift open in subconscious mimicry of hers as the spoon neared her mouth… There aren't many moments in a young boy's life as perfectly complete as that synchronicity.

So, as you pass through the various stages of early adult self-absorption and come out, in your early thirties, to find yourself in subway cars, hoping the little child in the stroller across from you will throw her toy in rage and frustration in your direction, so you can pick it up and get a chance to play with her a little bit, show the subway car's passengers, yourself included, how paternal you are, how unflappable, how playful—well, you begin to feel ready. Ready to go.

In the incredibly narrow sense of the term, though, when I found out I was to be a father, I wasn't ready. In that the plan was to be having a kid around now, as of this time of writing. Not fifteen months ago. In fact, a little under two years ago, my wife was getting ready for the gastroenterologist. Having spent the better part of two weeks throwing up all day long [details redacted by my wife…]. There was a stomach virus going around. A trip to the doctor. No dice. Days more spent throwing up. A trip to the gastroenterologist, clear suspicion of an ulcer, endoscopy scheduled. Then, the day before the endoscopy, the gastroenterologist, who had the presence of mind to order a full battery of tests, unlike the dim-witted GP the week before, gets to utter words that pass so rarely through the mouths of gastroenterologists….

"It's not an ulcer. You're pregnant."

This was the story I kept telling folks during those twenty hours in Frankfurt as phone call after phone call with my wife made it clear I was going to have to get the hell back to the United States. That story became a way of talking about the pregnancy, recognizing it, without really having to contend with the fact that things seemed to be going very wrong all of a sudden—a cute little anecdote to soothe myself, and allow me to not have to have to discuss what was going on. Plus, I barely did know what was going on, except that my wife was lying on the floor, in too much pain to stand, and I had been asking my sister to see if she could somehow, I don't know, get into, break into the apartment to help. Then our friends were mobilizing to get her to the hospital, and I was getting a first-thing-Friday-morning flight back to NYC but going to the airport itself, suitcase in hand, that very night to see if there was anything going to the U.S. sooner. (Word to the wise: no planes fly to the U.S. from Frankfurt later than 3:30 p.m. May this info be utterly useless to you.)

So readiness turns out to be the thing, then. Ready for anything. No: prepared for anything. No: accepting that you can't prepare. It just blows over you. So where I stood, after all this washed over me—back from the airport, having failed to get out that night, but needing to be en route to the airport by 6:00 a.m.—was in the lobby of the Frankfurter Hof, suitcase stashed, a glass of wine in each hand, bought by friends helping me self-medicate the anxiety. My sister and friend were back in NYC, trying to half carry my pregnant wife downstairs to get her to hospital (where they'll have to fight to have her admitted by utterly, socially and medically, benighted individuals unwilling to believe she wasn't a malingerer). I worried about my daughter: I just didn't know, I just didn't know. There weren't supposed to be any reasons to worry about her, except that when I left, there also weren't supposed to be any reasons to worry about my wife. Ready but utterly useless.

It was about five-thirty in the morning, then, when Jamie, a man who cuts a real swathe through the world of the Frankfurt Book Fair (and other worlds besides), a raucous character of immense talent, publisher of a small Scottish operation that, out of the blue, published Obama in the U.K. before he'd even announced his candidacy. He knew me hardly at all but even in my befuddled state, slightly beside myself with anxiety and wine, I could tell he was making a beeline for me. He'd heard of what was happening and wanted to let me know everything would be okay—little girls are strong, stronger than any of us men....

Which was indeed true. My wife would be in hospital for weeks and would endure much, yet not once was there the slightest hint that the tiny girl inside her was anything but tremendously robust. It took days for them to figure out what was wrong, in part because it took them far too long to recognize anything was wrong. In fact, it was four days before they took it upon themselves to do an MRI, which indicated that she had a stress fracture of her pelvis: as best any of us can figure out the little girl had been leaching calcium out of my wife to build her own self up. So much so that in the days that were to come, as we waited to see that her lungs would be ready for a cesarean birth, and my wife endured yet more slings and arrows, including one scary drop in blood pressure, the fetal heart monitor was as confident as ever, her heart vigorous, headlong. (As she is now, and to complete the picture and the rhyme, vigorous, headlong and headstrong. It is clear, even at this young age of sixteen months, that she is a girl who knows what she wants, is fearless and direct, knows only to go forward.)

But little girls were not just strong, Jamie continued that night. They're divine, said he, with a conspiratorial grin. His first child was a girl and years ago, when she was born, the musician/writer/lyricist Gil Scott-Heron (the guy who wrote *The Revolution Will Not Be Televised*) sent Jamie a note. Type-written, all caps, a little mad, many typos. A song of praise to little girls. "'Enjoy your miracle,' he told me," Jamie continued. "'Help the wife. Spend as much time with the child as honesty provides. That is how you show your appreciation to the spirits.'" And he stepped forward, closed his eyes, held me by the shoulders and began to recite.

Another sudden drop in my wife's blood pressure just before the C-section notwithstanding, the delivery was probably the most conventional, predictable and smooth event of all that had happened those three weeks at the hospital. Normalcy, after a fashion, had returned to our lives. Our daughter, well, I'm not writer enough to really tell you about what happens in your head, in your body when you first witness your child. Most of us know for our own selves what that's like, and the true writers in this volume will make sure those of you who don't can get a sense of what it's like. That strength of hers we witnessed in utero has continued ex utero, and so far it is the clearest trait of them all, physically and emotionally, especially in our society, which does so much to undermine and defeat strong women. I know it is my honor and my duty to do all that I can to maintain and preserve that strength of hers.

As impossibly dorky as it might seem, the folks I identify as the eagles under whose wings I think she can fly, the women who can reinforce my wife as she models for Sophia the confidence, the vehemence I want her to have, are the first ladies Michelle Obama and Hillary Clinton, ladies with whom it must be said my wife has far more in common than I with their husbands. Hillary's ordeals have been more public than Michelle's, but you know they've wills of steel; you know they've empathy; you know they've learned from experience how to combine the two, when to use more of one, when to put the other aside altogether; their grace and power are what I think of when I think of what I want for Sophia.

For I know Sophia will be a leader, though I wouldn't wish being president upon her: leading the country being so clearly a leadership where what you must give of yourself is so much more than you get back, but a farm, a university, a business, a laboratory, a sports team or, okay, a country if she so chooses, all those I know she's the protean strength to lead. Gosh, I just watched her, all of twenty months old, hurling herself through the basketball courts in my neighborhood—all 101st-percentile height and 97th-percentile weight of her, pure momentum, pure headlong joy, tripping, knees, hands, forehead to the ground, tears, anguish, up in my arms bawling, thirty seconds later, squirming out of my grasp down to the ground again, out the park, hurtling down the sidewalk, me scuttling to stay alongside, her grinning, new curls bounding, arms flailing, splat on the ground again, tears, up in my arms, writhing to get down on the ground again, into the water-spray fountain, shock of cold water, running out, circling, back in again, watching the big kids stick their faces into the jets of water, following, shocked, scared, out again, and in again, squealing out, diving in, and me never forgetting those words Jamie recited to me, welcoming me, a man about to head to the airport to rejoin his brave wife, a man about to join him in the glorious status of father-of-a-daughter:

> *Their love comes totally without reservation,*
> *Without pretense or nonsense a brand-new sensation*
> *Little girls trust their fathers through all situations*
> *This is how the dreams of an ultimate destination*
> *Maybe they don't know how they link generations*
> *And carry your immortality on to yet another station*
> *But somehow they must hear and feel God's vibrations*
> *And know that you are their connection to creation.*

THE GOALKEEPER
Brendan Halpin

It's cold and raining, as it usually is at the beginning of soccer season in New England. My daughter Kylie is in the goalkeeper's box, and a girl from the other team comes streaking up the field with the ball.

The attacker exudes confidence, and why wouldn't she? She's gotten this far. You can tell what the attacker is expecting—for Kylie, like most goalies her age, to fall back into the goal in a vain effort to protect it, thus allowing the attacker her choice of angles and shots.

Instead, Kylie comes charging out of the goal, falls at the attacker's feet and grabs the ball away from her. The attacker is stunned: she hasn't faced this kind of aggressive, fearless defense before. The other team will keep shooting, of course, but whatever cockiness they have usually evaporates after Kylie's first save.

I wish I could say that Kylie's outstanding play in the goal has consistently led to winning seasons for her team, but the truth is she's not perfect and, more important, her teams have often been cruelly scheduled against teams they are no match for, and so she's often been in the unenviable position of ensuring her team only loses by two goals.

I've always been deeply suspicious of sports in general. My parents were theater people, I was a theater person and, even if I had had a passion for sports, small, weak, and uncoordinated is not usually a formula for sports success.

But when I, widowed with one daughter, married Suzanne, divorced with one son and one daughter, I found myself parenting two gifted athletes. My daughter Rowen inherited her mom's track star body but appears to have also inherited her dad's sports apathy.

And so, as much as it would please me to report that the arts did the trick, I actually think it's soccer that has unlocked my relationship with Kylie.

Kylie was the toughest sell on the whole blended family. Rowen appreciated not being a bored only child anymore and seemed to welcome an adult female presence in her life. My new son, Casey, outnumbered for years, was happy to have another male on the team and enjoyed living with a grown-up who could relate to his love of video games and comic books. (He's since outgrown the comic books. I can't say the same.) And Kylie, well, she was pretty happy with just her mom and brother, and while she accepted Rowen, I seemed to be an unnecessary addition to the picture.

She let me know this in subtle ways: like the painting she made of a dog with two pups that read, "Three or four is a GOOD NUMBER FOR A FAMILY." Also by refusing to allow me to hug her and by crying pretty much nonstop whenever she found herself in a house where I was the only adult.

Because I am a mature adult, I saw the hurt behind all of Kylie's rejections and always approached her with patience and love.

Okay, that's a total lie. On many occasions, I would wade right into battle with her. If you really want to feel like an idiot, try engaging in a screaming match with an eight-year-old. If regular idiocy isn't sufficient and you want to feel like me, try *losing* a screaming match with an eight-year-old.

I had been parenting a daughter for eight and a half years

when Suzanne and I got married. I was a little nervous about parenting a boy, but I was pretty sure I had the whole daughter thing figured out.

But Casey and I bonded on a number of fronts, and adjusting to having a son was a breeze compared to parenting Kylie. She inverted most of the dad-daughter clichés. For example, instead of wanting to protect her from the boys of the world, I kind of wanted to protect them from her. I watched the way she was with me—hostile, then occasionally really kind, then inexplicably hostile again—and I feared mightily for her future boyfriends. I looked at the boys she professed to have crushes on in her grade and tried to imagine how they'd withstand that kind of treatment. I felt she would almost certainly destroy any of them. And yet, even as I feared for what she would do to fragile male egos, I admired the hell out of Kylie. She was, at age eight, something many of us aspire to be but precious few ever achieve: a badass.

If Kylie and I battled at first, we eventually reached a kind of uneasy détente. She went from hostility all the way to tolerance spiked with occasional (and immediately regretted) affection. On two occasions, she actually asked me if I would help chaperone her class on a field trip, and both times she seemed genuinely happy and proud to have me there. I was thrilled. After one field trip, she stayed in the hall after her class returned to the room. "Thank you," she said and ran up and gave me a hug and a kiss. I could not have been more shocked if she had suddenly sprouted wings.

I ran and told Suzanne immediately. "I really think we've turned a corner," I told her, convinced that Kylie had fully accepted me at last.

That was the last hug I received from her for two years.

Soccer, though, is what has really helped me to understand Kylie. I even think it's led to a breakthrough in our relationship.

This is not because I am able to help her with soccer in any way. Though I now commute by bicycle and lift weights regularly, I'm still short and not athletically gifted—okay, okay, I'm athletically cursed—and I'm spectacularly ill qualified to help anybody with sports.

So I'm not a coach—Suzanne did coach her team for a season, but that would have been completely beyond me. I am, though, a pretty reliable fan. In the past few years, I've been to more soccer games, indoor soccer games, and futsal games (another form of indoor soccer, played on a basketball court) than I can possibly count. I frequently wind up hoarse at the end.

And while Kylie plays a variety of positions, what she really excels at is goalie. Suzanne can't stand watching Kylie in the goal—she hates seeing all that pressure come down on Kylie's head, and it makes her so anxious she can barely watch.

I, however, love it. I get insanely proud of the way Kylie positions her defenders during corner kicks, and of the way she gobbles up shots that nobody else can stop. I love seeing the frustration on the faces of the other team and going, "Yeah, that's right! That's my girl! Take *that* back to the suburbs, bitch!"

Of course, I never said any of that aloud. One doesn't verbally abuse eleven-year-old girls even when their snotty suburban parents are annoying you on the sidelines. And, of course, if I'd ever shouted that Kylie was my girl, well, she might well have yelled that she is not, in fact, my girl as, biologically speaking, she isn't. This would humiliate me in front of the other parents, many of whom already regard me with a certain amount of amusement because I spend more time watching the game than shooting the breeze with them and because I cheer loudly and often.

I find myself nearly bursting with pride every time Kylie makes a save. This is not just because she's keeping her team in the game—it's because when she is diving at a ball with zero regard for her personal safety, I feel like I finally get her.

Kylie hates to let her team down, and she is competitive and tall. (At eleven, she's matched my five feet five inches; we're thinking she'll probably get to six feet, which is shy of her biological dad's height but a solid four inches taller than any ancestor of mine.) But I don't think this is why she's good at goalie. I think she's good at goalie because she has something to protect and she will be damned if she's going to let some girl she doesn't even know take it from her.

As I sat through game after game after game, I couldn't help but admire Kylie's toughness on defense even if I realized that at home, it was usually aimed at me. Kylie's deepest thoughts and feelings usually remain mysterious; she repels any attempts to get to them with the same ferocity she shows when attacking a soccer ball.

So this is just a theory, because she'd never tell me, or even Suzanne, this, but I think Kylie is heartbroken. Her parents divorced when she was two, and her father, still a huge presence in her life, moved three hundred miles away from her a few years later. While Casey struggles openly with his dad's absence, Kylie, on the surface, doesn't appear to be too bothered by the whole arrangement.

I distrust sports metaphors, but I really think after her dad moved away, Kylie's heart became her own personal soccer goal. She viewed every attempt to hug her, every attempt to get close to her as a shot on goal. She'd come out of the goal and repel the attack with shocking ferocity, leaving me shaken and afraid to shoot again. (The metaphor works as long as we keep it in the realm of figurative language and put aside the fact that I could never play soccer well enough to beat eleven-year-old female defenders and get a shot on goal.)

Sure, she'd let a few goals in—the field trips and other affectionate gestures. But Kylie is an exceptional goalie, and she does what all exceptional goalies do: when a goal gets through, she shakes it off, forgets the ball that just went through and focuses on getting to the next one.

I'm not going to say I found some magical way to get Kylie to open up to me, that I eventually cracked her code. All I did was show up. Well, that and cheer. And one time abuse a referee who was not calling fouls on any of the players kicking her in the head when she scooped up a ball. (Fortunately he was resolute in his determination to do absolutely nothing other than keep time, and he did not kick me out of the game, either.)

But I think this is really the key to parenting: just freaking show up. I've made worse mistakes parenting Kylie than I have with any of my other kids, and yet, at last, I feel that she's beginning to accept me as, at least, an adult she trusts, and possibly even loves, all because I just showed up.

It turns out that there's tremendous power in just being there, that my loud, probably embarrassing cheers of "Yeah, Ky!" when she made a save were actually telling her something else, something that allowed her to accept me at last.

The other night, Kylie gave me a hug. It was in the guise of hanging on me, but still, I'll take it. I feel, at last, like we kind of get each other. We are, after all, both loudmouths who put on cranky fronts to cover up the soft spots that still hurt sometimes. I suppose it's possible that she's just having a bad game, but I like to think that she finally feels like she doesn't have to come out of the goal and flatten me to stop the shot every time, that she recognizes I'm not an opponent but, rather, a teammate.

She's not a teenager yet, so I know we may be back on opposing sides soon enough, but, for now, I just appreciate what a great goalkeeper she is and appreciate that she's not bringing all her skills to bear against me.

LETTING GO
Carl Lennertz

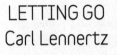

Among my many rules of life, some of which I adhere to and others not so much, is to try and do things a little differently than most people. I don't mean that I need to learn Chinese or to take my first parachute jump at fifty-five, but in nuanced ways I want to put into practice life's rituals askew by, let's say, ten degrees. Nothing radical or annoying; in fact, I am a pretty regular guy. But, being aware of my ordinariness, I don't want to fall into the usual traps that make life clichéd, including stereotypical child-raising practices. Our daughter can have all the chocolate and TV she wants, for instance, but get the homework done first. The occasional clothes shopping trip is fine, but logos are strongly discouraged. Text away, but do the dishes. I like to think that we've given her both freedom and strict guidelines. We've given her a ton of love but insisted on good manners. It's been going pretty well, even into the teen years.

First, let me say that our daughter is, by all measures, a great kid, though naturally I would say that. The evidence includes great grades, a neat group of friends and the ability to speak to adults comfortably. Additionally—and here's where I hope my life view comes in—she is both painfully normal and learning that things don't have to be the way others say they should be. She loves music, new bands and the Beatles. She has boyfriends of several nationalities; cool. She's class prez and science geek; that's my girl. Loves to shop and loves a great bargain. Frugal like her dad. But there's no ballet or violin; just her iPod, a lot of homework (we survived junior year, SATs, APs and all that together), movies, dates and coffee shops. And she hates vegetables; I did, too. She'll come around on her own.

A significant sign that our not-so-wee one wanted to shake things up was her decision, at the wise age of thirteen, to change schools. In New York City, a kid has the choice of a dozen high schools. (Being a small-town kid who went K-12 in one building, I marvel at this.) Most of her friends were going to go to high school in one place, but she decided a clean break was in order and took a test to go elsewhere. Elsewhere, as in an hour away, in a different borough, with no one she knew going there. A big step for her, and a giant step in our parental letting go.

Yes, yes, there had been many smaller steps in this separation already in the books. We all know them. First day of school, the first overnights at other houses, first dates. Life's passages are either marked by ceremonial walks down imposing aisles in churches or auditoriums, or they happen quietly and without swelling movie music. A walk down a driveway toward a friend's house, and then she disappears through the door. The walk from my car to her circle of girlfriends outside school before a fifth-grade dance. Walks big and small, all of them symbols of transition toward her adulthood and away from our constant care.

Believe it or not, I did not have a problem dealing with any of these; hell, I'd put her on planes by herself already. She got a note pinned to her jacket and off she went to a beloved godmother in Alabama, and there was a school trip to Turkey. I watched her form recede down the walkway, gave her a huge hug upon return, and knew this was all in the scheme of things, how it has to be. Walks, doors, journeys.

But I wasn't quite as sanguine about the daily morning and

evening subway ride by herself to high school in a so-so neighborhood. That changed the rules for me and brought safety issues to bear, but through the power of text messaging to signal safe arrivals and imminent departures, rules about no headphones and choosing busy streets to walk down and a convoy of friends after dark, we made it work. It is a fine line to walk when teaching someone that life is both beautiful and dangerous, to open up to the world as well as be on guard.

Which brings me to a party and my stakeout from midnight to 5:00 a.m., with the help of a jumbo iced coffee. Me, who hasn't stayed up for SNL since season five. Me, psychofather? Read on before you judge.

She was a sophomore and her boyfriend was a senior, so she was going with him to his last prom. All cool, another big occasion well in hand. But then came the news of an after-party at a house where the parents were away. Sorry, no way! Many tears and some negotiation later, I said this would only happen if I could be allowed to be down the street from the party in my comfy minivan. I was not to be an official chaperone, just someone proximate in the event of emergency. I knew these kids and knew they would behave well, but I told my daughter and her beau that experience has taught me that house parties take on a weird dynamic, that all can be fine one minute, and then a friend of a friend slips in a bottle of booze and off we go. Also, one cannot control what happens outside the bubble of the house, like a group of guys cruising by at 2:00 a.m. deciding to crash the party. Stuff happens. But I was willing to give it a go, knowing full well something would go awry, deciding it was better she experience it now in a relatively safe environment and, yes, with the old man down the street.

I will tell you now that all mostly did go well. A few cars slowed down at 1:00 and 2:00 a.m., but kept going. The kids listened to music inside or sat on the front steps talking. And, big shock, someone got into some vodka and had to have their hair held back over the toilet—or so I heard later. Good! I'm glad she saw the mess that clear liquid can cause. And I did see a tall teen, shirttails out, stumble down the steps and commence that telltale weave down the sidewalk, but he was rescued and returned to the nest.

It turns out I ended up having the more interesting adventure before the party even began. You see, I don't stay up past ten, as I am a very early riser. I knew I would need to get some sleep before manning my post at midnight. Since we actually lived an hour away from the party locale and the start time of the party was dependent on how late the prom went, I booked a room at a modest but new motel a few miles from the school so I could sleep and then be up and at the house in fifteen minutes. The hotel was not in a great area but I wasn't moving in. I just needed food and four hours of sleep.

I bought some Chinese food across the street and plopped on the bed, TV remote and a plastic cup of red wine in hand. I was going to make myself sleepy: MSG + tannins = soporofic. The plan was to conk out by eight and rouse at midnight, when I got the text message that they had left the prom for the after-party. I settled in, despite the fact that the door across the hall from mine sported some yellow crime scene tape—I am not making that up. But it was too late now; I had paid for the room and my door had double locks.

I was dozing off, my plan going perfectly, when a car, seemingly right outside my window, let loose with the loudest music I have heard since I was dragged to a Frank Zappa concert. I'm not sure if it was merengue or salsa, and under any other circumstance, I would've enjoyed this joyous noise, but not now, not tonight. I had a stakeout in a few hours.

Needless to say, I didn't fall sleep until about eleven, got an hour in before my teen's text alert, got in my minivan, went to a drive-through Dunkin' Donuts for the largest iced coffee they had, and I was on my way. Upon arrival, I got a wave from my daughter, and a few waves from her friends, who thought her father was sweet or nuts or, mostly, not theirs. I got a text from my daughter at 5:00 a.m. with the news they were locking the door and going to sleep, whereupon I went to a local diner for the best breakfast I've ever had and the first newspaper off the top of a just-delivered bundle tossed from a truck, just like in the movies.

That, in a nutshell, is the story of my great vigil, my folly. My wife and some friends said that I was nuts to even let her go, but gatherings of that size, with all their fun and foolish variables, are something she'll have to learn to navigate, especially come college, so I was okay with the all-nighter, hers and mine. I had coffee and music, and our offspring was chalking up another rite of passage.

I wouldn't change a thing about that night—even the crime scene tape and the three-foot woofers in that car outside my window—or about any of the adventures we have been on with this marvelous young person, now, really, almost an adult. She is just a few more heartbreaks and her first rent check away from full status.

Our next significant walks together—well, before the one down the aisle, which is so far away I can't even think about (and the courthouse is just fine with me, honey, being the father of the bride and footer of the bill)—will be the mundane ones from the van to her dorm room soon, carrying the everyday objects of a college student: pillows, pencils, computer, T-shirts and more. All done, hugs and goodbyes, and then she'll walk through another door by herself or with her roommate, and my wife and I will walk back to the van in the lot, and then, I'm sure of it, I will tear up for the first time in eighteen years about a silly old drop-off. She isn't coming home that night for dinner, or for many more nights to come. No battles over a messy room, no more grumpy teenager at 6:00 a.m. No more chats around the kitchen counter or watching TV together. All those normal, clichéd, stereotypical daily events of family life— I will miss them all.

There has been a roller coaster of little letting go's in the days between when I started this essay and when I finished it. First came her own senior prom. No stakeout, I just said "Have fun, be safe, and see you tomorrow sometime." I was asleep by 10:00 p.m. And, miracle of miracles, she was fine! A whirlwind two weeks followed: classmates' grad parties all over the city, sleepovers and the complete abandonment of a normal schedule. There was Father's Day and the sweetest darn card from her. Then the graduation ceremony, which was both totally predictable and totally wonderful, and a fun graduation barbecue with her friends and ours. Afterward, she went out with friends in the city till 1:00 a.m.; you know where I was, right? Asleep, happy in the thoughts that we have pretty much done all we can to help shape this person.

It's a measure of our mutual love, as well as understanding that it's time for a change, that she settled on a university a five-hour drive away. Not too far, not too near. No popping home on weekends, which I think is good, but we'll have holidays and maybe a visit to catch a football game each fall.

On her last day of high school, I did text her to say that today would mark her last "I'm here, Pops!" back to me upon a safe arrival. She texted back in all caps, but that was perfect. Over a thousand "I'm here" and "I'm home" texts in four years. The next four will probably bring 1 percent of that, if that. I'm not going to be a pest, honest. I'll be working a bit extra to pay the bills; she'll be studying and playing, finding her way with another new group of friends, finding her career path. She'll be letting go, too, of high school friends, her old routine, her old bedroom and our two cats, and of Mums and Pops, always around in some measure.

But I'm guessing—hoping—that most of the texts, both ways, will be simple I-love-yous. Actually, I am sure of it, more sure of that than anything else in life. And that is good. Letting go with one hand and holding on with the other. Those tiny digits we held tight crossing the street are now typing papers and texting messages home.

THE WHOLE WIDE WORLD
Claude Stanush

We are on the family ranch, the Half-Circle 45. My mother and I are sitting on some bales of hay in the middle of a large, brushy pasture. A short distance away is a windmill, the blades turning sporadically and creakily as they are hit by whiffs of wind. The sun is on the horizon; it will disappear in half an hour or so. My father is on his favorite horse, a sorrel with a streak of white down its forehead, and he tells us that he has to ride to another ranch, some miles away. It's serious business.

An hour goes by. Then another. Darkness has set in. Everything is pitch-black except for some tiny specks of light high up in the sky. All we hear are some squeaks of gears turning slowly as the wind hits the windmill. Not far away from us we hear the haunting screech of some animal. A dangerous one?

Who knows? Then there is something howling far in the distance. "Probably a coyote," my mother says. But I'm scared.

Oh, where is my father? Thrown from a horse? It happens on ranches, although my father is an expert horseman. Trouble at the other ranch? Who knows why he had to leave us like he did?

My mother tries to reassure me. "You know that other sound we heard? I bet that was Hooty the Owl." Of course I knew Hooty. "And that howl?" she went on. "That's Old Man Coyote out there. And the wind that's turning the windmill? That's Mother West Wind."

The calm way she mentioned those characters, everything

seemed natural, the way everything in nature sounds as it should sound. My mother was relaxed. I relaxed.

Two more hours passed before we heard, in the distance, the *clump clump* of a horse's hooves. Then the creak of saddle leather. That seemed perfectly natural to me now, but I hugged my mother, and when the horse and its rider appeared suddenly a few feet from us, I ran to greet my father, and later, when he took the saddle off, the horse's back was naturally covered with sweat—and I love the smell of that sweat.

I can still smell it. And I'm telling the story now because it's not only the story of the value of metaphor in life, but it's the background for all that follows—which is the story of a whole family of storytellers who believe that Hooty the Owl and Old Man Coyote and Mother West Wind are as real as horse sweat.

In the middle of the Great Depression in the 1930s, when my brother Frank was fourteen and I was ten, my father died, leaving my mother to become father as well as mother. We had a modest ranch with cattle, but there were three years of severe drought, the Mexican fever tick was rampant, and cattle were a half cent a pound. What savings our family had were lost completely in a bank failure. But in all of this, my mother was solid as a mesquite post—and we survived.

Stories are the heart and soul of life. They tell how we feel, think and act. Whether we're humans in the best sense or the worst. Good stories bare the heart and soul of human beings.

My family, the Stanush family, has a long history and tradition of storytelling. It began in Poland, where the people were under the subjection of the Prussian Empire. My grandfather was drafted by the Prussian army, and because he was an excellent horseman, he was chosen to be in the elite cavalry guarding the kaiser. My grandfather's future wife, my grandmother Mary Zygmond, was actually born on a sailing ship in the Atlantic

Ocean headed for the Americas. My grandparents and my great-grandparents were brave ranchers in South Texas at a time when it was still a dangerous land of Mexican and American outlaws, fierce Apache and Comanche Indians and something else they didn't have in Europe, rattlesnakes.

My mother, Mary Burda Stanush, was a great storyteller. One of her stories tells of how, when she was three years old, her father took her to see the Apache renegade Geronimo. The army had captured him and put him on display on Alamo Plaza in San Antonio. My mother wasn't a writer, but through her stories she could provoke laughter at one time and at another bring tears to the eyes.

I'm a storyteller, too, and so is my wife, Barbara (through poetry), but this story I'm telling now is less about us than about Michele, one of our daughters. Actually, we have two other daughters, Pamela and Julie, but there's a reason this particular story is primarily about Michele. She will probably be the one who will carry on the storytelling tradition after Barbara and I are dead.

There's one story from my life that has particularly inspired Michele. I was working at the *San Antonio Light* when I decided I wanted to work at *Life* magazine. On my vacation I took a train to New York and appeared at the office of executive editor Wilson Hicks, who did the hiring. The secretary told me to take a chair and when Mr. Hicks could see me that she would let me know. I sat in the chair and waited, and days went by without his calling me in. People in other offices felt sorry for me and brought me coffee and sandwiches.

Two weeks went by and he never called me and I sadly went home. For my next vacation, the next year I was back outside Mr. Hicks's office and, finally, after several days of waiting, he called me and asked me what I wanted. I told him I wanted to work for *Life*. He asked me what my qualifications were. I said "Well, first of all, perseverance."

He laughed. "Yes, I can see you have perseverance. But we don't have jobs for you."

My heart sank. I rode home on the train and resumed my job at the *Light*.

About a month later, while I was having lunch at the café across the street from the newspaper, a copyboy came running to tell me that I had a phone call from New York. It wasn't Mr. Hicks. It was his assistant. "We have a job for you in the Hollywood–Los Angeles office. We want you there in a week."

After my father died, we had a lot of hardships and things that were difficult. But when I was offered my first job for *Life*, I remember coming home and saying, "They want me to go out to Hollywood," and my mother said, "Go." That was her very first word. She never hesitated. She said, "Go." And I felt badly because we were living in this half attic in the south part of town and Grandma couldn't drive a car. She would be very limited in what she could do. I remember the day I left, it just broke my heart. I was going to leave her so lonely and by herself. But there was never a question with her that I would make the decision to do something that would benefit me. It was simply, "Do it." I believe there were a number of times when Michele was turned down for something initially and, thinking back to my story, she just hopped right back up and tried again.

Barbara and I were living in New York City when Michele was born in 1960. Barbara, a magna cum laude graduate of Duke University, was working for the Institute of International Education, in the arts division, whose mission was to bring artists, writers and other talented people to this country. I had worked thirteen years for *Life* but had recently resigned.

Michele turned out to be a healthy, beautiful baby, her only aberration a pair of big feet. "She must have Texas blood in her—she's going to be a tall girl," one nurse said. Of course, she was half-Texan, but we were living in New York and her first home was in one of those famous old brownstone buildings at 111 Waverly Place in the heart of Greenwich Village. The apartment, which had been a speakeasy in the 1920s, was in the basement of the building with a garden in the rear. It was just a few feet away from Henry James's Washington Square. Down the street was a former apartment of Edna St. Vincent Millay and across the street was the spot where Edgar Allen Poe had first recited his poem "The Raven."

I changed Michele's diapers and I read stories to her, and, like many children, she wanted some stories to be read to her over and over again. Stories like "Duck in the Truck," "Mother Mouse" and particularly the one about Little Bear climbing a tree and looking out over "the wide, wide world." Michele loved that part, except that she called it "the wide, wide *woild*." And so I started to read that section the way that she pronounced it: "the wide, wide *woild*." I had hoped that Michele would see that "whole wide world" and be a part of it.

We took Michele everywhere we went in New York—shopping, to parties, on the subway—and although she couldn't be aware of it, almost everything in New York at the time was lively and meaningful. At that time, the early 1960s, it was the world's capital in government (the United Nations), in the arts, finance and cultural exchange. (Years later, when Michele was working for a film company in New Jersey, she spent time in New York, visiting the sites we had told her about and imbibing some of the flavor of that time.)

When Michele was two, Barbara and I were looking for a change of experience and a less expensive cost of living and so we moved back to my hometown of San Antonio and eventually into a house on Maverick Hill, where there was plenty to stir the imagination.

Living on the Hill as an only child for some years and without neighborhood kids as playmates, Michele suffered from loneliness more than my wife and I realized. She did spend a lot of time with my mother, her grandmother, who kept her entertained and her fantasies enlarged with stories about her ancestors when they lived in Poland under cruel Prussian rule and then the hardships and dangers encountered when they came to Texas to become farmers and ranchers.

Michele's sisters, twins Pamela and Julie, were born when she was seven years old. She loved them, and they loved her, but they were different—good students but also good athletes. Julie wrote the family's first novel when she was eleven—the story of a boy and his horse.

We had interesting visitors galore on Maverick Hill, with all kinds of dramatic stories and conversation, and Michele was always on the edges, seldom speaking, but always listening, recording, enlarging her imagination. *Life* photographers and writers, who had been close friends in New York, came. So did Fred Gipson, author of *Old Yeller* and other books made into movies, who on one occasion brought his future young wife, Angelina, dressed in a leopard-skin miniskirt. And so did Willis and Joe Newton, old retired outlaws and champion bank and train robbers, whom I was interviewing for a book. Visiting us on Maverick Hill, they liked to eat Barbara's mustard greens with us, and in return, they brought jars of honey from hives they had at home. "We're too old to rob banks no more, but we can sure rob them beehives," Willis said.

I had been working on a novel version of the Newton Boys' story. Why? Because the story was more than that of some talented bank and train robbers. It was about a major turning point in American history, the 1920s, when this country was rapidly passing from an agricultural society, where the measure of value was land, to a technological, industrialized society, where the measure of value was money.

The fact that a feature film about the Newton Boys was about to be made gave me a new impetus to finish the novel, and I asked Michele if she wanted to work with me on it. The film, financed by 20th Century Fox, had top-notch actors, good music, and it was a lot of fun because director Richard Linklater let the whole Stanush family be a part of the filming in one way or another. I was in one very short scene—I played a grizzled farmer (they told me not to shave for three days) who was making a deposit in a small-town bank when the first robbery took place. Michele was also hired as an extra to play a school-marm.

By the time the filming was finished, however, we still had a long way to go on the novel. I had developed the story line, the main characters and their voices and many of the details of their robberies and capture. But I still had to fill in gaps and a lot of the details, like what life was like back in the 1920s, the way people dressed, the kind of cars they drove, the music they listened to and so on—the kind of detail that Michele was un-surpassed in getting. In doing research, she was like a blood-hound after its quarry, never stopping until she had acquired every aspect of a story, right down to the tiniest detail.

More important even than the details she supplied, however, Michele began to challenge my characterizations. She felt I had made Willis "too soft" and his wife, Louise, "too sweet." Didn't Willis have a vicious side to him? For example, hadn't he bitten the finger off of somebody that he was fighting? And wasn't his wife, Louise, "wilier and smarter" than I had portrayed her?

"You don't know women like I do," Michele told me.

Eventually, after many months of working together and reconciling differences, we thought we had produced a good book together. And when the book was published, *Kirkus Reviews* gave us a starred rating, with the comment, "This novel transcends biography since it's Willis' voice that will stay with you. Melding seamlessly, the Stanushes debut deliciously here with a combination Tom Jones and Billy the Kid…"

After we finished *All Honest Men,* Michele then did something totally unexpected—a project suggested by her mother, who had been a great help to me as a nuanced editor over many years. Michele went through some of my short stories that she loved and that had not yet been published in a book. She spent many hours checking details and editing. Then she went hunting for somebody to publish them. Someone was found and the stories appeared in a book entitled *Sometimes It's New York.* The cover—a photograph taken by my wife, Barbara—was of the building where we lived in New York and that, incidentally, was Michele's first home.

Most of all, this book was for me a gift of love. Love isn't something you can demand, or even expect, of children. It has to be spontaneously given. When Michele helped to compile my stories, it took a lot of work and time. And although Michele does a lot of things for Barbara and me, this collection of short stories has special meaning for me. Michele has told me that of all the writing projects she has been involved with in her life, this book is the one she is most proud of.

All three of our children are sensitive to the needs of others, and if someone were to ask me what influence these three have had on my life, I would say that, number one, is the gift of love, particularly love when it is most needed. One of the expressions of that love came four years ago, when I became desperately ill with a high fever—in the hospital, my head was covered with bags of ice to prevent damage to my brain—and my wife and all three of our daughters helped me through months of rehabilitation to regain my health.

It seems as if, in the relationship between parents and children, that independence and community are two sides of the same coin. Michele is currently helping me with a second novel, entitled *Piece of Cheese*, about a young artist struggling to survive in New York during the turbulent 1960s, when it seemed that everybody was revolting against something, even artists against art—at least the traditional art of the easel. She is also reviving a screenplay she wrote based on one of my short stories called "Holes." The original story was based on an old schoolmate of mine who made a fortune buying up natural holes in the ground, like caves, and selling them for a great variety of purposes, from garbage dumps to nightclubs. But she's also working on the first book of her own—that is, apart from me—with an occupational therapist whose life's work has been to tackle chronic pain without drugs or surgery. I'm glad she has been as determined to succeed as I was all those years ago at the offices of *Life*. Despite her shyness and introversion, she never gave up.

In 2004, Julie went with Barbara and me to Poland to visit villages where my grandparents came from. In the village churches, we saw the baptismal records for the Stanush and Burda families that went back hundreds of years. And I couldn't help the tears in my eyes as I looked at the tracks of the narrow-gauge railroad that took my grandparents to Danzig, Prussia, where a sailing boat was waiting to take them to Texas.

Pamela has also gotten interested in the family stories, and to add to them, she's started to record my story on tape—from birth to the present time. But the purpose is not simply to focus on our family. Our family, although the stories are interesting, is but a tiny, tiny, tiny part of the family of man *and* woman whose home is that "wide, wide *woild*" that Little Bear saw when he climbed up the tree.

LITTLE FIRES
Amitava Kumar

It is Father's Day today.

In the morning an excited voice in the kitchen told me to return to the bedroom. *Go back, Dad. Go back, mister.* But it was my wife who brought the tea while I pretended to be asleep. Attached to the handle of the teacup was a paper flower with the words "I Love You, Dad." Giggles from behind her mother's nightgown, and then the presentation of gifts, including a pair of boxer shorts imprinted with the maps of countries, which, who knows, she'll perhaps visit someday, maybe even with her parents.

We had a little celebration around breakfast but I have been in pain. My joints are swollen, as if someone has poured cement into them. Waves of fatigue wash over me, and I feel unsteady, like I'm in the sand with the tide running out. The doctor thinks it could be rheumatoid arthritis, a condition that, thankfully, isn't common in my family. The other possibility, he thinks, is Lyme disease. It would have come from a tick that had bitten me when I was in the park with my daughter. After examining me, he once again asked my age, and having noted the number down, he drew a circle around it. Yesterday, first thing in the morning, I had to go to a facility where I gave my blood and urine for the tests that the doctor has ordered.

But I think he is being dire. I'm pretty sure I know what the trouble is—and why I'm in this state. Earlier in the week, I had returned from a literary festival in Chicago around one at night.

Perhaps because of the exhaustion I was feeling from a busy day, I left one of my bags on the train; I didn't go to sleep till two more hours had passed, and was then up a few short hours later, when my daughter woke me up with kisses. I fed her breakfast and helped her change into her day clothes. My wife was going to drive her to summer camp. When they waved me goodbye, I jogged beside the car in my slippers. My daughter began to laugh. This absurd ritual that we participate in, particularly because it annoys her mother, is an old joke between us. But soon I was overdoing it. I had switched to a comic high-stepping action, so as to look like a demented ostrich. Seeing that my daughter had stretched out her hand through the window, my wife slowed down but I urged her to go even faster. And I kept up for a while, although I had not had any exercise for ages. My little girl in her car seat was by now bent over with laughter, and when they turned onto the main street, I could still hear her happily screaming, "Daddy, Daddy."

By night, my ankles had become heavy, and I began to think of them as being waterlogged. My knees had stiffened into a posture of immobility. I bent down to take the butter out of the fridge and the pain knocked my breath out. The next day I didn't feel like getting out of bed. Today, even my neck is suffering from a familiar ache. At varying hours during the night, I hear the question "Dad, can I come into your bed?" She climbs in between her mother and me. By morning, my daughter's curly head is pressed right against my neck and I find myself sleeping awkwardly on the edge of the mattress. Now when I open my eyes, but very often even before that, I'm aware of a throbbing pain. Sometimes my arm, more often my neck, sometimes my head. I am forty-six. It sometimes feels that my father, who is in his seventies, must be waking up each morning feeling better than I do.

Next week the result of the blood and urine test will have come in. I will be going back to the doctor. I have no idea what he will tell me, but I know that I'll never be able to say to him that my problem is that I love my daughter in a way that is both excessive and perhaps harmful to me.

When our daughter was about to be born, I chose for her a short name—Ila. Ila's mother is Muslim; I am Hindu. We got married when our two countries, India and Pakistan, were fighting a war. Ila is a Hindu name; it is also the opposite of her mother's last name, Ali.

Ila Ali. A friend of mine said it would be a name that would sway in the breeze all day. I had noticed that it formed a palindrome. Ila's name mirrored her mother's and yet kept its difference. I liked that.

Which is all to say that even before she was born, Ila had become, like many other kids, a site of complicated, and often silly, fantasies on the part of her parents.

Ila is now six. Around the time of her birth, I chanced upon an essay by Raymond Carver called "Fires." It is a memoir produced, I suppose, in response to a question about literary influences. In a characteristic move, Carver declares that more than books and writers, it was other things in his messy, real world that had affected his work. In particular, his children. The memory of those years, when his kids were growing up still bothered Carver. Sitting in the basement of my in-laws' house in Toronto, while waiting to become a new father, I read that when he looked back at his years as a young father, there was no area untouched by what he called his children's "heavy and baleful influence." That his two children were the greatest single influence on his life.

Around the time that I first read "Fires," I was also starting to draw the outline of a first novel. I began to think that I would write about the birth of my daughter. My wife underwent a long, painful labor. The novel began with a man in a prison near my hometown in India. I tried to imagine him witnessing a birth in a prison, not a human being giving birth, but an animal. Say, a dog. The distance from actual experience, its transformation into something removed from actuality, seemed to me the proper task of the novelist. On the day of my daughter's birth, I made the following entry in my journal: "The bitch had been sullen and sluggish through the long afternoon."

When I sat down at a makeshift desk in a room adjoining the one in which my wife was sleeping, I saw in my mind the man in prison, looking down into the dusty yard. He was watching a dog circling a clump of banana trees in distress. The animal tries to bite and lick a bone. The man stays at the window and realizes, the discovery filling him with tenderness, that what the dog is licking is a newborn puppy.

Now when I look back on it, I wonder whether some of Carver's "dirty realism" (or what Tess Gallagher, Carver's second wife, has called his "benign menace") hadn't crept into my presentation of Ila's arrival as an animal birth witnessed in a prison. In any case, when the novel was published, the scene I have described above found its way into its pages. But there were many times during the writing of the book when I wished I had more time to write. Perhaps all writers complain about time—there is never enough time, and in the years following that first encounter with Carver's essay, I have often gone back to it like an alcoholic returning to drink. As far as I am concerned, despite or perhaps because of my hunger for it, that piece is like poison.

For the truth is that I also love my daughter so much that anything sweet or tender reminds me of her. I don't only mean a child on a street in strange city, who can suddenly induce heartache because she's wearing a dress of a style and color I associate with my daughter, but even a bird calling in an overhead branch, *ku-hu, ku-hu*. I remember being in a small town in India a couple years after Ila had been born. In a dark front yard of a house where I had come to conduct a late-night interview, two young servants were busy with a black cow that was about to give birth. Lanterns swinging in their hands, the youths explained that the last time one of the cows had given birth, it had been in the middle of the night. No one was around to take care of the calf. In that crowded stall, the mother had accidentally trampled her newborn to death.

As I watched, fifteen minutes later, the calf arrived, its legs thin and crooked as in a child's drawing. I could think only of Ila as I gazed at the lovely little animal in front of me: she was also the child whose drawings had given me a way to look at it that night. The creature's arrival filled me with a sudden elation and it also made me miss my daughter terribly. It is the same when I'm in the train coming back from New York City, hoping to be home before she goes to bed. To participate in the ritual of preparing her for sleep, and then lying down next to her to read a story, offers me great joy. I will not exchange it for another hour of writing. At such moments, I have traded Raymond Carver for Wallace Stevens. When asked by Marianne Moore to turn in a piece on William Carlos Williams, Stevens said no, explaining in his letter: "...there is a baby at home. All lights are out at nine. At present there are no poems, no reviews. I am sorry."

Such grace. And, however impermanently, that sense of patience and grace is also mine.

I say impermanently not only because, in my case, the feeling of sweet resignation that Stevens is describing gives way, sometimes, to the rage that Carver is articulating. That does happen, but what I have in mind is this: I put Ila to sleep and lie awake in the dark for a while. The lights are, indeed, out at nine, but not for long. I come out of the room and make my way slowly upstairs to sit down and write.

On occasion, I write about Ila. As I am doing right now. This is what writers do—they write about the world, and because their children often loom large in their world, they end up putting them into their stories, too.

Carver certainly did. He wrote a poem to his daughter that invoked a similar effort by W. B. Yeats, except that instead of wanting his daughter to be plain, he wanted her to be sober. "You're a beautiful drunk, daughter. But you're a drunk." These are two lines that appear near the middle of what is certainly not among Carver's better poems. In this poem, Papa is preaching against alcoholism. As in an AA meeting, there's great value put on confessions of one's own sins, the daughter being asked why she hasn't learned from all the mistakes her parents made. The poem goes on to document the daughter's degradation and her injuries at the hand of the man she loves. It's all gritty and intense, but I wonder what Carver's daughter herself thought of her father laying out in full public view the intimate picture of her sorry life.

I ask this as if I feel aggrieved; I'm not. I ask only as a member of the offending class. The offending class of writers. Once, when Ila was two, my wife was nursing her. Ila turned away from one breast to the other, saying, "This one not working." I remember asking myself how long it would be before I used that in my writing.

Ila would come back from preschool and bring bits of her strange, alluring world to me. Everything she said I'd store like postcards from a fictional place. In my journal is a note that shows that when Ila was three, she pored over a map and asked me,

"Where's California? California lives in the desert, right, Dad?" I thought that was precious but a part of me must have also believed that I could use that line in a novel. But even as I look at some of the other entries I have made in my journal, I see that there is another impulse also at work.

Consider the line that Ila offered at bedtime on April 18, 2007, when she was a few months short of four: "I know only two things. That I have to wear loose clothes when I go to sleep, and that we have to be nice to each other." These are not notes for a novel: instead, these are memos to self. "Shape up," these memos say. There are several entries in this vein in my journal. I find myself reflecting, not only on my daughter's sweetness, but also on my secret desire to be the person that my daughter thinks I am. This becomes clearer to me when I read in another entry that after a ten-hour journey, when Ila and I are picked up late at the train station by her mother and I complain about the time we have spent waiting in the cold, Ila silences the apologies by saying, "You were on time, Mom. You were on time."

My daughter thinks I am the person who will take her to Disney World. Who am I to pretend to be otherwise? This was a couple of years ago. My wife, who is an economist, refused to come with us. She said something like "It is a corrupt consumerist trap; you cannot possibly take Ila there." I enjoyed the trip very much. I confess I had mixed motives for visiting Florida. In the pages of the *New York Times,* Thomas Friedman had written that post–September 11 America had become hostile to visitors and our government was exporting fear, not hope. More specifically, Friedman had complained, "If Disney World can remain an open, welcoming place, with increased but invisible security, why can't America?" Friedman's remark sparked my curiosity. I suddenly felt that I could excuse my extravagance.

Once there I noticed that bags were searched before entry

but there wasn't much more that I could observe. This becoming a research trip was unlikely. It wasn't as if while rushing from the Caribbean Beach Resort to the Magic Kingdom, I could touch Mickey Mouse's elbow and ask, "Say, where are the hidden cameras?" Not only that. Even if I had found the answer to that question, perhaps all I'd have wanted to find next was whether the cameras would reveal where the lines for the rides were shorter.

Frankly, I couldn't have been happier than doing what I had really come to do. From morning to night, nervous about a thousand things, I took my child in a rented stroller from one overpriced event to another. There was tea with Sleeping Beauty. There were endless encounters with people in cute, but no doubt hellishly hot, stuffed-animal costumes. We met patient princesses who held their smiles while parents of the kids standing next to them figured out how to use a simple digital camera. I was anxious that in the heat my daughter looked sunburned and thirsty. But I was happy not to have to think about work. I was on holiday with my happy child.

It is not always like this. I can be in another city for work, perhaps on my way to an interview, but I'll be searching with one eye for a toy shop. There was a time when I would take the train to New York City to attend a terrorism trial—but even while rushing to catch the subway, I'd stop at a kids' store in Grand Central Station to buy a little gift for Ila. I was often late in court, and when I took a seat on a bench near the door, a witness would already be halfway into a story about illegal funds. I would hear about where the money went, but have no idea about where the money came from!

Such happenings leave me conflicted. Not about the plain fate of being a father—although one evening when she was four, Ila looked up from a game she was playing with me and asked, "Are you tired to having a child?"—but about how I deal with my responsibilities. Last October, I was in Beijing searching for clues to two writers' lives early in the twentieth century. I went to museums and libraries, and even to cemeteries, but required more information for what I wanted to write. A lot of work needed to be done. Instead of pounding the pavement in search of people who would provide me what I needed, I found myself one morning in Beijing's Hongqiao Market, looking for a Chinese costume for Ila. Her instructions had been precise. She had watched *Mulan* on TV, and wanted what Mulan was wearing. Earlier, I had stopped at a store called Cinderella but it sold only bridal dresses; Hongqiao Market didn't disappoint, it was full of goods that we think of as stereotypically Chinese. The shops were packed with haggling Americans, and salesgirls who, in a show of intimacy, would each grab my arm and shriek, "Very cheap, very cheap." I had a list of things I needed to buy, which included a Chinese doll and a paper kite; on the back was the outline of two little soles because, as you might be aware, Mulan also wore distinctly Chinese shoes. I had to search for these items with care but what was also exhausting was the pressure to bargain. For thirty yuan, one could buy a cup of green tea, and, more than once, I sat down to sip tea and collect my wits. And during those breaks, I asked myself whether I shouldn't have actually been conducting interviews at the Beijing Normal University. The answer was perhaps yes, but what was undeniable was the elation I felt as I ticked off what I had purchased on the list. It was my best day in China.

In January 2004 a Seattle paper reported that a conference was going to be held in Yakima, Carver's hometown, to honor the writer's memory. The keynote speaker was Vance Carver, the writer's forty-five-year-old son. The younger Carver had declared his intention to remove the misconceptions about his father's early family life, about the bad years before the writer sobered up and did the work that earned him his name. The younger Carver had told the newspaper that those years his father had spent as a family man hadn't all been dark years.

The detail that caught my eye in that news item was Vance Carver's mention of a famous story of his father's called "The Compartment." This was the first story of Carver's that I had read. A middle-aged man named Myers is on a train, going to visit his son whom he hasn't seen for eight years. En route, the man discovers that someone has stolen the expensive wristwatch he had bought for his son. The mood has soured, and the man realizes he never wanted to meet the boy or make small talk with him. Then, more and more things go wrong, as they inevitably will in Carver's fiction, and it becomes clear that Myers isn't going to see his son, anyway.

In the news story Vance Carver had pointed out that "The Compartment" was based on a trip that he had taken to Paris with his father. But that wasn't all. He also said that his father had transformed what had been a pleasant memory into a dark tale of the troubled relationship between a parent and his progeny. And yet, he said that he had liked the story but simply wanted people to know his relationship with his father didn't resemble what we encounter in the story. Such pathos, such poignance! It is not only parents who have fantasies about their children. The opposite is also true.

But that is beside the point. I don't myself know what I want to believe more. That the lives of the Carver children weren't always as miserable as their father's writings had suggested, or that so clear and steadfast was Carver's vision of reality that his imagination turned all he touched to something squalid. Here I have a private fantasy of my own, which is a writer's fantasy, fatuous and self-serving, and it goes something like this: Carver was good at hiding the drunkenness and his frustration from his kids when they were growing up, but when he sat down to write, he hid nothing and tried his best to cut close to the bone. Of course, a writer's greatest fantasy is that he or she will keep writing well. When Carver was doing that, a few years before he died of cancer, he claimed in an interview that he had regained his children.

At the end, Carver seemed to have found a balance in his life. I haven't found that place yet. But perhaps because I haven't felt myself at the end of my tether, at least not for too long. I also haven't scripted for my life bleak little narratives of destruction. But I think of Carver often. One night we were sleeping at a friend's house. I woke up Ila at night and asked her to come to the bathroom with me so that she could pee. But she refused. I was afraid she was going to wet the bed. I tried again and again, and lost my temper when she crossed her arms and angrily turned to face the wall. I put out the light and said I wasn't going to lie down with her anymore; she could sleep by herself. Ila began to cry then, and when I put on the light a few moments later, she was standing on the floor. Her hands were stretched out in the dark; her eyes were still shut, and tears were streaming down her cheeks. Such shame. The squalor of love, the play of power. That is probably what made me think of Carver, although in him one would find no quick redemption through swift kisses. There is little search for forgiveness in his writing, only the clear putting down of the right words for all the wrong things in life. He came to mind the other day again, when I found myself thinking that there is a word in the English language for loving one's wife too much, but none for lavishing too much affection on one's daughter.

RECKLESS IN LOVE
Richard Farrell

My daughter Siobhan is riding in the backseat of her friend's car. She's nineteen and home for the summer. With hardly any effort, Siobhan has just barely finished her first year of college at Seton Hall in South Orange, New Jersey. She tells her older brother that the second semester introduced an inability to calculate the correct equation between parties and classes.

She's wearing her seat belt.

Siobhan's friend Shelly is driving. Shelly's mom bought the car for her as a high school graduation present the previous summer. Shelly went to the University of Maine and dropped out after the first semester. Shelly doesn't believe in seat belts.

Moments earlier, Kate called "shotgun" and claims the front seat. Kate is Siobhan's best friend and sits directly in front of her. Kate attended community college in Concord, New Hampshire, for one semester but didn't really like it. Kate's seat belt is broken; wearing it isn't even an option.

Chelsea is in the backseat behind the driver. Siobhan had been the last one picked up. Chelsea had just finished her first year of college, a small school in Charlotte, North Carolina. Chelsea had removed her seat belt when she slid over. In the moment, she forgot to fasten the seat belt in her new position.

It's only 7:00 p.m. The sun's glow is fierce, almost blinding. The four friends are on their way to Burger King. They debate about what to do. The night is young and they're all bored. Siobhan suggests taking a ride to Massachusetts to see her brother. Somebody else suggests they go to their friend Danielle's house because her mom's not home. A Bob Dylan song blasts out of the radio.

I'm back in Los Angeles. Most people only get one chance to get their story right in this town. I'm a heroin addict in recovery. In another lifetime I was pure evil. But that's another story. I'm here today to sell my memoir to Hollywood. Twelve years ago, I made my first run at it. Harry Ufland, who had produced *Snow Falling on Cedars, One True Thing,* and *Crazy/Beautiful,* loved my story of redemption and purchased the rights. Brendan Fraser was going to play me and Academy Award–nominated screenwriter Anna Hamilton Phelan was going to write the script.

It failed. Brendan backed out and Anna never got a handle on the script.

Today, almost eleven years later, I just left a two-hour meeting at the Gotham Group on Sunset Boulevard. I love Sunset Boulevard, an endless row of flash and glamour, billboards attached high on buildings, digitally turning beauty and glimmer into riveting imagination and ceaseless dreams. I want to live here, to drive the Strip every night at sunset, and suck in the vivid magnetism or gesture of what I could become.

I'm not an ex-junkie on Sunset Boulevard. I'm a writer.

My memoir, *What's Left of Us,* is set to be released in two weeks. An op-ed piece I wrote for the *Los Angeles Times* is going to run tomorrow morning. Everything is lining up for me. I force myself not to get too excited, to always remember that this town has a never-ending supply of fairy dust. Nothing out here is what it seems.

My last meeting was the fifth during my five-day trip. I'd gotten a consensus; in one way or another, everybody said, "This book is gonna make a great movie." It's 4:00 p.m., the twentysomething part-time actor and full-time valet at Hotel Roosevelt recognizes me. He's seen me with actor Christian Bale and thinks I'm somebody. "Hey, my man. How's ya day?" he asks as he extends his fist. I put out my right fist; we pound and blow it up. I'm cool for fifty-two. The other night at the pool he told me he dreams every night of being somebody. I think of my daughter, Siobhan, and want to tell him, "You are somebody, kid."

I hear the phone ringing in my room as I exit the elevator. I don't run anymore; for years I always anticipated the worst news whenever the phone rang. I had to answer, to find out what happened. Now, I just accept things as they are. I struggle with my room card. A beautiful blonde in a string bikini opens the door next to me.

This town makes me horny.

The phone begins to ring again just as the light goes green on my door. I decide to let it ring. Yesterday, I got out of the shower soaking wet because the phone rang ten times, back-to-back, with just small breaths of quiet between rings. It was Siobhan; she wanted to ask me about the Fourth of July. She figured it was far better to keep ringing—why leave a message and have me call back when I'm available on something as important as "Can I go to the New Jersey coast for the weekend?"

Finally the phone stops.

I love this hotel. Like me, it's haunted by ghosts from the past. And like me it's just been done over, old on the outside but new on the inside. Not much in the room, a picture of Marilyn Monroe hangs on my brick wall. I love the desk, long, black, vacant of anything but a desk light and solid black phone. It sits comfortably next to a giant window holding a snapshot of the Hollywood Hills. Each morning I'm amazed at how it lights up my view.

I wonder if it was my beautiful new wife, Melissa, who called. I miss her. I get horny just talking to her. She's fifteen years younger, long legs, great ass, and the best thing that ever happened to me. I feel bad. I talked her into taking a self-portrait. She was so embarrassed. A smile broke across my face. She said, "I have to shave first." I picture her in our bedroom, sitting on the edge of the bed, trying to get the right angle with her cell-phone camera.

She said she'd send it only if I promised not to put it out on the Internet. Of course, I said no way and joked about making her famous. The picture was perfect. I'd masturbated to it before I'd left for my meetings. For a quick second, I hope she didn't think I was weird for asking her to do it. I was straight with her, told her what I was going to use it for.

There is no flashing red light on the hotel phone. Siobhan never leaves messages. I decide to sit and get to work, and my computer lets me know I have twenty-eight new e-mails. Melissa's picture remains minimized along the bottom row of my screen.

The phone rings.

"Hello."

"Richie?"

"Hey, Melissa, I was just thinking about you."

Dead silence. Wait, she's crying. Oh my God, what an asshole I am. I'm so messed up. I could have masturbated to anything. Why did I have to ask her to do something like this?

"Melissa, I'm so sorry I asked you for the picture."

"Rich, I have bad news."

Bad news? What? I can't make out her voice. Did she say "bad news"? What could have happened? I should have answered the phone earlier.

"Melissa, what's wrong?" My voice is shaking.

"Siobhan has been in a serious car accident."

She goes on but nothing but the words "Siobhan" and "serious" bounce inside my brain like a BB in a metal boxcar. I stand. Window open, the phone's handle rests softly on my computer's keyboard. Outside, a young couple has climbed out on the roof below—they're kissing. Melissa's voice is muffled.

My eyes go blind. Siobhan's face takes me back. I'd gotten in late that night. Siobhan's mom and I were still together. Debbie was beautiful, American Indian, tall, dark and bipolar. And she refused to take her medication. Siobhan was only eleven. The fight was violent, mostly Debbie screaming at me. She accused me of having an affair. I was. Siobhan woke up and defended me. Debbie kicked us both out of the house, threatened to call the police if we weren't out in five minutes.

It was two in the morning. Siobhan sobbed and rested her head on my lap as we drove together to my mother's home a few miles away. She kept asking if things were going to be okay. "I just want you and Mommy to be happy," she said. I couldn't respond. I slowly stroked her strawberry-blond hair. "Dad." She rolled her head toward me. She wanted an answer. Her eyes were emerald-green and her pearl-white skin seemed to make them glow in the grayish moonlight.

I got custody of her in the divorce settlement. Debbie self-destructed. She tried to kill me once. Put Siobhan in danger during a weekend visit. The police called me. They had Siobhan. The judge refused to even allow Debbie supervised visits.

My baby girl was twelve when she came out of the bathroom and told me she had "her friend." I remember the fear on her face. She was bleeding and asked me what she should do. "Well, I think…maybe, um." I couldn't stop stuttering. Of course, I knew what was happening. I wasn't an idiot. I just had no idea what to say to Siobhan. Something was surreal about the moment. I loved this little girl. She was my whole life. Everything was spinning too fast; I didn't want her to become a woman just yet.

She cried alone in the bathroom as I dialed the local pharmacist. Funny, the explanation was easier than I thought. She gave me the tightest hug and laughed when she took a pad into the bathroom. "Dad," she said, "I know how to put them on."

I am distracted by the young couple's passion building against the air-conditioner units sitting on the rooftop, kissing, grinding, hands everywhere. But their intensity couldn't pull me away. Siobhan was flying down the field after a small, white, hard plastic field hockey ball. Her athletic gait was no match for the defender heading in the same direction only yards away.

It was Siobhan's first high school play-off game in the state tournament. In one fluid motion, Siobhan raised her wooden stick high, sucked in the space around her, grunted and nailed the ball. The ball rocketed across the field at the exact instant Siobhan's opponent attempted to bodycheck her. The collision was fierce. Arms and legs backwards into the air, Siobhan's opponent was knocked out cold on the field. Seconds later, Siobhan's teammate caught the pass and drove it past the goalie.

When I got onto the field, her coach was asking her questions. I broke the huddle of teammates circling her. Her nose was bleeding, tears rolled awkwardly sideways, filling her ears, and she called out, "Daddy." As if in a vacuum, I reached down and cradled her. I couldn't speak. To me, right then, her eyes, looking back at me, were the same as the first moment I saw her. "I just want everything to be okay, Daddy," she cried.

"Are they all right?" I screamed into the phone.

"I don't know," Melissa responded.

"What do you mean you don't know?"

"Rich, the EMT only said, 'We have your daughter. She's been in a serious car accident. We're taking her to Southern New Hampshire Medical Center.' They told me I should go there immediately."

"But is she okay?"

The girls never had time to scream. In the blink of an eye, the car's front end exploded from the impact of a pickup truck. Like a ride at an amusement park, the car began the first of its three 360-degree spins. Glass, blood, piss, shit and panic filled the inside space that music had occupied seconds earlier.

The car was traveling south on Armory Road in our hometown. A few minutes earlier, a young man in his early thirties climbed into the cab of his pickup truck and headed north on the same road. There was an intersection. The light turned yellow. Shelly thought she could beat the red. She stepped on the gas pedal. The young man was in a rush to get home. He thought his truck could beat the light. But he turned left in the middle of the intersection.

The car's front end folded like an accordion. Shelly broke her ankle. The dashboard cut into Kate's legs and her head bounced off the inside roof. The music had stopped. The young man in the pickup was in trouble. The car's final spin was halted by the impact of another car thirty yards away.

No sounds. Nothing but terror. Chelsea's helpless body had flown around and around inside the car like a toy top. Her body came to rest on Siobhan. Sheer madness took control inside the KIA; Siobhan was pinned. Chelsea's face was resting on Siobhan's head. The smell of puke and shit activated Siobhan's gag reflex. She turned. Chelsea's eyes were vacant. Blood dripped on Siobhan's face from someplace on Chelsea's head. A gurgling sound mixed with fresh vomit filtered from Chelsea's diaphragm.

Chelsea was dead?

Siobhan's call came shortly after midnight. She knew I'd be up writing. "Dad. Question," she said. I immediately removed myself from the scene that had enveloped me for hours. Whenever Siobhan began a conversation like that, one of two things was about to happen. She was either in trouble or about to do something her young brain hadn't really considered.

"Dad, I don't know if I really want to be a nurse. Can I change majors?"

"What do you want to change it to?"

"I don't know. I don't know, but this is hard."

"Hard as in difficult or hard as in I have to study too much?"

"Daddy, I gotta go. My friend wants me to walk her to a party. Can you put some money in my Pirate Points account?"

I reached down and picked the phone receiver off the desk. Melissa had gone. The couple outside had gone. They must have taken to the inside to finish what they couldn't control on the rooftop. I sit and consider how many miles I am from the medical center. I'm completely helpless, trapped, as if I'm pinned on my back inside a car, my friend is dead and I can't get out to help her.

Melissa's picture remains on the bottom bar of my computer. I can't see it but it's still vivid in my mind. I love Melissa. She's given Siobhan a mother's love for the past five years. Siobhan's mom, Debbie, had found several new ways to self-destruct, and Siobhan hadn't seen her in years. I consider opening the picture. Sex always relieves stress. But a wave of Siobhan's love washes over me; I do not even remotely feel sexual. Will I ever see Siobhan again? Jesus Christ, Sunset Boulevard will never look the same again.

My cell phone rings.

"Hey, Daddy."

It's Siobhan. I fight back tears. She's alive. Her voice sounds like she's seen something I saw when I was covering the war in Bosnia as a journalist. She says everybody in the car is going to live. Chelsea was revived at the scene. They took her to another trauma center after the fire department removed the girls from the car. Nobody knows the young man's condition; he was unresponsive at the scene.

"Daddy," she cries, "I just want everything to be okay."

I'd like to tell her it will be. But I'd be lying. Only one thing is certain right now. I can't tell her the truth. I cannot tell her that there is no such thing as okay. There is just life. Sometimes it will be good and other times it will be bad. The only option we have is to live life as it comes, one day at a time.

But that's a hell of a lot better than being dead.

THE KITTEN GANG
Nick Taylor

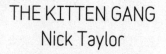

One of the most famous clichés about my line of work is that writers are always working. A writer who vacations in Europe, for example, is not simply bingeing on Bordeaux and Camembert but "gathering material." And when a writer lies in bed at four in the morning, unable to sleep, he is never simply paying the price for the double espresso he drunkenly ordered at the end of dinner, but rather "sorting through" the plot of his novel.

Perhaps. But couldn't you say the same for people in other occupations? Doctors truly never stop working. Every acquaintance with a cough wants a free consultation. Compared to doctors, writers have it good. No one stops us on the street for an impromptu short story.

No one, that is, except the little people who live in our homes.

Seven in the morning and I'm across the breakfast table from my five-year-old. I am still in my robe, but my workday is about to commence—just as soon as Violet finishes her toast. She lifts a slice of white bread to her face, pressing her mouth into the center to extract the choice part without ever biting through crust. She wipes blueberry jam off her cheeks with the back of her hand.

"Daddy?" she says at last. "Will you tell me a kitten gang story?"

I tug on my coffee. I don't want to do it. But before you

impugn me for refusing a bright-eyed child such an innocent and wholesome pleasure, I ask you to consider how you would react if your own child asked you to start working before breakfast.

Like the mayor's daughter, who runs for class president, or the banker's, who looks for change in coin returns, the writer's daughter wants to imitate her parents. She wants to *participate.* Which is painless enough for the mayor and the banker. But it makes storytelling hard for me.

It was Violet, actually, who invented the "kitten gang"—the characters in these morning stories. One night several years ago I read her a picture book about a house cat giving birth in a little girl's bedroom closet, and Violet asked why our own cat, an ornery ten-year-old named (appropriately) for the female protagonist of Bram Stoker's *Dracula,* had never produced a litter of her own. I explained that the veterinarian had given Mina an operation so that she would never have babies. This seemed like a terrible injustice to Violet, so as an act of charity, she invented a litter of four kittens for Mina on the spot. Like a mother licking her newborns, Violet described for me each member of the kitten gang in precise physical and psychological detail: Snow, Cream, Night and Dawn, four distinct looks, four identifiable personalities. It took her all of five minutes. She never once stopped to think. Never corrected herself. Out came the kittens, fully formed, like Greek goddesses. We should all be so lucky.

The stories are built on a formula, like most children's tales. The phone rings early in the morning in the kitty house, and Mina picks it up. It's the boss of some place of business—the supermarket, the car wash, the firehouse and so on—who is in dire straits because his employees are all out sick. Can Mina help out? Sure she can. She volunteers her children. So they load up the KitiVan and drive to the job site. After a long day's work, during which the resourceful kittens solve numerous problems with their specialized feline skills—a whole bag of carrots, don't you know, can be peeled in seconds by sharp kitty claws—the gang is taken down to city hall, where the mayor gives them each a medal.

Scholars of the picture book genre will recognize this last bit from *Curious George* by Margret and H. A. Rey. Remember that a good artist borrows, and a great one steals. At five years old, all use is fair use.

I put down my mug. "So the phone rings," I say, "and Mina answers."

"No!" Violet interrupts. "Mina is in the shower. Tom answers the phone."

I forgot to mention Tom, the kittens' father. He's a tabby, a fighter, has only one eye. Lives in a gutter.

"Okay, Tom answers, and the voice says, 'Help! This is the theater manager! All my ticket rippers are out sick!' And so Tom says, 'No problem—I'll send the kitten gang.'"

"But the KitiVan won't start!"

"Right. The van won't start, so Tom has to call a tow truck...."

"But the truck driver is sick!"

I look across the table. Violet's eyes are sparkling with invention.

"The tow-truck driver is sick...."

"No, no, no—actually what happened is that the van started up again. Tom was just using the wrong key!"

I read a magazine article many years ago about the reclusive American novelist Thomas Pynchon, who apparently warmed up for each day's writing, while he was working on the novel *Vineland* in the rural woods of northern California, by composing letters, under a pseudonym, to the editor of the local newspaper. I have read the letters, and I have read *Vineland,* and I vastly preferred the former. Pynchon's wit was in full effect when played against the little crises of Redwood Country— much more than against the tapestry of hippie conspiracy theories that served as the basis for *Vineland.*

I worry that my own work suffers the same fate: I write historical novels, but perhaps I should be publishing kitten gang stories. My mind is fresh at seven o'clock in the morning, and the words come freely under pressure from my demanding coauthor. In an hour I will be showered, shaved and sitting at my desk, working for pay. But I will be alone. And perhaps I will have missed my calling.

Violet takes down her bike helmet from the shelf by the door. I pull on my shirt and lace up my running shoes. The elementary school is two blocks from our house. We used to walk it, but a few months ago Violet began riding her bike without training wheels. I have to jog beside her to keep up. I try to finish the story between breaths.

"So the kittens are dressed in their uniforms and the manager gives each of them a job. Snow runs the projector, because she's the oldest and the projector is a dangerous machine."

Violet nods in full appreciation of this fact. Strapped onto her tiny skull, the sleek, aerodynamic bike helmet looks like a sombrero. No matter how many times I cinch the chin strap, it's never tight enough. Her enormous, glistening brown eyes light our way.

"Cream sells the popcorn," I explain.

"I hate popcorn!"

"You don't have to eat it. She sells soda, too. And candy."

"You mean meat candy? For cats?"

"That's right. And Night and Dawn rip the tickets."

We pull up in front of the school yard. Violet dismounts, walks to the far side of her belled and beflowered bicycle and toes the kickstand. I unclip her helmet and she tucks her hair behind her ears.

"Do you want to hear the end of the story?" I ask.

She peers around me, inside the fence. A few children are already free of their jackets and dangling from the monkey bars.

"Later, Daddy. I promise. Or you can finish it tomorrow."

For a moment, I am crushed. Rarely do writers come face-to-face with their audience, and with good reason: it hurts too much to be snapped shut.

"Are you sure? I could be quick."

Tilting her head back so that her face receives the morning sun, she puckers her lips. I take the hint.

I have tried to explain the kitten gang to friends, and although they laugh in all the right spots and usually compliment Violet's imagination, the conversation always veers to a place I regret. "How sad it is," they say with furrowed brows, "that poor Violet, the only child, has to invent playmates. How sad."

My wife substantially agrees, though for a different reason. How sad, she says, that graduate school came calling for her and we had to put off conceiving a sibling for Violet. And how sad that in those five years something went wrong with her fallopian tubes, and we may have missed our window for having another child. Which makes it doubly sad that, owing to my flexible schedule, I performed the bulk of Violet's rearing— an opportunity that my wife may now never enjoy. I agree that this is sad, and if I had to do it over again, I would have put my writing career on hold and gone back to programming computers at least until Violet was fledged and my wife was satisfied with her role in the process. I am told that not many men get the opportunity I had. But no one seems to understand the converse: that not many women *lose* that opportunity. That is sad.

But the kitten gang? The kitten gang is not sad. On the contrary—the kitten gang is a triumph. In our family, those imaginary kittens and their highly derivative tales are not a sign of absence but rather a manifestation of a rich and unique presence. My wife and I have always favored abstract possessions over tangible ones—intellectual property over the "real" kind. For example, in the lead-up to our wedding, when most couples would have been out shopping for their first home, we were scrambling to finish an album of songs we wrote and recorded in our bedroom. We gave away the disc as a wedding favor. Nine years later we are still renters, and somehow our daughter has caught on that we prefer ideas to things. Most children buy Dad a tie for Father's Day. This year, Violet wrote me a story. Nothing could have made me happier.

For my wife and me, the question of whether our daughter was going to be able to appreciate our values was always a more important question than the number of children we would have. Parents of only children sometimes talk about the pressure they feel to have another. This is real—I can't think of any couples from our childbirthing class who do not already have second babies, and thirds. But the bigger issue, for us, has been the guilt of not providing a sibling for Violet. She is a remarkably empathetic little girl, and she has told us many times how much she wants to have a sister or brother. We nod and tell her that we never intended for her to be an only child. She understands that we have been trying to get pregnant—she even knows, thanks to my wife's commitment to full disclosure, exactly how this occurs—and I want to believe she accepts the fact that it hasn't happened. In the meantime, we have tried to give her the benefit of our values, and of course all our love.

Before Violet was born, my father-in-law described how he felt when his first child (my wife) was born: "You have this family unit of two, you and your wife, and then one day it grows, and you are three instead of two. You bud."

I'm reminded of this image—budding—when I think about Violet composing a kitten gang story. We are not clones, she and I, but the apple doesn't fall far from the tree. Still, I worry that my wife and I may have a distorted perception of her: she may not be as much like us as we think, or at least not yet. For example, a few months ago we let her watch some of *Grey Gardens,* the 1975 documentary about two old women, mother and daughter, living out their days in a squalid Hamptons mansion. "That will be you and me, sweetie," my wife told her after the scene where Little Edie serves her mother a plate of cat food "pâté." Violet turned away from the television in horror. "No, Mommy!" she cried. "I don't want to eat cat food!" Tears began to well up. "I am *not* going to live with you my whole life!" Then she looked at me. *Tell me she's joking,* her expression seemed to say. I kept a straight face. Finally, my wife broke down and told her she was kidding. With the pressure off, they shared a good laugh about eating ice cream from a carton with a knife and feeding raccoons in the attic.

Does it make me a bad father that I kept her on the hook? Flannery O'Connor famously said that if you survive childhood, you have enough material to last the rest of your life. I have to believe that siblings played some role in Ms. O'Connor's calculation. My sister certainly provided material for me. But Violet will never be able to draw on that source. So maybe when I torture her with the possibility of a *Grey Gardens*–like existence, I am trying to compensate for her sibling-less childhood. My wife would say this is nonsense—that we're just making her tough, and that teasing is good for the soul. I want to believe her, but it seems like a big risk, considering we have only one chance to get it right.

The fact is, Violet will not be exactly like either of us. And it has nothing to do with us letting her watch *Grey Gardens*. The problem with my father-in-law's analogy of parenting is that budding is asexual: a baby hydra is an exact genetic copy of its parent. Humans reproduce sexually (thank God!), which means that each child is a mix of two parents' genetic material. Violet could end up like either one of us, or both, or neither.

Though as a father I fear this uncertainty *(Will she be like my wife's great-aunt, the one who ended up in the padded room?)*, as a writer I am grateful for it. Without the suspense of discovery parenting would be duller than most of us would like to admit. And with all due respect to Flannery O'Connor, I am not done gathering material.

BLINK OF AN EYE
Robert Dugoni

I heard the spray of the shower through the closed door, reached to turn the knob and found it locked. That three-inch-thick piece of wood never seemed so solid, so impenetrable, as it did that morning, and I stood there feeling a keen sense of loss.

Catherine had always taken to the shower in our master bedroom. There's a bathroom just outside her bedroom door, but for some unknown reason that tile-and-grout tub-and-shower combo just wasn't the same as the one in Mom and Dad's room.

My wife entered the room, looking harried and concerned, as was the case every morning when we went through the ritual of getting the kids up and out the door for school. I know marriage counselors blame many failed marriages on finances, infidelity and religious differences, but I'm a firm believer that the morning ritual has contributed to its fair share, as well. That morning was particularly stressful because it was one of those weird "in-service" days for the teachers, which meant the kids would be getting out of school early and my wife and I were trying to coordinate pickup and my son's request to see a movie with his friends in the afternoon.

"What are you doing?"

"The door's locked."

She walked to where I stood and jiggled the handle, as if I were incapable of determining for myself whether a door was truly locked.

"Catherine?" she called out, with her mouth pressed closer to the door. "Catherine!"

There are times when I will just sit and listen to my daughter, her squeaky little voice as melodious and pleasing to me as the sound of a stream babbling over rocks. This was not one of those moments.

"What!"

"You locked the door," my wife shouted, stating the obvious.

"What?"

"Unlock the door! Daddy has to get ready for work and we're late. You need to eat breakfast."

I heard the lock click and my wife pulled open the door, fanning the steam. "Have you gone over your spelling words?"

I did not immediately enter, unconvinced that my eight-year-old daughter had locked the door by mistake.

"Go ahead," my wife said, stepping out to make room for me. Our house was built in the 1960s and for some reason the architect decided that a bathroom the size of a postage stamp would suffice. The term *master bathroom* has never been so misleading.

"Go ahead," she said, sounding like one of the impatient customs officials at the Canadian border crossings.

I stepped in and turned to the small alcove with the sink, wiped the condensation from the mirror, and began to shave, my daughter hidden behind the shower curtain.

"Baby," I called out.

"Yeah?" she squeaked.

"Why did you lock the door?"

"I don't know," she said, confirming my suspicion it had not been an accident.

The spray of the shower ceased and the buzz of my electric razor filled the room like a swarm of bees. I watched in the cleared spot in the mirror as a tiny, tanned arm reached from behind the curtain and pulled one of the powder blue towels from the aluminum bar.

When my daughter materialized, she looked to be the same little girl I had awakened that morning with a kiss on the cheek, but I knew she was not. She had wrapped the blue towel around her midsection, leaving exposed only her head to her shoulders on one end and her legs to her feet on the other.

"You need to get going," I said. "Mom's getting upset. Do you have your school clothes?"

"No," she said, and I looked down at her discarded garments on the bathroom floor—not pajamas, but a pair of sweatpants and the brown T-shirt from a horseback riding trip to Idaho.

"Did you sleep in your clothes again?"

Her eyebrows arched and her eyes widened, lips spreading into an impish grin. "Maybe."

"Catherine," I said, and she broke out in her unique little laugh.

I tell people my son, Joe, is my conscience, constantly reminding me of the proper way to behave. Catherine, on the other hand, has always been my angel. She melted my heart the moment my wife gave that one final push and Catherine burst forth into this world.

Joe was born very early in the morning after a long and arduous labor. When the doctor placed him on his mother's stomach, he looked at me as if I were an actor who had just missed his cue to deliver the most important line in the show. Eyes wide, he gently flicked Joe's engorged testicles.

"It's a boy!" I blurted, perhaps better late than never.

But, of course, there had been none of that with Catherine. In addition to the difference in genitalia, she came into this world at a reasonable hour in the evening after a far more reasonable labor. Whereas her brother had blond curls and rosy skin, the crown of her head was a mat of black hair, and her complexion olive. Her face was scrunched, as if annoyed with the whole birthing process. She looked like my ninety-five-year-old Italian grandmother, Nonie.

When I held her in the palms of my hands, I remember having to sit, feeling light-headed with the thought that this was not just anyone's little girl. This was my little girl. I had heard the adage—you know, the one about when you have a boy, you only have to worry about one penis. With a daughter you have to worry about a hundred. But that night I realized there was truth amidst the humor and it filled me with a sense of dread I never felt with the birth of Joe.

I put down my razor. "I'll get your clothes," I said, ever the pushover, and walked down the hall toward her room.

My wife intercepted me, returning to further inspect the troop's progress. "Is she out yet?"

"I'm getting her clothes."

"I told her to bring them in with her."

I shrugged.

As I reentered the bathroom, carrying Catherine's school uniform, blue-and-green plaid skirt, white blouse and navy blue sweatshirt with the school letters stitched on the front, my wife was yanking the towel around Catherine's body, apparently wanting to use it to dry her hair, but Catherine held on tight.

"Catherine, darn it, let go."

I handed my wife a second towel from the rack. "Here, use this one."

She took it, rubbing Catherine's head vigorously, then stopping to look at me. "Are you getting in the shower?"

"Why don't you get dressed outside?" I said to Catherine and she left, still clutching her towel.

"Remember you have the father-daughter sock hop tonight?" my wife said.

I didn't, of course, but I stuck to the rules in the man code—never ask for directions and never admit you forgot an event your wife has told you three times to place on your calendar because it's important.

"Of course," I said.

I closed the door and turned on the shower but I did not immediately step in, considering instead the black-and-white framed photograph hanging on one of the walls. In it, I'm standing in a shower, and on my shoulder, no bigger than a football, is my little girl, her black hair prominent, eyes staring attentively at the camera lens. As the years passed, Catherine continued to shower with me and with her mother, sometimes all of us together. I'd wash her hair, using the shampoo to mold it into a Mohawk or some creation from a Dr. Seuss book, and Catherine would pull back the curtain to look at herself in the mirror and giggle.

I knew the day would come when modesty, self-consciousness and self-awareness would replace that child's naïveté and the showers would stop. In fact they had ended well before she turned eight. But that had been my decision. Catherine had showed little sign of modesty up until that morning. I knew it was inevitable, as it had been with my son and his mother, nature's way of helping children to understand what is appropriate, and to respect their body so that others will respect it, as well. I also knew there would come a day when discussions on certain subjects would be better left between Catherine and her mother, and friends have warned me about the hormonal teenage years. As my friend Robert explains it, "The aliens snatch your daughter's brain when she turns thirteen, and you become the most embarrassing, annoying person on the planet for the next six years. Then the aliens give back the brain and you're great again." I think Einstein said something similar.

Still, as I stood in the shower that morning, I felt the sense of loss overwhelm me and I bowed my head, allowing the spray to beat on my neck and wash away my tears.

I returned home from my office at close to five o'clock that evening. Fighting to meet a publishing deadline, I had squeezed in as many writing hours as I could.

"Did you talk to Mom?" my son asked as soon as I walked in the door.

"No, what about?"

"I was at the movies today and I saw all the girls in Catherine's class. It was a party."

"What?"

He told me the name of the little girl who had the birthday. We know the family well.

"Catherine wasn't invited?"

Joe shook his head. "And when her dad saw me, he turned around really quick."

"How many girls were there?"

"A lot, Dad," he said and I could tell now that Joe was upset.

They fight a lot, as most siblings do. It's ridiculous, really, given the three-year age difference and the fact that Joe's big for his age while Catherine is a peanut. But I've also witnessed tender moments indicating they love each other and Joe is fiercely protective if anyone bothers her. It makes no sense, I know, for him to defend her against others for doing the same things he does to annoy her, but whoever said the brother-sister relationship made sense?

My wife was in the backyard, driving the ride mower and wearing a pair of earmuffs. I motioned to her to catch her attention and she turned off the mower and removed the muffs.

"Joe told me about the birthday party."

She was much calmer about it than I was. "I'm sure it was just one of those things where she could only take a few girls."

"Joe said the whole class was there."

My wife relented, a bit. "Not the whole class…I don't know."

"Aren't they friends?"

"I thought so."

"Does Catherine know?"

"Someone mentioned it at school."

"Where is she?"

"In her room getting ready for the dance."

It broke my heart to think that my little girl had been left out, but if Catherine's feelings had been hurt, she didn't show it. I found her in her room, the walls painted pink with colorful butterflies and adorned with pictures of horses, photographs of her in school plays and a lot of horse-show ribbons. I'd tell you the color of the throw rug, but we haven't seen it in years, buried under an avalanche of magical clothes, stuffed animals, books and toys. We say they're magical because no matter how often her mother and I put them away, they somehow magically make their way back to the center of the room and Catherine never knows how it happened.

Catherine stood on her bed, swinging her hips and watching the pink poodle skirt with the black-and-white guitar that her mother had sewn swish back and forth in the mirror of the antique dresser. She also wore a white sweater, only the top button buttoned, and her mother had pulled her hair back in a ponytail, leaving bangs. She looked like a young Olivia Newton-John in *Grease*.

"Wow," I said, entering. "Don't you look beauteous!"

She smiled and jumped down from the bed, her Mary Jane shoes tapping the one clear spot amidst the mess.

She gave me a hug, so excited she giggled. "Hi, Daddy."

"You all ready to go?"

"Yep."

"Then I'd better get changed."

This dance was one of those money-raising events bought at the school auction where alcohol and guilt have forced more than one attendee to sign up for things they wake up wishing they hadn't. I once bought a $2,000 trip to run with the bulls in Pamplona. And I'm afraid to even get on a horse! At least it was a tax write-off. But I digress.

Anyway, I had been planning to wear a pair of jeans and a button-down shirt. I knew most fathers would. But then I thought about my little girl, who had not been invited to the birthday party and who was all dressed up and excited to go to the dance with her daddy.

I went to my closet and pulled out a pair of khaki pants and a thin black belt, pulled on a T-shirt and slipped into a pair of black penny loafers. In my bathroom I emptied half a tube of gel in the palm of my hand and worked my hair into the best ducktail I could, leaving a small "Elvis" curl in the center of my forehead. As a finishing touch I drew a heart-shaped tattoo on my arm with red lipstick and added my daughter's name in the middle. When I emerged, Catherine said I looked weird, but did so with a huge smile.

We entered the school gymnasium together and I knew instantly it would be one of those moments that would remain forever etched in my memory. There are a few, like the time Catherine and I strolled at night through the twinkling lights of a Phoenix resort, Catherine beguiling in her little blue dress, or the time I sat watching her face light up during a production of *Wicked* at the Ford Center in Chicago.

The gym had been decorated with tiny lights and made to look like a 1950s diner, complete with deejay. Catherine never stopped between the entrance and the dance floor. She walked right to the center and held out her hand, my cue to join her. It did not matter that there was no one else yet dancing or that everyone stood watching. She wanted to dance, and that night she had eyes only for her daddy, something I was keenly aware also would not last. We crocodile rocked to Elton John and twisted and shouted to Elvis and Buddy Holly, and when the music slowed, she stood on my shoes and we swayed to Frankie Valli and the Four Seasons.

When we finally took a break to rest my aching feet, we sat off to the side at one of the tables, drinking a root beer and sharing a large pretzel. She focused on the dance floor while I focused on her. I wanted to tell her not to be in a rush to grow up, that life goes by in the blink of an eye, that she would only get one chance to be a child. I wanted to tell her that when our childhood ends, so does that wonderful naïveté that allows us to believe, against all reason, in things like Santa Claus and the Easter Bunny, and gives us the freedom to skip down the street or to burst into song for no particular reason. I wanted to tell her that each year the harsh reality of life steals a little bit more of that child's innocence until all that is left is the harsh reality of life. I wanted to tell her that friends will turn their backs on her and disappoint her. And that girls will plot against her simply because she's pretty and smart. I wanted to tell her that boys will say nasty things and more than one will break her heart. I wanted to tell her that she'll worry about things like work and finances and mortgages and car payments.

What I really wanted to do was to hold her tight, as I used to in the shower, and shield her from all the pain that comes with growing up.

Then she leaned to the side and rested her head on my arm, gripping my bicep, giving it a squeeze.

"I love you, Daddy," she said.

And I smiled. Wisdom seems to have a way of finding us at moments when we need it most, and it found me then. I smiled because at that moment I realized it really isn't about what I would tell her. It's really about what she wants most to hear, what we all want to hear.

"I love you, too, angel," I replied.

THRIFT-STORE BANDITS
Mike Adamick

My mom stood before a rack of dusty clothes. Her fingers combed through the prints and tweeds, the florals and smocks, the shifts and disowned, sweat-stained blouses, while I kicked my feet on the dirt-speckled Formica tiles beside her, whining about going home. The store smelled like an attic and the kind of overly floral pancake makeup reserved for dead people. Every time she shifted the rack, I fought against a sneeze.

"I like this one," she said, holding up a gaudy blouse. "What do you think?"

I shrugged. "Can't we just go?"

She moved on to a pair of worn black shoes, holding them up and letting her eyebrows ask the question for her, while I frowned at her achingly dull taste in footwear. I glanced toward the windows, watching the sidewalk for friends—ready to dive beneath the display of vintage vinyl records or hide inside one of the circular clothes racks.

"Oh, just have a look around," she told me. "You never know what little treasure you'll find."

And it was true. As much as I hated to admit it, my heart sometimes quickened among the aisles of all her favorite thrift stores. Over time, I discovered that the good stuff could be found at the dusty, pocket-sized store run by graying volunteers of the St. Vincent de Paul Society, while the Salvation Army was usually good for sticky furniture and the Goodwill was better suited for nice clothes and purses. At a time when most of my peers were just coming into the realization that the Gap at our local mall consisted of one season of stripes and plaids after the other, I was learning to tell the difference between a real Fendi handbag and a fake one—schooled by a cagey thrift-store veteran. My mom and I were always talking about the expensive art sometimes left abandoned in the corners, and I learned to walk up close to paintings and examine the canvas for real brushstrokes of oil or acrylic. I'd press my nose to the pictures, studying the way the oily glops were spread thin or cut off by brushes or sharp palette knives—a rainbow of indiscernible wispy strokes. Then I'd take a few slow steps back and watch as the colors spread out, took shape—all the brilliant shades commingling and becoming whole, some fulgent gem developing before my eyes.

One day while wandering the aisles, I found a pair of unused roller skates. They were still in the box. When I saw the flawless blue wheels and the creamy white leather, I gasped and glanced over my shoulder, wondering if anyone else had noticed. They were so perfect and gleaming that it must have been a mistake, I thought. Who would throw away new skates?

I spotted my mom across the store and held up the box, guarding it almost. Sure, they were girls' skates, but they were new and cost three dollars. That kind of find was worth whatever school yard beatings were headed my way. Even from across the room, I could see my mom smile and wink, holding up one thumb of approval. And then she curled her finger, calling me over. "Look at this," she whispered, showing me the tag inside a purse. "Gucci."

We didn't say anything, the both of us. We glanced around and shared an amazed smile before hurrying to the counter as if someone were going to catch us, as if someone would realize we had both found something too good and were about to get

213

away with it. When we got outside, we laughed out loud, two thrift-store bandits exchanging squeals of delight the whole way home.

"See?" she said. "Treasure."

Years later, as an at-home parent myself, I often think about our times driving around the city, stopping in odd shops and thrift stores—the two of us embarking, heads down and gloomy, on some mundane, day-to-day errand, only to turn it into some wondrous adventure, our lips breaking into smiles at the sudden magic.

When my wife and I bought our first home in San Francisco, one of the biggest selling points was that there was a Salvation Army a few short blocks away. While the Realtor used her hands to describe household amenities like central heating, two-car parking and original hardwood floors, my head swam with all the abandoned, cast-off clothes and books and vintage gewgaws and knickknacks located just a few minutes away. About the same time I started staying home to raise our daughter, Emmeline, my wife and I took up sewing. Thrift stores, we quickly learned, were an excellent source of cheap fabric, and soon I was walking out of the store with oversize women's skirts and 1970s-era sport coats—all of which would be cut up and stitched together again, transformed into children's clothes for our daughter. Emme and I hit up the Salvation Army so often that soon she started referring to it as both the "toy store"— because I let her browse the ancient Fisher-Price™ farms and airports and pick through the stuffed animal bins—and the "fabric store," because that's where the bulk of her clothes came from.

We end a lot of dull, boring days at the thrift store, usually coming home laden with sacks of toys or oversize, discounted clothes we could turn into dresses. On one trip home, we were both exhausted after a long day at the playground. It was hot. I was sweating through my shirt and struggling under the weight of a few purchases: a pair of jeans for me, a shirt for her and an armload of books. Instead of carrying her the last few blocks as I usually do, I put her down and forced her to walk. By her reaction, you might have thought I had conscripted her for some baby Bataan March. Her cries could be heard for blocks. And then, suddenly, they stopped. I turned around and saw her crouching on a dirty square of gray, gum-pocked sidewalk, the unhelpful shade of a thin tree falling on one of her legs.

"Look, Daddy," Emme said, pointing at the ground. "What is it?"

I had to walk closer and crouch down myself to see it—a tiny bird so new and frail it had yet to grow any feathers at all. Its belly was purple and bulging, pushed outward by the day's heat and some wild internal cosmos of dying gases. Its eyes, which probably never opened, were closed and its pale pink beak was just barely open, as if to speak some final oath.

"What is it, Daddy?"

I said simply that it was a baby bird and hoped that would be the end of it. *How do you explain death to a toddler?* I wondered. Was she ready? Was I?

"Is it sleeping?" Emme asked.

I dodged the question.

"I think it fell out of this tree," I told her, pointing upward.

Emme thought it over for a moment, leaning ever closer to the frail, inert creature.

"Oh," she finally said, "I think its momma will come back for it."

"You do?"

"Uh-huh," she said. "The momma always comes back."

I grabbed her hand and said we'd better go.

"We're too big and I think we're scaring the momma away," I said, trying to move down the sidewalk. My bags were heavy and we still had a few more blocks to go in the noontime heat. In my head, I was calculating the time it would take to walk home, feed Emme some lunch, put her on the toilet and read a book together before putting her down for a nap. It had been a long day: we both needed one.

"No, Daddy," she said. "Let's wait and see what happens."

Cars rattled by and leaves and gutter junk began to roll in a tiny breeze that felt cool on my burned neck. I checked my watch. Then I put my hands on my hips and said, "Emmeline, come on, kid—it's time to go home." But she just remained, her body doubled over and her neck craned to the side.

"It's not moving, Daddy," she said.

"No?"

"No," she said. "I think it's sleeping."

Emme watched it for a few moments longer and as much as I wanted to get home, I suddenly found I couldn't move. Some moments Emme looks exactly like me—her nose painted on with some upward brushstroke that gives us the appearance of pugs. Then a moment later, something changes—her lips grow fuller, her eyes less worried and she looks exactly like her mother. It must have been the thin shade playing on her features, but standing there, watching her up close, it was as if I could see an entire family portrait spreading across her face: a grandma's blue eyes, a grandpa's smile, a deceased uncle's wispy blondish-red hair. *Who is this person developing before me?* I wondered. *Who is this bent creature drawn in a sfumato of people, all of them blurring the lines between who she is made of and who she might become?*

Suddenly, she stood up. She looked at the tree above her,

squinting her eyes into the sun and holding a hand up to shade herself.

"Momma bird!" she called. "Momma bird! Get down here!"

"Emmeline," I said, walking over and taking her hand, "it's okay. She will come. She will come."

I hauled her a few steps down the sidewalk, toward home. She fought back, stretching her arm in my grip and looking back toward the tree.

"Momma bird! Your baby's waiting, Momma bird!"

When we finally arrived home and went through our usual midday routine, the monotony of it familiar to us both, I set her gently in her crib and brushed a wisp of hair out of her eyes.

"Daddy," she whispered, reaching up a hand to mirror my movements. "Daddy, do you think the momma bird came back?"

I paused a moment too long, trying to find the words, when she closed her eyes.

"Me, too," she said, rolling over and falling instantly asleep, as if struck by some quiet spell.

Usually our days aren't so dramatic. We go to playgrounds together. We visit museums. Emme loves to feed the ducks at the zoo. We've found that if we stick to an exacting schedule, Emme seems to sleep better and generally be happier, and so our days sometimes bleed into the next, each one barely different from the last. We get up, eat breakfast, embark on some adventure, and then hurry back for nap time. After that, she eats a small cup of yogurt while I do the dishes and then we play games or make crafts. Sometimes she sits on my lap while we make her dresses or shirts at the sewing machine. Dana arrives home after a while, we eat dinner and then it's bedtime.

My single guy friends used to be jealous of my chosen vocation, announcing, "You can do anything you want all day!"

And then I'd fill them in on our exacting schedule and I would see this glint in their eyes, this faraway look I could tell was full of pods and office cubicles, these wearisome locales that probably never looked so charming to them.

I've found that even the smallest things can break up the monotony and throw off our schedule. One late afternoon, Emme and I were in the kitchen after her nap. She was eating her regular yogurt while I was doing the dishes, when suddenly I let out what, in hindsight, was probably a terribly loud curse for a terribly tiny cut.

"Daddy, what happened!?" Emme said, pushing her yogurt away and pulling up her hands as if to protect herself. "Daddy, why are you yelling?"

"I'm sorry, kiddo, I'm sorry," I said, grabbing a wad of paper towels and wrapping my thumb in them. The knife had clattered to the floor, and together with my impromptu afternoon vocabulary lesson, the whole scene must have appeared all too dramatic to a still-groggy toddler. Her eyes were as wide and unblinking as golf balls.

"It's just a cut—I cut myself," I told her, watching as the paper towels grew red under the applied pressure. I glanced at Emme—she was still frightened. Maybe it was the sudden blood loss that made me disoriented and loopy, but it probably wasn't a good idea to hold up the crimson towels so she'd see it wasn't really so bad.

"See? It's nothing."

It took me five long minutes to quiet her screams before I could run to the bathroom for a Band-Aid.

Later, after the bleeding stopped and I cleaned up the mess, we headed upstairs to the sewing machine so we could make a dress for her. I knew she'd curl up on my lap and feel comforted again in my arms as together we pushed the buttons on the machine and worked magic on someone else's disowned clothes. On the way up the stairs, she stopped and turned to face me.

"Daddy?"

"Yes?"

"Daddy, why did you scream?"

I scratched my neck and could feel my face flush.

"Well, I wouldn't call it a scream, per se."

"No, Daddy," she said. "It was a big scream."

"What?"

"It was a big, loud scream like the kids," she insisted.

"What kids?"

"The kids at preschool."

"I screamed just like the kids at preschool?"

"Uh-huh," she said. "When they get hurt."

I told her to just keep going, that we'd make her a shirt and forget about the whole thing.

But she stopped again, this time at the top of the staircase.

"No, I mean it—let's just forget about it."

"Daddy?"

"Yes?"

"Daddy, what was that word you said when you screamed?"

I was still stuck on that other word.

"A scream? Really?"

Emme nodded her head and grabbed my hand.

"It's okay, Daddy," she said. "You'll feel better soon."

The phone rang and fortunately knocked her off the subject. My mom, a teacher, called to say she had just started summer break and was hoping to get together to see her granddaughter. We made plans to go shopping the next day in a tony suburb across the bay.

"You should see some of the stores!" my mom said, growing excited.

I knew immediately she wasn't talking about the Macy's or Nordstrom, which stoke most people's shopping giddiness. Her house is still filled with "finds"—instead of purses and blouses, however, she had turned her attention to her Emme, filling the available space in her home with baubles and baskets, tiny doll chairs, ancient woven strollers and rocking horses for my daughter. It was a wonderland of discarded children's bounty.

We met the next day outside one of her favorite thrift stores. She grabbed Emme's hand and I watched as they pushed quickly through the door together, stopping for a moment to take a look around and breathe in the scene, as if they could smell the deals hiding in the circular racks or slumping on the shelves. My nose caught a familiar aroma when the door opened, something overly floral and haunting. Two elderly volunteers with thin blue glasses stood behind a glass counter, their fingers working over a cash register they claimed was broken.

"It's just a piece of junk," one of them snorted, looking over her glasses. "And so dirty. God, these people."

My mom carried Emme, while I thumbed through the racks, fighting a sneeze. I found a pink woolen jacket I thought would make a good hat and came close to buying a green polka-dot apron that, with a few snips and stitches, would become a lovely summer smock for Emme. My mom and my daughter played with the toys and sat next to each other on enormous green velvet recliners marked Sold. I noticed one of the clerks glared at them from behind her glasses. My mom ignored the look, while Emme started to rock in her chair.

"Good job," my mom said loudly. "Way to go!"

My mom and I spent the next half hour trading Emme between us, showing her books and old records, toys and T-shirts, worn jeans, brand-new picture frames, a lonely bicycle wheel and assorted castoffs huddled in the corners.

My mom held up a garish blue bowl.

"What do you think of this, Emme?"

I found a blue-and-white flower shirt for Emme and went to pay for it.

"Is that all?" the clerk huffed at the glass counter.

We didn't find anything of value. I bought the two-dollar shirt for Emmeline, and my mom considered buying the blue bowl but then apparently wised up. But standing there, searching my brain for something witty and cutting to say in response to the rude clerk, I was distracted. I heard my mom oink like a pig. I heard Emme laugh. I saw them flip through a stack of books and play with the clothes tags. I thought that one day Emme might wander the aisles by herself and maybe learn to tell the difference between gold and brass, silver and plain old steel. I thought she might enjoy hunting for old coats and dresses we could buy together and turn into something new for her to wear.

From across the room, I saw her face and thought immediately of those old paintings in the wet corners, their oily glops appearing so disjointed and splintered up close, and how if you took a step back, you could see the whole picture. We share so much every day, spend so much time together, that it's sometimes difficult to see all the little pieces of our days commingle and become whole within her: the playgrounds and nap-time routines, the first glimpses of death on a lonely sidewalk, the thrift stores and the slow realization that a father is not the strongest man in the world and just might, sometimes, scream out loud like a preschooler. Watching her from across the room, it suddenly appeared that something had changed. Her grandpa's face had disappeared. Her mother's smile was gone. My own nose was nowhere to be found. From a distance, it was as if I were watching the brushstrokes spread out, become clear—as if I were watching the pieces fall into place in this new, distinct person developing before my eyes.

It broke me, in a way, to realize she'd grow up, get bigger. She would become wise. She might someday fight against riding around the city to yet another hand-me-down store. Maybe she'd whine for candy. Maybe she'd just give in and discover a "find" of her own in the dank aisles. Standing there, I studied her developing face, heard her laugh, and I smiled at the thought that I was passing on the lessons my mother had unknowingly gifted me. I closed my eyes for a moment and hoped that after all our time together and our time to come, my daughter, too, might come to realize that there's magic in the everyday, that spells are sometimes cast in the ordinary, and that as far as treasure goes, sharing something is just as sweet as finding it.

The blue-haired clerk looked over her glasses and rapped her knuckles on the counter, clearing her throat.

"I said is that all?"

"What else is there?" I asked, handing over two dollars before finding my mom and my daughter on the recliners. Along the way, I stopped to pick up the green polka-dot apron.

"What do you think of this, Emme?"

She frowned and shook her head. I picked her up and hugged her, carrying her to a circular rack, where together we picked through the clothes.

"Ooh," I said. "How about this? Or this?"

DISASSEMBLING MY CHILDHOOD
Dan Beachy-Quick

My father called to say a gift was on its way. It was for my three-year-old daughter, but I'd be interested in it, too. More than interested. This gift, he said, would "blow your mind." It would "knock your socks off." My father loves my daughter past bounds, loves her wildly, adoringly—a love that often finds expression in gifts. I've come to anticipate such gifts with a healthy amount of wariness. Each present is heartfelt, undoubtedly, but are often things my wife and I would tend not to purchase ourselves: plaid dresses with white-lace collars that looked as if they might be the uniform to a preschool prep school, teddy bears larger than the children trying to hold them. The last such gift, sent a few months before, for no occasion other than kindness, was a porcelain music box within which a poem, printed in gilt cursive, read: "I was never so blessed / as the day you were born." It was gift meant to be precious. It had all the clues that speak to a child of its value: the milky-white material with a heft to it, the brass filigree around its edge, airbrushed flowers on the lid, morning glories, maybe, but pinker, larger— orchids perhaps. The poem begins as a dedication, with a florid *FOR* emblazoned in gold on the inside cover, and where my daughter's name should next appear (the precious is always personal) was a small piece of paper on which my father had typed my daughter's name, Hana, in italicized Times New Roman. He taped her name in on a scrap of copier paper. Then the golden engraving began again.

When Hana turned the key in the box, the hidden metal cylinder began to spin and out came the song, in the tinny pin-pricks of the medium's music, "You Are So Beautiful." When the box is shut, the music stops, the poem is hidden. Sometimes I find Hana on her bed with the box open, listening to the music in strange reverie. She loves it; I, of course, have my questions.

I told Hana that Grandpa had sent a present that should arrive in a few days and she, being at the age where the idea of a "gift" or a "surprise" is the finest thing in the world, began her anticipatory questions. "Is it here, Daddy?" ad infinitum, until the package would actually arrive. Her excitement is con-tagious enough for me to feel excited; it's an enthusiasm I can't help but stoke with my own repeatedly uttered "Soon, it will be here soon." The best part of waiting for the gift to come is asking Hana what she thinks it might be. "An elephant." "A macaroni bowl without macaroni." Nothing else gives me such a sense of how astonishing desire is. Desire gives equal weight to things of radically different worth. Hana would cycle through the possibilities at every meal. "A teddy bear." "A piece of glass." "Crayons." "A cloud." Desire erases boundaries by easing through them. Desire is wonder in motion. Desire finds that reality's border is loosely guarded. Someone—"reason's viceroy"—is always asleep at his post. My three-year-old girl knows already what many poets would do well to learn: desire pushes through the limit of what is possible; it does not recog-nize it and retreat.

A cloud in a box would blow my mind, would knock my socks off. I hoped the gift was a cloud in a box. I was curious; I had my doubts.

My parents divorced when I was three years old—the age my daughter is now. I have very few memories of my parents together, my life before my parents' divorce. My father letting me sip the foam from his beer as I sat on the brown-shag steps that led from the kitchen down to the living room. His yellow car. A small, mean dog named Porsche. I fear I might be making these things up. My mother raised me by herself in Colorado. I had no siblings. I would spend my summers in Ithaca, New York, with my father and my grandparents, with whom he lived. My father taught courses like Business Management and Entrepreneurship, things that inspired little wonder in me. What did seem wonderful was spending the summer in the same house my father himself grew up in. We would sleep in the same bedroom, a bed on each side of the room. At the head of my bed the wall was papered in a wilderness scene: the woods at sunset, the color of the sky changing from orange to yellow as the sun set between the trees. There were deer in the woods whose ears were pricked up as if they were listening for a footstep in the forest; I would go to sleep thinking I was entering the woods, getting lost in the dark. I liked to pretend, every summer I arrived, that I couldn't remember how the house was put together, which room led to which, and would ask for a "tour." Reassembling the house was reassembling the kid—the kid I was in the summers, so different than who I was with my mother during the school year. The kid who wandered through the woods, who had adventures, who idolized the dad he hardly knew.

Becoming a father myself was an experience that didn't so much shatter my expectations as make me realize I had no expectations to shatter. I didn't know what it was to be a father, because I grew up without one. The summers?—those were a different life. The sudden realization of that vacancy in me, that blank resource, shattered me. Who should I be, who could I be, for this little girl who would need me? It was a question that tormented me in those earliest days when Hana, colicky and crying for hours, could not be comforted through those sleep-less summer nights, when my wife and I would wake together to try to calm our baby, when I felt desperate, when I wanted to call someone, anyone, my father, and say, "What's the answer? What should I do?" But there was no answer.

Hana grew out of her colic at three months and began sleeping through the night. This wasn't a feat of parenting but of biology. I was happy, grimly happy, that we all survived. Things got easier—they're still getting easier. But moments still come when the same fear suddenly blurs the outline of my image of myself: this father I am who knows how to be a father. Then the man I picture in my head when I think of myself as my daughter's father disappears, and there is no image at all. Just some emptiness riddled by nameless feeling. And I find in myself the same sense as years ago when I held my bawling infant and asked not, "Who is this child?" but asked instead, "Who am I?"

Hana and I set the large, thin, envelope between us on the floor the day the gift arrived. The envelope was sealed too tightly for Hana to open it, metal clasp and tape, so I tore it open and took out the contents. "What is it?" Hana asked, voice wonder filled, expectant, hopeful.

What I took out was a picture of myself. I'd seen the photo countless times hanging on the wall of my grandmother's house in Ithaca. I saw it every summer I went to be with my dad—a photo taken from one of the first of those summers. It is, un-doubtedly, the best picture ever taken of me. I'm a little boy, maybe five or six. I'm walking on the stone path outside the house that goes past the bougainvillea bushes whose scent seems heavier than the blossoms. I'm not wearing a shirt. I've been in the sun and my shoulders are golden. I'm walking away from the camera and looking back over my shoulder, smiling. My hair is blond. My eyes look only like black smudges beneath my forehead. My mouth, too, is dark where it is open. This photo, more than any other memento of my childhood, defined that time for me. When I think of myself as a child, this is the image that comes to mind. For me, it was a photo of the summer happiness that could have been permanent.

"What is it, Daddy?"

"This is a picture of me when I was a little kid."

"Oh." I figured she wouldn't be interested for very long in the photo, but she kept holding it, looking at it, examining it with a minute attention I found slightly uncanny. I figured that it must have been strange for her to see me when I was more or less her own age. Then she held the picture out to me and said, "Look, Daddy. Grandpa sent me a puzzle."

She was right. A thin line coursed throughout the photo, a jigsaw line that cut through the picture. I'd never spent enough time looking at it to notice. I just glanced at the picture behind its frame as I walked down the hall, the image whole in my mind, taking root in my memory, gaining definition there, gaining permanence. Now, holding the picture in my hands, my daughter sitting on the floor beside me, I could see that the image—this image of my own face so many years ago, this image that memory made whole—had cut into it the lines by which it could be taken apart. And that's what we did. I popped it out of its frame, and Hana and I pushed the puzzle pieces, one by one, out from the picture. It had never been disassembled before. A little point of cardboard held each piece to the whole, a little resistance to push through. I tried hard not to think about the process and mostly failed. Sitting on the floor, taking apart my childhood self, this picture of me that looked up at us as we dismantled it, piece by piece, with the daughter I was trying to raise so she couldn't be taken apart so. All the little pieces. We spread them on the floor. We found the circular edge and assembled it: skin tones to skin tones, and the impressionistic background of blurry grass and rocks and flowers. We continued to reassemble the photo. And when I had again a sunlit torso, and my right arm again jutted forward below my face—except I had no face, except my arm didn't yet attach to my shoulder—Hana stood up and left, the puzzle not half-done.

I wanted to call her back; I wanted to say, "We're not done." I wanted to say, "You can't leave me like this!" but say it in a tone so she knew I was joking. But I wouldn't be joking. I knew I wouldn't be. So I said nothing at all. I felt like a child myself, sitting on the floor next to the undone puzzle. I felt like a child with a child of his own. Parenthood, for me, is inextricably caught in the paradox of being a father and a child at once—a child with a child, a father with a father. A paradox is another form a puzzle takes, one that desire is powerless to solve. It is a condition and not a game. One just recognizes that puzzle in oneself, as oneself—or, at least, I do. Parenthood, unlike childhood, is a puzzle into which no pieces have yet been cut. I know it can be taken apart but I don't know how to do it myself. And until it's taken apart, how will I know how to put it back together again? It is uncanny, unnerving. It feels almost like fate. In fate, the pieces never seem to fit—and then they do. I have a daughter. Her name is Hana. That's the first amazing, impossible piece.

I'd like to say when Hana left me and the puzzle incomplete that she returned with the music box in her hands. That's what I desired, that recognition of the moment, these gifts through which, uncomfortably, we recognize who we are. To hear that tinny music would be a form of kinship, a kind of understanding. I desired it past reason, but it didn't happen. She came back into the room to ask for something. A glass of water? There I was, still spread across the floor. I was looking for the dark smudges that were my eyes. And there was my daughter, calling my name. Not my name. Calling me Daddy. There was my daughter.

I was in pieces on the floor.

She was a name in a box.

MILES TO GO BEFORE I SLEEP
David Teague

On the day she was born, when darkness fell, twelve hours in and everyone still, the old order defunct, Annabel ascendant, through my brain flickered visions of jump rope, basketball, ballet, hopscotch, the 200 butterfly, fractions, mean girls who would stockpile every mustard stain on every skirt and every botched haircut and every hard-boiled egg in every lunch bag to humiliate her with, if only they could, though they were doomed to fail, the miserable lip-glossed freaks, because she'd be so tall, pretty and able to hit left-handed layups. I watched a future me mutter, "What're you doing in my driveway, boy?" and the caterpillar-lipped juvenile flee rather than answer. I considered the fleet, durable and miraculous soul inhabiting the baby girl in my arms, whom, if I'd had one, I would've eaten with a spoon.

Skipping. Leave-in conditioner. Like a chimp with a transistor radio, I inventoried the mysteries to which I'd never been privy, but now at least might haunt the vestibule of, peeking in, holding Annabel's hand as she scampered down the sidewalk, or brushing the tangles out of her hair, when she finally grew some.

Outside the hospital streetlights, headlights, store lights, taillights, stoplights, brake lights inhabited their fixed or moving places more and more, until the constellation set and I thought, *We're going to have such a good time.*

Annabel didn't do too much when she was brand-new, so

early on there was time to anticipate standing in line to ride the Sea Dragon, and sending her to collect sticks for the campfire, which I would try to kindle with the cardboard box her sleeping bag had come in, and when that petered out to no avail, would douse in camp stove gasoline and toss a match at, leaving her to admire the surprisingly slow *whoooomp* of the resulting explosion. I imagined being, as long as that fire burned, Annabel's guarantee against...everything.

This daydreaming went on for a while, and then, around 9:00 p.m. of her fourth day, Annabel's mother, Marisa, her brother, Charles, and I started to wonder when she'd sleep. Or maybe stop screaming. At ten o'clock, we wondered if it would be by eleven. At eleven, midnight. At midnight we hoped for one. At one, for dawn.

Fifth night, the same. Ditto the sixth.

On Annabel's seventh morning, as the sun rose, we wondered if these nights would last a month.

Soon we realized we were facing two.

In the third month, we were sure Annabel would sleep by September, when she turned half a year old. Or at least quit howling for a few hours here and there.

By September we were telling ourselves her sleeplessness wouldn't stretch past a year.

At some point, a low-grade panic began to rumble through the substrate of our family. To our exhausted eyes, the world looked as grainy as an ancient TV show starring, say, Jackie Gleason.

We consulted certain experts, who said to put her in her crib. Let her cry. A little longer each time. Annabel would figure it out.

So we did. Before long, we were approaching four hours per session. Annabel was our tiny warm machine smelling of baby soap and new hair with lungs of tool-grade steel. The monotony of her misery was the worst of it, its ceaseless rhythm, until at 2:00 a.m. we occupied an incessant squall lit by a smear of sixty-watt bulb beside her crib, the entire family knee-deep in psychosis and stumbling. We had to work tomorrow, go to school tomorrow. And tomorrow and tomorrow (crept through at that petty pace).

We tried to explain it to her doctor. "Some babies cry like that," he advised. "It's not fun. But it won't hurt." He also said we could call Annabel's affliction colic, some people classified it thus, and we proceeded to learn from the Internet that a high percentage of colicky babies go on to earn PhDs.

The pediatrician was wrong about one thing. It did hurt. Annabel's mother knew it. Her brother knew it. I knew it.

Annabel's problem was that sleep is the little death, and around its edges lurk fidgets, heebie-jeebies, gremlins, goblins, gargoyles, frights, night terrors and existential dread. If you want to argue that four-day-old infants, six-month-olds, toddlers are not burdened by existential dread, fine. But I guarantee you Annabel had some training-wheel version of it even on her fourth night of life, which was linked by a thin black tendril to every subsequent night, until, when she was three, avoiding sleep while the summertime sun hung on crazily at 9:00 p.m. and the ten-year-olds hollered on their bicycles outside, Annabel asked, "Will I be able to talk to you when you're dead?"

I took that breath you take, buying time, plugging as many leaks as I could in the fairy tale, the one where we live forever in one another's hearts, no matter what, and just as I was about to lay it on her, Annabel warned, "And don't tell me about a voice I can hear in my heart...."

There was never any help for it.

But back in Annabel's early days we were still blissfully ignorant of this, and in our doomed optimism, we somehow managed to beat the thing back, whatever it was. If we held Annabel (no sitting), and did knee bends (no standing) constantly (no stopping), she might not sleep, but at least, in her small, racked body, a dab of ease seemed to diffuse. And what really brought her solace was to be carried. Across the room and back, across the room and back. We didn't live in a big house, so pretty soon Annabel and I took it to the street.

For the first few blocks, she kept wigging out on her infant grief. Inhabitants of the nearby Casa Fermi, men and women whiling away their twilight years by performing the diminishing rituals of the elderly in a building named for one of the fathers of the atom bomb, regarded our comings and goings impassively from their cement-canopied piazza. They gazed with the bemused magnanimity of the forgotten as Annabel's screams echoed through the quilted night.

When I came eyeball-to-eyeball with two cops one morning about two, I realized the sleepless residents of the Casa Fermi had been doing more than watching. The tall cop said, "This must be the guy," and the short cop hiccuped at the wisdom of this, fingering the handcuffs dangling from his overstressed police belt. They were in no hurry to let me in on the joke, or to indicate if it was a joke, or even to step aside so I could pass, so I was left with no choice but to ask, "What guy?"

Whereupon it came to light that a squad of ladies from the Casa Fermi had been able to ascertain by (a) the outlandish way I held Annabel (colic grip, a trick I'd picked up in Lamaze class) and (b) her continual godforsaken caterwauling that I was not her father and had, ergo, kidnapped her. Which they duly reported.

"Yahahahahaha!" laughed the tall cop. "Now get that kid in bed!" Because Annabel now appeared to be asleep in my arms.

Of course it wasn't that easy. Sometime later that night, somewhere in Philadelphia, there would come a point when the spell cohered, when Annabel passed from asleep but not asleep to the place all children deserve to go at night, and I would know it by a shudder the same size as her body. Then I could scuttle home, unlock the door with one hand, and lay her down with her crescent eyes, small breathing, spiritual feet, and Marisa and I would linger above her to enjoy solace for the baby and grace for us, but you can bet we got out of that bedroom in a heartbeat if she so much as twitched.

On Lombard Street, South Street and in Elfreth's Alley, Annabel began to notice it, underneath the mohawk she'd been sporting since birth, fat, fat baby girl, coffee beans for eyes, stuck in biscuit dough, grabbing, grabbing, grabbing for the things in front of her. She saw it before I did, even though this was what I'd wanted to show her since the second she was born, the tiny best friend I'd been awaiting my whole life: the world is a knockout.

I was still pretty sure I would lose my mind, and my job, and go bankrupt, and default on my mortgage, and my other mortgage, and develop the habit of weeping in public, but after we walked and walked, once all the lights were out except the ones that would stay on till morning, once only taxis went abroad, once the front doors were locked three times from inside, Annabel and I liked it.

There was an opera singer. There always is. One night, a few years before Annabel was born, this opera singer's husband had picked our doorstep on which to detain a homeless guy who'd pissed him off somehow, and the husband ended up dying of a heart attack. Right there. On our stoop. That lady could sing, though.

We saw a preacher writing in his notebook in the tiny little house nobody knew about in the alleyway behind his church.

And every night around two, a bereft and distracted woman appeared on a stool outside her house, which featured plywood where the windows should've been, and sat amid a scrum of men who had a vile investment in her. At some point, as we passed and repassed her on the far side of the street, a red snow cone appeared in her hands, and after it did, the men, four or five of them, ranged farther afield, as far as the next street corner, but not before deputizing one of their number to knock the snow cone halfway up the wall of her house if she started enjoying it too much.

Eventually, the men disappeared for the night. Left alone, the woman read a book; maybe it was the same book every night, maybe not, with a title along the lines of *Лучше больше чувства*. I'd like to say I caught her eye, or that she looked at Annabel and smiled, but you know better than that; she stared into space, ruing some small turning that would have landed her in a different place, what had or hadn't happened in another country. Her regretful smile, her chin stuck out, a question to contemplate. Why does everything, always, have to hurt?

Was there once somebody she'd imagined would keep her safe, the bedrock apparition of little girls, the imprint in the air named Daddy? It's an impossible job, a doomed endeavor, a figment, and any idiot should be able to see this, but given the aroma of Annabel's scalp, of course I'd already plunged in like leaping into the heart of a dust devil churning down a highway in the panhandle of Oklahoma.

Annabel is seven and she still can't sleep. Mornings, in her room, I find all her lights on, books strewn across her covers, stacked beside her bed, on the table, books and books she's read—how hard she's worked, how long she's been alone, how afraid she's felt, how quiet she's kept while the rest of us slept. Sometime when Annabel was in kindergarten, I gave up and let her start facing night by herself. I couldn't keep her company anymore.

Through Philadelphia, we walked.

Annabel liked the corner store at night, lit like a fishbowl, redolent of produce, Doublemint gum, and wax, exclamations of one kind or another lapping the truncated aisles. Every night we bought something different—milk, matches, mousetraps—because the ex-cop behind the counter didn't have much patience for folks who entered without intent to buy, not even if they were three months old and toted by their daddy.

I don't know what we picked up that night. Milk, bananas, Cheerios.

As soon as we set foot out the door, they churned around the corner the wrong way on Thirteenth, plowed into traffic on Lombard, streaked between parked cars, regrouped on the sidewalk in front of the Casa Fermi and, like a swarm of bees in *Tom and Jerry,* kept right on sizzling like an arrow through the night.

At first, it looked like nothing more than ordinary buffoonery. One guy pedaled a bike, the other three seethed around him, and there was no obvious point to it, although the dynamic seemed to be taking the form of them against him. The guy on the bike, Annabel and I knew. He had a job sweeping peanut shells out the door of a bar on Pine Street. He couldn't talk very well. If he had a home, it was free, or cost five dollars a night. He bought Sugar Babies in the cop store, stuck them all in his mouth at once, and, while barreling through the dark streets on his orange ten-speed, chewed them back into sugar.

While Annabel and I watched, the three guys on foot

pounced like hyenas bringing down a gazelle, and as soon as they had him on the pavement, they began kicking the life out of him.

"They're gonna kill him!" I shouted at the counter guy. "Call the cops!" The old, fat dude glanced out the door of his little store and contemplated the scrum on the sidewalk heaving like a particularly aggravated patch of the North Sea and returned to his *People* magazine, wisdom accrued in twenty-five years on the force.

That beating had a rhythm, a rise and fall, swell and de-crescendo, a pace that promised to endure. It was just getting started when I got to our door, grabbed my phone, dialed 911 and told the police what was happening, who was doing it, and what they looked like. One, for instance, was tall, chubby, and wore a striped shirt. I mentioned that an ambulance would probably be in order, too, and it was. I ended up spending half an hour in it.

Somewhere, a cosmic fuse blew. The assault stopped. They stood up, leaving the ten-speed guy in a pool of blood, teeth and bicycle parts, and they moseyed down the street, rolling on their legs a little oddly, as if they stood on the deck of their very own ship, and their heads lolled around while they looked for more stuff to mess up.

Here come the cops! Lights blazing! Chirpers chirping! Annabel watched, reaching for them and kicking like mad. Two cars stopped. Policemen squeezed out and, leaving their doors dangling open, ambled over to peer down at the guy on the sidewalk.

Three more cars came blasting up Lombard, slowed down so the cops inside could peer at the cops peering at the guy on the sidewalk, and then kept blowing down the block, toward the miscreants. And pulled up even with them. And blared on past.

And kept going. Right through the red light at Broad Street. And the one at Fifteenth, and the one at Sixteenth.

Annabel lay quietly in my arms, considering all this.

While he waited to cross Broad, the kid in the striped shirt picked up a rock and shattered the window of a parking meter. When the light changed and the little green walk–signal man hitched up his hind elbow and shoved off across his municipally owned Lite-Brite, lacking for nothing in the world except hands and feet, the three guys who had transmuted Annabel's peace into idiocy crossed uneventfully at the hash marks and began fading into the night.

I took Annabel inside to her mother. "I've got to see about something" was my claim.

Catching up with the jackasses wasn't hard. They weren't moving very fast, since they felt compelled to check for unlocked front doors about every third house, kick over news-paper boxes whenever the opportunity arose, and spit on the ground quite a bit.

The chubby one had his shirt off by now, liberating much sweat. Solid caveman stuff. The guy on his right looked like the jerk who needs his ass beat and in fact gets his ass beat in *The Karate Kid,* down to the hair spray and the polo shirt.

And the third, lagging behind, reminded me of this cat I once knew named Randall who always seemed ready to burst out of his skin, even in study hall, and got thrown off the football team for excessive violence at practice (in Arkansas!), and at one point got in the habit of dialing random male classmates, making appointments to meet for a blow job, and beating them sense-less when they showed up.

Later people asked me what I was thinking. I always answered, "I don't know," even though I do know, exactly. I believed my outrage would prevail.

But that's getting ahead of the story. When the time came to hold these bozos accountable for what they'd done, before a judge and jury, I guess I was thinking, I wanted an airtight case. So when they stopped to mill mindlessly in the mouth of an alley near Fifteenth Street, I stepped up and asked, "Did you guys just beat up the little dude on the bike?" Angling for a confession. My question was met, briefly, by silence, while they tried to make sense of what I'd just asked, or to figure out why I'd asked it, or to examine some of the reasons for and against answering, or maybe just to remember what they'd been doing 145 seconds before.

The chubby one snickered. He was still holding his shirt. "Yeah," he said, and for a second he seemed to be expecting a high five.

"I was out there carrying my daughter," I said. The logic of this response seemed solid to me. I pulled out my phone and started dialing.

Vince asked what I was doing.

I told him, "Calling the cops."

We all took a moment to glance down the street and watch the blue lights pop off of the concrete façade of the Casa Fermi and listen to police chatter fizz out of radio speakers. The cops were farther away than I'd have estimated only a few seconds before. And then Randall, striking like a water moccasin, slapped my cell phone into the gutter, where it shattered. I took a moment to contemplate what a dark, dark place I'd chosen.

I'm pretty sure I could have run and gotten somewhere safe.

But these guys were not going to steal the world from my daughter and get off lightly.

"See this belt buckle?" asked Randall, hitching it up for my benefit. For some reason, along with his khaki shorts, flip-flops and rowing shirt, he appeared to be wearing a rodeo-championship belt. "I'm gonna beat your ass with it."

It was a strange thing to say. I still think about it. Why, in a street assault, would you take the time to do an impersonation of somebody's dad before the beating commences? I stared down the street in the direction of the cop lights some more, pondering this question, while Randall stood in front of me and Vince and the chubby guy circled behind. Then, while I wasn't watching, Randall broke my nose.

"Not really what Annabel needed from you," Marisa observed nine hours later, after I'd sat in the ambulance, identified two of the three perps (Randall eluded capture that night and forever afterward), and sworn an affidavit.

And Marisa was right. But if I saw those guys today, I would crush them to powder, take that night back, and give it to Annabel.

Nightetime

Nightetime
Peaceful Dark
sleeping reading listening
bed Mom dad home
walking creaking cuddling
scared tired
Nightetime
Annabel Teague (Age 7)

THE RIGHTS
Thomas Beller

I

We are on our way to a party—my wife, my daughter, my mother, me and the babysitter, who is going to take my daughter home after an hour or so at the party. My daughter likes parties. She's two. This one is at the National Arts Club on Gramercy Park. My wife lived nearby when we met. After our second date she took me, with her key, to the park to sit on a bench in the dark. Another life. Except that both then and now it was May, the air newly soft.

I have taken an unusual route. A gamble. There is traffic. This is a party for which I am a host and I don't want to be late. I'm wearing a jacket and tie. The tie is, I am pretty sure, an old tie of my father's. I do everything I can to suppress the anxiety and free-floating exasperation that come with being stuck in traffic on the way to a party. Then the traffic lets up. We arrive and, like magic, find a parking space right on the park. We get out of the car, all of us dressed up, and I start to hurry to the party with my daughter in my arms.

"How do I look?" I say to her. I am trying to be lighthearted and chatty, but it sounds needy. A father shouldn't be needy of a two-year-old. I don't know at what age you can start being needy of your own child, or showing it. Not two.

"Concerned," she says.

"I do?" I say and laugh, amazed. "Really? Wow! Where did

you learn that word?" I take a few more steps with her bobbing on my hip. "And how are you?"

"Confused!" she said, and now it's her turn to laugh.

II

We live part of the year in New Orleans, where our front yard is adorned by a small but productive rosebush. My daughter, a toddler with rosy cheeks, always marches straight over to it and reaches for the petals.

The flowers found on a rosebush are so different from the coy, coiled, secretive stems in flower stores. On the bush the rose opens and expands and then expands farther, effusive and fragrant. Like a baby's emotions, it holds nothing back.

My daughter moves to it with her customary urgency and reaches for the lush flowers, and I stand above her, bent over, like a house enclosing her, and tell her to be gentle with the beautiful flower. I love these kinds of moments, when I am an unseen structure to my daughter. Of course, I love it when I fill her eyes. But then there are moments like this when I am not the subject of her gaze but provide, somehow, the context.

Her fingers move from the petals to the thorns. I tell her to be careful of the sharp thorns. I can see her breathing and contemplating these opposing forces as she stands before the rosebush, sorting out the ecology of beauty and danger.

III

In the process of selling a story or essay for publication in a magazine or book, contracts are drawn up that touch on matters beyond what sum of money will be paid. The fine print of these contracts involves rights, such as TV and film rights. These rights are often negotiated in advance, so before there is a single word on a blank page, there is haggling over who owns the rights to make a movie about whatever ends up on that page.

My daughter is not a blank page. Quite the opposite. I have found that various tidbits, phrases, remarks she has made find their way into my writing. If I am selling movie rights to something that includes tidbits by or about my daughter, what exactly does that mean?

And why should I even mention the fine print in an essay about my two-year-old daughter? Maybe because there is fine print in that relationship, too, written in invisible ink that, over time, becomes visible: The fine print that delineates what is mine from what is hers, that separates her from me. I hear the primal need for this distinction every time I hear her say the word "Mine!" It's so rude, so naked in its aggression, so total and totalitarian. In her current contractual arrangements with the world this word is applied to just about every toy in the sandbox, every piece of food on every plate.

Who gets to tell the story? Who is allowed to? Who is obliged to? Who wishes not to but cannot help themselves? Who wishes to but cannot bring themselves to do it? Who is lost and spinning around, looking to the heavens, asking, "What is the story I should be telling?" A question for which there is no answer, unless maybe a two-year-old blurts it out.

IV

My father resides, or perhaps I should say is buried, atop a gorgeously landscaped hill in Westchester in the company of many other gravestones. Some of them have recognizable names like Guggenheim and Gershwin. My mother and I visit his grave once a year, in spring. There are dogwoods and azalea bushes, flora of incredible variety and delicacy, huge looming oak and pine and a perfectly manicured lawn. I like to joke, on our annual visit on the anniversary of my father's death, that this is the most prestigious address with which I am affiliated.

Ever since he died, or ever since he started dying in a visible way, which was around three or four months before he actually did die of cancer, just when I was about to turn ten, there has been this tension in me between plain, unadorned feelings of sadness and fear, on one hand, and wanting to make jokes. In the dark, sad months leading up to his death, when he was alive, but shaky, I was willfully buoyant and jokey with him, as though cancer was a mood I could cheer him out of.

It's no joke to be perched on the side of a very steep hill, at the age of nine, watching your mother crouched down beside an open hole in the ground into which everyone has just thrown a flower. A kind of halo of grief surrounds her and shimmers above her in the unseasonable heat, and your father's best friend bends down on one knee and holds her shoulder patiently, patting it and holding it. In hindsight I see this gesture of Arnie's as both consoling and, perhaps, given the odd kind of crouch my mom is in, and her grief, a precaution against her falling into the grave.

There was a dogwood tree planted next to my father's grave but it died a few years after he did, and an azalea bush, which still lives. My mother always asks the people who maintain the cemetery—who keep it manicured and in a state of gorgeousness—not to trim this bush. She wants it wild. Every year we arrive and, halfway up that hill from the road, she looks up, catching her breath, and says, "They trimmed the azalea." She is both disappointed and also faintly amused. It's become part of the ritual of our attendance.

We are always laden with picnic supplies. My mother is a champion picnicker. She brings a basket, a blanket, strawberries and cherries and grapes and peaches, cold cuts from Zabar's, baguettes, bread, mustard, orange juice, water, chocolate and many white flowers. This last visit my mother looked up halfway up the hill and said, "Oh, look at that."

The azalea bush had not been trimmed. It sat there resplendently bushy and unkempt, crowding the simple granite stone with my father's name on it—Alexander Beller—and beneath it the austere, familiar numbers 1922–1975.

Why, having started off thinking about my daughter, am I going on about my father's grave? I'm not talking about my father, his pensive humor, the feeling of his arm dangling around my shoulders, pulling me close, his blue socks tipped with gold thread pointed upward during one of his mysterious naps, but rather referring to a piece of ground where, if you think about it literally, which sometimes I do and sometimes I don't, there is a box within which is a badly decomposed body. Why should I be thinking about that?

In becoming parents, we meet our parents again. In some way, we meet them for the first time. And if you didn't really know one of your parents that well, then the dialog that springs up—What were you like when I was the kid? Oh, here is what it's like to stand in the place you once stood!—becomes not so much a reunion on different terms, but a whole new acquaintance.

This last visit to the cemetery—a few days before the party at the National Arts Club—was unusual. It was just my mother and I walking up the hill, which is how it always had been for decades, until I started bringing my wife. When I first brought her along, I couldn't suppress the feeling that this was a slightly macabre version of introducing your spouse to your parent and vice versa. Part of the mythology of my marriage is that my mother and I are the chaotic disorganized ones, and my wife and my father are more organized and like things being in place. She was meeting her ally.

And then we had a baby. Did we bring our tiny infant to the top of that hill? Yes. The following year, when she was a year and a few months, we brought her, too, and I posed her balanced on top of the headstone and made her hand trace the name carved into the granite.

But this year, the year of the bushy azalea, we had a live wire on our hands, a person who spoke and remembered and asked questions. A person who could see, hear, talk, think. What to tell her about why we were taking her to the top of a steep hill to have a picnic next to a stone with a name and numbers on it? Was I in such a rush to introduce my daughter to the concept, and the fact, that fathers die?

For the first time I saw how being religious could be helpful in raising a kid. We could roll out the heaven concept, say he was up there somewhere, looking down and eat sandwiches while she frolicked and we—my wife in particular—worried that she would tumble down the steep hill, perhaps smacking into one of the new mausoleums at the bottom. But we are not religious—though it is a Jewish cemetery, which brings up all kinds of thorny questions about my wife and daughter. Can they be buried there? No? An outrage! But then do I want to be making plans for this argument now? When there are so many arguments to have in the meantime?—and so this option was not available.

Should we bring my daughter to have this lovely picnic, to see the lovely view? Should I bring my little inquisitive girl to my father's grave?

Whatever benefits there would be from the nice picnic could not compete with the negative possibilities of opening up in my daughter the cavern of horror and dread associated with death. But death is too easy a way of putting it. Beyond the concept was the physical fact that my father was under the ground beneath that stone. Down there unable to see or breathe. Dead. But then the physical fact wasn't it, either, as I contemplated it further. She is consciously aware that her mother has two parents and her father only one, but now she will have met, or located, the other one. The person in the ground was the father of me, who is the father of her. And if my father could be dead and underground in the dark with no air to breathe and no one to talk to, then her father could also be there. Which was not a thought I wanted to rush into existence for her. Even if it had rushed into existence for me.

Up on the hill in the year of the bushy bush I had drifted into one of those meandering ruminations that I allow myself in the company of my mother. When my father was diagnosed with cancer, he was told he could live anywhere from two to twenty-five years.

"If he lived a few more years, it would have been so different," I said.

"Yes, very different," said my mother.

"But you know, even two more years, I would have been twelve. It's not like it would have all been nice and good. He would have had the money I wanted for things. He would have been the one to say no to things. He would have been my problem!"

"And your strength," said my mom.

The last time I saw him, I was about to turn ten and he was in a hospital room. I had been summoned by my mother to the hospital and I went with a terrible sadness. Not because my father was in the hospital but because I was going to miss a boxing match. What I remember from this moment was the night ride in the taxi, the sight of my father lying, asleep or unconscious, in bed, his friend Ray Raskin standing on the other side of the bed. Ray was a figure of comedy and lightness for me. All through my youth he always gave me a piece of gum whenever I saw him. I called him my "Gum Uncle." He was mostly bald and what little hair he had was always a bit unkempt. He wore bifocals that hung low on his nose, and he peered down through them to look at my father gravely, but when he looked across the bed at me, his eyes looked over the rims, and his eyebrows rose, and he scrunched up his mouth as though to acknowledge that this situation was not too hot, but it was still somehow within the realm of the good humor that always accompanied my Gum Uncle. At the funeral I still recall the sound of Ray breaking into sobs in the silence of the chapel, or whatever it was, and this signaling to me that the situation was indeed serious.

I had done everything in my power to keep it from being serious in those last months. I had kept an almost manically light tone, jumping around and calling my father "Pops," when I had previously only called him "Papa." My mother had bought him an electric razor, an act of optimism or denial, depending on how you look at it. Though if your husband is dying of cancer, is there really a difference? I took it out to the hall to plug it in and try to use it.

One other memory from that night—an image pertaining to the boxing match. It was a promo image from the network, featuring Muhammad Ali. I wasn't a huge boxing fan or Ali fan, but I absorbed the sense of drama surrounding Ali and was swept up in it. I wanted to see the fight. And now I could not, and it was torture to tear myself away from my neighbor's TV just an hour or so before it began. Looking into it now, I see that Ali had a fight on May 16, 1975, and that must have been the night in question, because my father died early in the morning of May 18.

It was Ali against Jerry Quarry. Ali, needless to say, won. I spent the weekend with family friends on Fire Island. When I returned, my mother, ashen faced, came to their door and summoned me to our apartment, where I did not want to go. We were watching the Mets. Rusty Staub was at the plate. I insisted on staying to see what happened. He struck out. Then my mother and I sat together in the kitchen and she told me the news. "Oh, but I prayed!" I said and banged my fist on the table.

Recently, while playing with my daughter, I had the most striking sensation while she looked at me, laughing. She was on the bed and I was above her and she was stalling for time before I put her diaper on, and I was doing something to make her laugh, I forget what. At some point she started demanding that I "make a house." She wanted to go "in Daddy's house," which meant I was to arrange myself on my hands and knees with my arms on either side of her. If she was standing, I was to bend at the waist and make a kind of A-frame above her, an exaggerated version of what I had done while she stared at the rose bush.

After I made the house, she would scamper out from under me and say, "Close the door!" Then she demanded, "Open the door!" and she went back in.

Somehow in the midst of this she kicked me in the nose. I retaliated by shoving my nose into her chest and ribs. I am always roughhousing with her, throwing her around. She was laughing uproariously. I sat up.

Her eyes flashed as she was looking up at me and laughing. There is something in a child's laughter that opens you up to the universe in its totality, shooting you into its mysterious depths. Sometimes you can go along for the ride. And sometimes you can't. And sometimes you think you are on that ride up and into the unbridled laughter and then, at a certain altitude, consciousness returns, and it's like a dream—how did I get all the way up here? And what is all this I see!

A spear of pain moved through me, which was also kind of delicious. *She needs me,* I thought. Obvious, simple, it goes without saying, but this was an understanding that bypassed the intellectual, even the emotional. It was a flash of perception that I felt in my chest, and it encompassed a fantasy of my absence. What my absence would do to her, how it would hurt her. How the absence hurts even more than the departure, as my father's absence had hurt me.

Looking down at her looking at me looking at her. The spear in my chest said, "She would be hurt! That laughter would be hurt!" The laughter, and the person, would evolve and reappear but it would be different, its shape changed, her shape changed, as mine had been. And then I imagined, or felt, my father grappling with that same thought, though not of the hypothetical variety, but rather the cold facts of the blood test, the cancer, the absurd and arbitrary spectrum of two to twenty-five years to live. It turns out he had eight.

In parenthood you meet your parents all over again. I saw myself at two, laughing and looking up at my own laughing father. And I saw myself at two through the eyes of my father, at forty-two, having already begun rounds of chemo and radiation, keeping it a secret from his colleagues, his friends, his son.

In that moment I had a recognition of what my father must have been going through as he enjoyed playing and laughing with me, and how I must surely have seen this, seen something, picked up on something, however subliminally or unconsciously. That something now registered somewhere in my eyes as they looked at my daughter laughing at me, looking up at me, picking up the faint echo.

V

My daughter has invented a new game in the elevator of my mother's building, where I grew up. The building has become somewhat fancy but it's more or less the same. I used to get into the elevator and turn to say goodbye to my mom, who would stand on the landing, and then the door would close and I would descend. Every now and then, when I was a kid, I would shout, "Bye!" really loud and my mother would say "Bye!" which would come down to me very faintly. I remembered this when my daughter found herself in my arms, in the same descending elevator, having just watched the door close on my mother. Her face lit up with mischievous delight and she yelled, "Nana!"

And I heard my mother's voice call out her name.

"Nana!" she yelled again. And again the voice came to us, fainter now.

She yelled out "Nana" at every floor on the way down. Long after we stopped hearing the response, she was still yelling the name. When we got to the lobby, just before the door opened, she yelled her name one more time. This is always the moment she squirms free from me and bolts out into the lobby and then the street, screaming "Hello!" to whoever is there. Now she turned to me pensively.

"I don't think she can hear us anymore," she said.

VI

She redeems everything. Just running toward me, she redeems everything, snaps my attention to where it ought to be, to life, its pleasures, the immediacy of the moment. Divine comedy tumbles effortlessly from her. One day recently, while eating a cookie after dinner, she looked at me and brought the half-eaten cookie to her brow.

"Daddy," she said matter of factly. "There's a cookie stuck to my eyebrow."

I pulled her hand away, and with it the cookie.

"I fixed it," I said.

She looked at the cookie for a moment, then brought it to her nose. "Daddy," she said. "There's a cookie stuck to my nose."

Recently, in the playground, she watched a very fit guy do acrobatics on a tetherball pole, holding himself out perpendicular to the pole, his body very straight.

"Daddy, you do that!" she said.

I broke it to her, as gently as I could, that I could not do that.

"You're a big guy," she said. "You can do it!"

Her sense of faith was sweet, but it was the encouragement that really struck me like a blow. Because somewhere down deep I often wonder—I am sure every father does if they are honest—whether I can really do it. Be a father. Make a house. Keep that which needs to be separate, separate, and that which needs to be together, together. And part of that will mean saying no to her, fighting with her, this willful force of nature. I will have to be her problem in order to be her strength.

A STORY FOR MY DAUGHTER
T. Colin Dodd

There is a stereotype of the distant father. Not to be confused with the absent father, the distant father is there, but not there. Quiet, taciturn, dutiful and sometimes loving (but rarely, if ever, affectionate), the distant father has none of the damaging glamour of the absent father. No jail time, no military service, no secret life, no second family. The distant father does his job. He shows up; he just doesn't bring a lot with him.

One might imagine dozens of interesting reasons why these fathers are so remote, hiding in plain sight, but no one really cares enough to figure them out. Lots of grown children ponder the impact of distant fathers on their adult lives, their relationships with other adults, but not many really try to understand how their dads ended up that way. The essence of the distant father is that he doesn't stir up a whole lot of trouble and not much curiosity, either.

Of all the things I worried about when my wife was pregnant, I never for one minute worried about being a distant father. I worried about being a provider, a role model, a moral compass, a help rather than a hindrance, but I never imagined that I would ever have trouble connecting with my child. When I found out we were going to have a girl, whatever dim worries I had about possible father-son conflict evaporated and I started to imagine what a great father I would be to a little girl.

It's hard to remember it now, but I felt so secure that my benevolent patriarchy would be notable for its intimacy, an intimacy that I would create. I was going to start by serenading her in the crib, and then enchant her by reading all the Caldecott Medal winners to her using goofy voices when necessary. When she was old enough, I would tell her amazing stories, and finally, with my credibility established, I was going to be able to teach her enough about life and boys and the ways of the world to give her insight and confidence in this boy-infested world.

My daughter was going to know how beautiful and smart she was, because I was going to tell her. It was all too easy to imagine—a series of effortless conversations, each one building on the one before, giving her every kind, happy, reassuring, entertaining word she needed until she didn't need them from me anymore, and then a few extra for good measure. I was going to be in the moment with her, every moment, every step of the way. My truth would be her truth because I would give it to her. I was going to matter.

To get ready, I practiced sweet lullaby riffs and bought a dog-eared book about raising girls at the used bookstore. The book was several years old, but seemed enlightened enough. Unfortunately, the introduction was bleak. The author talked about how hard young women had it growing up in our society. That wasn't news to me, but the details were more than I was really ready for as an expectant father. It was a grim few pages full of statistics about eating disorders, suicide attempts, date rape, hormonal imbalances, self-esteem issues, authority issues, anger issues, silence in math class, body-image disorders, anxiety disorders, cutting, pack-mentality cruelty, economic marginalization, diminished opportunities, sexual experimentation, pregnancy and substance abuse. I put the book down fairly quickly without thinking that I might be making my first retreating step toward fatherly distance. It was a lot easier to practice lullabies than deal with all that. Besides, she wasn't even born yet.

It was a few weeks after she was born before I finally got the chance to bring out my guitar. I had been practicing the same riff for months, making it into sort of an instrumental lullaby (I never got around to writing any lyrics), so in that moment, I felt more than ready. Never mind that I had intended to write a dozen or so lullabies (with words) before she was born, but had not managed my time well enough for that. It was showtime, and if I only had one lullaby to sing, at least I wrote it. How many dads did that? I also thought it was pretty good. The melody was as close to lovely as I had ever come, and I was well rehearsed and ready for my imagined fatherhood to begin in earnest. You could even say I was *anxious* to play for her.

I strummed the first chord, and Ava's eyes widened. She looked up at me from the couch where she was resting on a towel with her huge (allegedly unseeing) infant eyes, as if to say, "You've got my attention. I am listening, Dad. Go on. Please. Begin." But I was a little out of tune, so I stopped and attempted to tune the guitar by ear. That ended up making it worse, so I walked away, leaving her alone on the couch, staring at the ceiling fan, to find my tuner. Five minutes later, I was still fumbling in front of her, flop sweat breaking out on my forehead, tuning and detuning nervously. I sensed she was growing impatient. She looked a little agitated, but that could have been gas. My fingers were shaking. *What was that?* Finally ready, I took a deep breath and started again.

Almost immediately, she began to cry. I played right on through, courageously, the way you're supposed to win over a hostile audience, but the music didn't soothe her. She began kicking her legs and flailing her arms. I was afraid she was going to wake her mother, so I stopped playing, put down the guitar and picked her up.

It had to be a diaper, right? Or was she hungry? I couldn't discern the different cries the way my wife could. She snuggled into me and stopped crying. I rocked her for a minute or two, got her a bottle, checked her diaper. Then I rested her back on the couch, reshouldered my guitar and started again. This time she wailed. My wife woke up and stumbled in, looking at me wearing a guitar, playing to a crying baby.

"Nice," she said.

My wife picked her up, and the crying stopped. Adding insult to injury, she began to sing, softly, sweetly in her very pretty voice, and you could see Ava's tiny muscles relaxing as she melted into her mother. I took my guitar off and set it in the corner, where it gathered dust for the next year or so.

When Ava got older, story time didn't come much easier. Being away at work most of the day, bedtime was my time to shine. But I realized fairly soon that I wasn't such a good reader when it came to reading aloud. Even in front of an adoring baby, my own flesh and blood, a captive audience, I felt a strange sense of performance anxiety. I stumbled over very familiar words. I read in a monotone that didn't sound like me when I read books in my head to myself, and I often missed commas or periods, so I had to restart simple sentences to find the sense in them. Sometimes it's hard to know that something is a question until you get to the question mark. I also had a bad habit of falling asleep in midsentence, which usually prompted Ava to smack me back into reading.

Because I had to concentrate to coherently read very simple stories, it was more or less impossible for me to use funny voices. At least that was my excuse for not trying harder. As Ava got older, I did improve at reading, but actually holding her attention was always elusive, and the stories never sounded as good as they did when my wife read them. My wife was masterful at voices and knowing how to read so that what came next had more impact. On those nights that I listened to her read, I was as impressed as I was jealous.

By the time my daughter was four, she was sufficiently bored when I read to her that she began asking me to just tell her the stories, off the top of my head. "Tell me a story," she would say, and I would find myself stammering, stumbling. "Once upon a time, there were three bears...." And then I would realize that, despite reading them to her dozens of times, I had not really internalized the plot of *Goldilocks and The Three Bears,* or *Hansel and Gretel* or any of her other favorites. Some stories, like *Where the Wild Things Are,* are untellable when separated from their illustrations. I would stop and start and try to wing it, but that never quite worked. Try telling *Hansel and Gretel* without the stepmother sometime.

"Why did their daddy leave them in the woods?"

"He was really poor. He didn't have enough money to feed them, I guess."

"So he leaves them in the woods? Alone?"

"Um...yeah...he...did."

This was very frustrating, and I was very disappointed in myself. Repeated failure at story time made me worry about the future. If I couldn't pull off bedtime stories, how was I going to handle the birds and the bees? If I was nervous playing the guitar for her, or had stage fright telling a story from memory, how was I going to be able to toast her at her wedding? I felt unable to connect, to register, to matter. Instead, I felt constantly rebuffed, thwarted by my own ineptitude. The things I naturally knew to do, and wanted to do to connect with my young daughter, I was no good at. Added to the usual frustration of her not following directions, or not listening to me when I told her not to do something, I often felt like I was disappearing.

I wanted it too much. I wanted to matter to her too much, and I couldn't get out of my own way to let it happen. As with any unrequited desire, the only escape was to not care, but that was not an option. I could feel the pull of retreat, and understood perfectly why so many fathers, especially with daughters, pull back. The disappointment of feeling like you aren't as great as you imagined you would be is just sometimes too bitter. The longer it lasted, the more I wanted to step back, to withdraw, so that I might cruise for the rest of her childhood on the power of my salvaged dignity, but for some reason, I didn't. I couldn't. By luck or by grace, I couldn't give up.

When she was five, a few weeks into kindergarten, Ava asked me to just make up stories, preferably ghost stories.

"Just make them up?"

Oh, great. That should have been easy for me, but I knew it wouldn't be. I'm from Kentucky, the dark and bloody ground, where the entire culture is built upon the idea that the very land, the trees and mountains and rivers are haunted. I grew up hearing that the Cherokee and the Shawnee wouldn't even live there, reserving it for sacred hunting only, because they believed it belonged to the animals and the spirit world. If anything should have been in my blood, it should have been the ability to conjure a good ghost story for a five-year-old girl.

Again, I was at a loss, completely unable to deliver, but I was also very tired of feeling this way, so I thought hard. I sat up on the edge of the bed and closed my eyes, trying to remember just one good ghost story.

The only real ghost story I could sort of remember was about a girl who lived near Mammoth Cave. I had to improvise, but I told it this way. The girl fell in love with her teacher, who, in turn, fell in love with someone else more appropriate for him. Heartbroken, the girl lured him into Mammoth Cave for a tour, and after taking him way back through a maze of passages, into the deepest chambers, she doused her lantern and slowly, silently walked away, leaving him screaming in the dark. He was never found. She kept the secret until her deathbed, and they say that to this day, if you're down in the cave and turn off your light, you can hear him screaming off in the dark distance, "Missy! Missy, come get me! Don't leave me down here."

Ava's eyes were wide, really wide, utterly terrified, and for a minute I thought I had made a huge mistake. What kind of a story was this to tell a little girl?

"But if she was in love with him, why did she do that?"

"I don't know. When you're in love, sometimes you get really angry at the person you're in love with, and you do crazy things. Especially if you think they don't love you back."

Too much information, I thought as I was saying it.

"Yeah, sometimes I feel that way about Aaron," she said solemnly. "But I would never do that to him."

"Good," I said. "Who's Aaron?"

Ava hid her face in her pillow and said, "We're not going to talk about that."

Despite the brush-off about Aaron, I went downstairs elated. I had finally told a good story. I felt like a Broadway star who had just delivered the performance of a lifetime, whose next move was to go to Sardi's to hang out until the reviews in the morning papers hit the news stands.

"Who's Aaron?" I asked my wife.

"He's a boy at school, and Ava likes him, but he likes Mathilde and Margaret. It's complicated."

Prompted by Ava, over the next several weeks, I spun an incredible ghost/love-triangle story involving the ghost of Blackbeard, the ghost of the New Orleans pirate Jean Lafitte, and their "girlfriend," the voodoo priestess Marie Laveau. The conflict is essentially within Marie, who loves both pirates but thinks she would be better off with someone who is actually flesh and blood, alive, like she is. The cast of supporting characters included Daniel Boone, Buddy Bolden, Louis Armstrong, Mark Twain, William Faulkner and Virginia Dare. Twain and Faulkner are ghost-hunting detectives, who track Laveau across the Caribbean. Buddy Bolden and Louis Armstrong give a lot of bad advice to the lovesick pirates and help Laveau escape from them when she wants to. Daniel Boone is there to help the pirates cross the Smoky Mountains in search of Marie, who has been kidnapped by the Shawnee.

The plot ranged across time and geography, through the temporal and spiritual worlds, but Blackbeard and Lafitte never give up as they moon over their beloved Laveau, enlisting the others to travel through time on Mississippi riverboats and pirate ships to help them find Marie wherever she is hiding and woo her away from one another. Marie put spells on everybody at one time or another, and was good at vanishing without a trace whenever things got too heavy. It wasn't so much a ghost story as a supernatural soap opera.

Ava ate it up and often asked me to tell her the next chapter in the mornings, as she got ready for school. She asked lots of questions on the way to kindergarten, but the best one was, "Why don't they just give up?"

"Because they can't," I told her. "Love is like magic. It won't let you quit until you're ready to quit."

"That doesn't mean it's good, though," she told me.

"True. That's true," I said.

That night, Virginia Dare was introduced into the story. With help from one of Marie Laveau's potions, the ghost of the first Englishwoman born in the New World falls in love with Blackbeard. She does her best to steal his attentions away from Marie, and in the name of resolution, she succeeds. Jean Lafitte and Marie end up together, and in the end, the principals and supporting characters all have a big pirate voodoo dance party in Key West and become friends, having shared so many adventures in the pursuit of love.

A few months later, out of nowhere, it seemed, Ava started to learn how to read, so story time gravitated back to books, which held a new fascination for her. Pulling words off the page by herself was now more of a thrill than listening to me make things up for her. One night, she asked if she could just read on her own and put herself to sleep. She turned on her flashlight and asked me to turn off the light on my way out.

"Sure," I said, getting up. I turned off the light and looked back at her, knees up, flashlight propped on the pillow next to her head. "I'll be right downstairs if you need me."

"I know, Daddy," she said without looking up.

CONTRIBUTORS' NOTES

 **Mike Adamick** is a stay-at-home dad living in San Francisco with his wife, Dana, and daughter, Emmeline. He enjoys old-school wooden playgrounds with dented metal slides, tea parties, playing dress up, finger painting and, above all, nap time. His writing regularly appears on National Public Radio, KQED Radio, and Babble.com and in the *San Francisco Chronicle,* as well as his own blog, Cry It Out: Memoirs of a Stay-at-Home Dad. When he's not writing, he can be found at his sewing machine, making dresses like the one in this picture.

 **Swan Adamson's** recent novels include *My Three Husbands, Confessions of a Pregnant Princess,* and *Memoirs Are Made of This.* He is also a playwright (*The Dads Try to Get Married* and *Domestic Manners of the Americans*) and (as Donald Olson) a prolific travel writer. He has just completed a new novel called *Mischief's Millions: The Super-Rich Adventures of Lenora Holmesley's Super-Rich Lap Dog.*

 **Steve Almond** is the author of five books, none of them quite as good as he'd hoped. His new book about music, *Bang Your Heart,* will be out in spring of 2010. He lives outside Boston with his wife, two children, and mounting debt.

Dean Bakopoulos's first novel, *Please Don't Come Back from the Moon,* was a *New York Times* Notable Book in 2005. His second novel, *My American Unhappiness,* is forthcoming from Houghton Mifflin Harcourt. He is currently at work on a book of nonfiction titled *The Hangover: Waking Up in the Age of Consequences.* The winner of a 2008 Guggenheim Fellowship and a 2006 National Endowment for the Arts grant, he is on the faculty of Iowa State University's MFA Program in Creative Writing & Environment and lives with his family in Ames, Iowa.

Robert Bausch is the author of six novels and one collection of short stories. His novel *A Hole in the Earth,* about a father and daughter, was a *New York Times* Notable Book. He teaches writing and literature at Northern Virginia Community College in Woodbridge, Virginia. He also teaches at the Writer's Center in Bethesda, Maryland.

Dan Beachy-Quick is the author of four books of poetry, most recently *This Nest, Swift Passerine.* He is also the author of a book of interlinked essays on Melville's *Moby-Dick,* called *A Whaler's Dictionary.* He is the recent recipient of a Lannan Foundation residency and teaches in the MFA Writing Program at Colorado State University.

Thomas Beller is the author of two works of fiction, *Seduction Theory* and *The Sleep-Over Artist,* and a collection of personal essays, *How To Be a Man. The Sleep-Over Artist* was a *New York Times* Notable Book and a *Los*

Angeles Times Best Book 2000, and *How To Be a Man* was a *New York Times* Editor's Pick and Amazon book of the month. His most recent book is the anthology *Lost and Found: Stories from New York*. He is a former staff writer at *The New Yorker* and the *Cambodia Daily*. His short stories have appeared in *The New Yorker, Elle, Harper's Bazaar, Ploughshares,* the *Southwest Review* and *Best American Short Stories;* and his journalism and essays in *Vogue,* the *New York Times, Oxford American,* and *Spin.* A founder and editor of *Open City* magazine and Mrbellersneighborhood.com, he teaches creative writing at Tulane University.

 **Chris Bohjalian** is the author of twelve novels, including *Midwives, The Double Bind,* and *Skeletons at the Feast.* His new book, *Secrets of Eden,* was just published. Visit him at www.chrisbohjalian.com.

 **Rand Richards Cooper** is the author of a novel, *The Last to Go,* and a story collection, *Big As Life.* His fiction has appeared in *Harper's,* the *Atlantic, Esquire,* and many other magazines; his short story "Johnny Hamburger" was included in *Best American Short Stories 2003. The Last to Go* was produced for television by ABC. Cooper has been Writer in Residence at Amherst and Emerson colleges. A longtime contributing editor for *Bon Appétit,* he received a 2002 Lowell Thomas Gold Medal Award from the Society of American Travel Writers. He writes a column, "Dad on a Lark," for Wondertime.com and is working on a memoir about later-life fatherhood.

T. Colin Dodd lives in Carrboro, North Carolina, with his wife and two daughters. He works for an open-source software company, writing pretty much anything they need.

Robert Dugoni is the author of three novels, including *Wrongful Death* (Touchstone/Fireside, 2009), a sequel to his *New York Times* bestselling debut, *The Jury Master* (Warner Books, 2006). He is also the author of *Damage Control* (Warner Books, 2007), a *Parade* Magazine Book Pick and Booksense Notable Book Pick, as well as the nonfiction exposé *The Cyanide Canary*, a Washington Post Best Book of the Year Selection and the Idaho Book of the Year. His novels have been published in eighteen countries and received national acclaim. For additional information, please visit www.robertdugoni.com.

Trey Ellis is a novelist, screenwriter, essayist, and blogger on the HuffingtonPost.com and an assistant professor of film at Columbia University. He is the author of the novels *Platitudes, Home Repairs,* and *Right Here, Right Now,* and the memoir *Bedtime Stories: Adventures in the Land of Single-Fatherhood.* His work for the screen includes the Emmy-nominated *Tuskegee Airmen* and *Good Fences,* which was short-listed for the PEN Award for Best Teleplay of the year. His essays have appeared in the *New York Times, Playboy,* the *Washington Post,* the *Los Angeles Times,* and *Vanity Fair* and he has contributed audio commentary to NPR's *All Things Considered.* His first play, *Fly,* was produced and performed at the Lincoln Center Institute.

Richard Farrell is an author, filmmaker, journalist, and adjunct professor of English at the University of Massachusetts in Lowell. His documentary, *High on Crack Street,* aired on HBO and received Columbia University's duPont Award. He is the coauthor of *A Criminal and an Irishman: The Inside Story of the Mob-IRA Connection.* He is one of the screenwriters for the upcoming film *The Fighter,* which stars Christian Bale and Mark Wahlberg. His memoir, *What's Left of Us,* was published by Citadel Press. He makes his home in Milford, New Hampshire.

Eric Goodman is the author of four novels, most recently *Child of My Right Hand.* He directs the Creative Writing Program at Miami University in Oxford, Ohio.

James Griffioen is a former corporate litigator turned writer, photographer, and stay-at-home dad in Detroit, Michigan. Every day thousands of people around the world visit his Web site sweetjuniper.com. His photography has been featured in *Harper's, Vice, Landscape Architecture,* and *New York,* among other publications. He has appeared on American Public Media's *The Story* with Dick Gordon, CBC's national arts and culture radio program Q, as well as in the *Wall Street Journal,* the *Washington Post,* and newyorker.com. He is currently at work on a book of essays.

Brendan Halpin is the author of two memoirs and four novels for adults, including the Alex–Award winning *Donorboy.* He also writes novels for young adults, including *Forever Changes* and the forthcoming

Shutout and *The Half Life of Planets,* cowritten with Emily Franklin. Brendan works as a teacher and lives in Boston with his wife, Suzanne, and their children Casey, Rowen, and Kylie.

Laird Hunt is the author of four novels, including *The Exquisite* and the recently published *Ray of the Star.* His writings, reviews, and translations have appeared in the United States and abroad in, among other places, *McSweeney's, Ploughshares, Bomb, Bookforum, Grand Street, The Believer, Fence, Conjunctions,* and *Brick.* He has held residencies at the Camargo Foundation and the MacDowell Colony and is currently on faculty in the creative writing program at the University of Denver.

Michael Kearns is an award-winning writer-performer who lives in Los Angeles with his daughter, Tia. He is the author of six theater books, more than a dozen produced plays, and numerous solo performance pieces, and his work is widely anthologized. As an actor-writer-director-producer- fund-raiser-journalist-teacher, his work surrounding HIV/AIDS— spanning more than a quarter of a century—is encyclopedic in its comprehensiveness, including work as an actor in film and television.

Amitava Kumar is the author of *Husband of a Fanatic, Bombay–London–New York,* and *Passport Photos.* His novel *Home Products* was short-listed for India's premier literary prize, the Crossword Book Award. His latest book, *A Foreigner Carrying in the Crook of His Arm a Tiny Bomb,* is a writer's report on the global war on terror. Kumar is professor of English at Vassar College. He lives in Poughkeepsie with his wife and daughter.

 **Carl Lennertz** has been in bookselling and publishing since the death of disco, first in bookstores and then as a book sales rep. As marketing director for Knopf, Pantheon and Vintage, Carl worked with Richard Ford, Anne Rice, Carl Hiaasen, and many others. In 1999, Lennertz joined the American Booksellers on a national marketing campaign, and in 2003, he returned to publishing as VP/ Marketing for HarperCollins. In 2004, Shaye Areheart Books published his book about growing up in a small town and then raising a child in New York City, *Cursed by a Happy Childhood: Letters from a Dad to a Daughter.*

 **Richard Nash** is an independent publishing consultant and entrepreneur. For most of the past decade, he ran the iconic indie Soft Skull Press, for which he was awarded the Association of American Publishers' Miriam Bass Award for Creativity in Independent Publishing in 2005. Books he edited and published landed on bestseller lists from the *Boston Globe* to the *Singapore Straits-Times* and on Best of the Year lists from the *Guardian* to the *Toronto Globe & Mail* to the *Los Angeles Times.* It is strange to be published, rather than to publish, but he's not surprised his daughter was the reason.

 **Daniel Raeburn** is the author of the book *Chris Ware.* His essays have appeared in *The Baffler, Tin House, The New Yorker,* and elsewhere. He lives on the south side of Chicago with his wife, Rebekah, and their daughter, Willa.

David G.W. Scott's poems have appeared in numerous literary publications, including *Poet Lore, Euphony,* the *Madison Review, West Branch, New Delta Review, The Lyric,* the *Greensboro Review,* and in *Red, White, and Blues* (University of Iowa Press). Winner of The Irene Leache Memorial Foundation's award in free verse poetry, he is also a recipient of a fellowship in fiction and poetry from the Delaware Division of the Arts. He received a PEN Discovery Award for Fiction in 2004. His essays have appeared in *About What Was Lost: Twenty Writers on Miscarriage, Healing, and Hope, Baltimore* magazine, and *Delaware Today* magazine. He lives in Tallahassee, Florida, with his wife, writer Julianna Baggott, and their four children.

Rob Spillman is editor and cofounder of *Tin House,* a ten-year-old bicoastal (Brooklyn, New York and Portland, Oregon) literary magazine. His writing has appeared in *Bookforum,* the *Boston Review, Connoisseur, Details, GQ, Nerve,* the *New York Times Book Review, Real Simple, Rolling Stone, Salon, Spin, Sports Illustrated, Vanity Fair, Vogue,* and *Worth,* among other magazines, newspapers, and essay collections. He is also the editor of *Gods and Soldiers: The Penguin Anthology of Contemporary African Writing,* which was published in April 2009.

Claude Stanush began his career as a newspaperman in his hometown of San Antonio, Texas. He went on to work for *Life* magazine, successively as Hollywood correspondent, science writer, religion editor, chief of correspondents in Washington, D.C., and associate editor in New York City. Accolades for his *Life*

stories include awards from the World Council of Churches and the American Association for the Advancement of Science; another *Life* essay inspired the feature film *The Lusty Men,* starring Robert Mitchum. A documentary film, *The Newton Boys: Portrait of an Outlaw Gang,* created with David Middleton, won the gold medal in its category at the Texas Film Festival and the International Film Festival in the Virgin Islands; the two men also edited an oral history on the Newtons. Stanush was a co-screenwriter on *The Newton Boys* (Twentieth Century Fox), a 1998 feature film. In addition, he has a book of newspaper essays, *The World in My Head;* two collections of short stories, *The Balanced Rock* and *Sometimes It's New York;* and, in collaboration with his daughter Michele, a biographical novel entitled *All Honest Men.* Other honors for his fiction include a creative writing award from the National Endowment for the Arts as well as the J. Frank Dobie Award and Fellowship.

Nick Taylor's first novel, *The Disagreement,* is now available in paperback. He lives with his wife and daughter in the San Francisco Bay Area, where he teaches creative writing at San Jose State University. Visit him on the Web at www.readthedisagreement.com.

David Teague lives in Wilmington, Delaware, with Annabel, Annabel's big brother Charles, and Annabel's mother, the novelist Marisa de los Santos. He is associate professor of English at the University of Delaware, creative director of IntEloquence Language Design, and author of two children's books forthcoming from Hyperion, *Franklin's*

Big Deal and *Billy Hightower*. Five nights out of seven, he and Annabel sleep just fine.

 **Robert Wilder** is the author of two critically acclaimed books of essays: *Tales From The Teachers' Lounge* and *Daddy Needs a Drink*, both of which have been optioned for television and film. He has published essays in *Newsweek, Details, Salon, Parenting, Creative Nonfiction, Working Mother,* and elsewhere. He has been a commentator for NPR's *Morning Edition, On Point,* and other national and regional radio programs, including the *Daddy Needs a Drink Minute,* which airs twice weekly on KBAC FM. Wilder's column, also titled "Daddy Needs A Drink," is printed monthly in the *Santa Fe Reporter.* Wilder is the recipient of the 2009 Innovations in Reading Award, given by the National Book Foundation. He lives in Santa Fe, New Mexico, with his wife, Lala, and their two children, Poppy and London. Visit his Web site at www.robertwilder.com.

ACKNOWLEDGMENTS

Thank you to my whip-smart agent, Emmanuelle Alspaugh, who very well may be the best one in the 212 area code.

For my incredible editor, Ann Leslie Tuttle, and her impeccable instincts, I'm very grateful to have found such a wise editor in you.

To Shara Alexander, a great publicity queen, so talented and determined.

My gratitude and admiration go to the fearless contributors for baring their hearts and minds on these pages. Your daughters are blessed to have such proud papas in their lives.

For Kimberley Askew, the truest friend I've ever known.

To the talented Dilyara Breyer, thank you for everything, including my lovely Web site design.

For their exceptional taste in men and writers, Julianna Baggott, Marisa de los Santos, Lauren Cerand, Kimberley Askew, Ellen Sussman, Deborah Brody, Jacquelyn Mitchard, Joyce Maynard, Martha Witt, Louise Jarvis Flynn, Emmanuelle Alspaugh, Emily Franklin and Susan Wiggs.

To my "book club" buddies for your delightful company and encouragement: Amy Dunnigan, Liz Smith, Susan Butler, Wendy Reichardt, Sara Bogolin Sonnet, Nysa Wong Kline, Ana Galofre Smith, Shelby Brock, Ritu Metzger, Tommie Jolly, Cheryl Cechvala, Selda Sarigol Heavner, Barbara Yien and Mary Ann Murray.

For my in-laws, who have always shown me enormous support, and my parents and grandparents, I love you.

For my husband and daughter, the very embodiment of a father and daughter in love. As I write this, they are backpacking in the glorious High Sierras. I imagine them dirty from the trail, refreshed by a deep blue lake swim, and sitting by a campfire in the glow of their mutual admiration. I'm lucky to have them in my life.

CREDITS AND PERMISSIONS

ESSAYS

"For Grace, as She Grows into Her Name" © Chris Bohjalian, 2010

"What Next, Papa?" © Steve Almond, 2010

"Vessels" by Daniel Raeburn originally appeared in *The New Yorker* on May 1, 2006.

"On Inexplicable Weeping" © Dean Bakopoulos, 2010

"Punk Rock Roadie Dad" © Rob Spillman, 2010

"Coaching Phoebe" © David G.W. Scott, 2010

"El Corazón" © James Griffioen, 2010

"The Man on the Stairs" © Robert Wilder, 2010

"Confessions of a Faux Pa" © Swan Adamson, 2010

"Do I Dote?" © Eric Goodman, 2010

"Late-Onset Fatherhood" © Rand Richards Cooper, 2010

"A Kind of Miracle" © Robert Bausch, 2010

"Kaleidoscope" © Laird Hunt, 2010

"Bloodless But Not Loveless" © Michael Kearns, 2010

"To Be Read By Ava on Her Eighteenth Birthday" © Trey Ellis, 2010

"Headstrong, Headlong" © Richard Nash, 2010

"The Goalkeeper" © Brendan Halpin, 2010

"Letting Go" © Carl Lennertz, 2010

"The Whole Wide World" © Claude Stanush, 2010

"Little Fires" © Amitava Kumar, 2010

"Reckless in Love" © Richard Farrell, 2010

"The Kitten Gang" © Nick Taylor, 2010

"Blink of an Eye" © Robert Dugoni, 2010

"Thrift-Store Bandits" © Mike Adamick, 2010

PHOTOS

ABOUT THE EDITOR

Andrea N. Richesin is the editor of *Because I Love Her: 34 Women Writers Reflect on the Mother-Daughter Bond* (Harlequin, 2009) and *The May Queen: Women on Life, Love, Work, and Pulling It All Together in Your 30s* (Tarcher/Penguin, 2006) and a forthcoming anthology on first love. Her anthologies have been excerpted and praised in the *New York Times*, the *San Francisco Chronicle*, the *Boston Globe*, *Parenting*, *Redbook*, *Cosmopolitan*, *Bust*, *Daily Candy* and *Babble*. She lives with her husband and daughter in northern California. Visit her online at **www.nickirichesin.com**.